PILGRIMAGE

JUNE HAGER

PILGRIMAGE

A CHRONICLE OF CHRISTIANITY
THROUGH THE CHURCHES
OF ROME

JUNE HAGER

PHOTOGRAPHY BY GRZEGORZ GALAZKA

WEIDENFELD & NICOLSON
LONDON

This book is dedicated to Robert Moynihan,
who first had the idea for the Churches of Rome Pilgrimage
and made its realization possible

Half Title: This bas-relief, probably the front section of an early Christian sarcophagus
and now at the entrance of the Domitilla Catacomb, shows the Good Shepherd as a youth in classical garb.

Title Page: Habakkuk and the Angel, a Baroque statue by Gianlorenzo Bernini (1598–1680),
is located in the Chigi Chapel of S. Maria del Popolo.

First published in the United Kingdom in 1999 by Weidenfeld & Nicolson

Distributed in the United States of America by Sterling Series Publishing Co., Inc. 387 Park Avenue South, New York, NY 10016-8810

A CIP catalogue record for this book is available from the British Library
ISBN 0 297 82517 8

Designed by: Anthony Cohen
Edited by: Annie Lee
Set in: Adobe Caslon
Printed in: Italy

Weidenfeld & Nicolson Ltd
Illustrated Division
The Orion Publishing Group Ltd
Wellington House
125 Strand
London WC2R OBB

CONTENTS

CARDINAL'S PREFACE

The Year 2000. At its very mention, thoughts turn instinctively towards the future. Apocalyptic images contrast strangely with the dreams of a world in which peace will finally reign. In the frenzy of preparations and speculations, the very reason why there *is* a Year 2000 almost seems forgotten. The turn of the millennium marks nothing less than the anniversary of the eruption of God into human history, into time and space, with the birth of Jesus. Jesus was born, grew up, carried out his mission and died in places well known to us today: Bethlehem, Nazareth, Jerusalem, Capernaum. He did indeed announce the coming of a new era and commissioned a small and fragile group of disciples to preach this Good News to the entire world, at that time in Western history centred in Rome.

Pilgrimage: A Chronicle of Christianity Through the Churches of Rome seizes precisely the heart of the Jubilee celebration of the Year 2000. Peter, to whom Jesus had entrusted the primacy of service, and Paul, the Apostle of the Gentiles, were martyred in Rome. John, the beloved Apostle, and Mark, the companion of Paul, left memories of their presence there. These and other such names have rung in Roman ears through the centuries. The Church in Rome today can, in fact, trace its ancestry directly back to the earliest days of Christianity. But it is not merely a question of some sort of spiritual archaeological dig. The churches of Rome express the ongoing life of a traditionally cosmopolitan people, starting from small groups of courageous men and women who gathered in houses to listen to the Good News, to proclaim it to others, and to celebrate the Eucharist together. The steadfast faith of these early Christians led many of them to martyrdom. The places of their burial too became sacred places for remembrance and celebration. And so on through the ages to the very eve of the Year 2000 and beyond.

A sign of the dynamism of this spiritual history expressed in stone is the genius of a people who, yes, built new churches at each epoch but who also continued to gather in earlier ones, adapting them, modifying them according to the cultural or liturgical needs and the artistic expressions of their day. To take but one example, the basilica of St Mary Major, which dates back to the fourth century, now has a stained-glass window from the 1990s: deliberately set as sign and symbol of the vitality of the faith across the centuries.

Pilgrimage helps us to seize this vitality and to grasp the significance of a sacred place that is limited in space but not in time. The churches here presented are still in use; they are not ecclesiastical museums. Each one, however, bears the mark of the epoch that gave it birth: from the earliest ages of the Church in Rome to the recognition of Christianity as the religion of the Roman Empire, from quasi-fortresses to a mirror of an apparently mundane society and on to the churches of the Counter-Reformation. And so it is with each succeeding period. The churches of recent times, often on the outskirts of an ever-expanding city, express the needs of a new population, far from the historical centre, but just as Roman as those who walked the Forum, passing the place, marked by a church, where Peter was imprisoned.

The churches of Rome also bear witness to the amazing inspiration that artists have drawn from the Christian faith. The history of Western art can, to a degree, be traced on their walls. Who would dare attempt to list the names of all the artists who have designed or decorated churches, who have paved their floors so exquisitely or built the tombs of saints and sinners alike?

Pilgrimage has been published in the light of the Year 2000. While a Jubilee is always a time of celebration, one in honour of the birth of Christ is incomparably more. Throughout his life, Jesus listened to the passage from Leviticus which sets the terms of Jubilee. It was read out regularly in the Synagogue. A Jubilee is a time for restoring the fullness of their dignity to those who have suffered injustice, for freeing slaves, forgiving debts, pardoning wrong. Even the land is to lie fallow in a sign that a Jubilee year is one totally dedicated to the Lord. If the churches of Rome reflect the ongoing history of Christianity, they are also reminders of what it means to live out this faith in a new millennium. It is a call to live true Jubilee in the concrete situation of today. *Pilgrimage* is a unique help in understanding this. It is a book to be savoured, to be read and reread slowly, but also to be contemplated, thanks to the magnificent photographs which accompany the text. Its interest is not limited to Rome alone. It holds significance not only for all those spiritual Romes, whatever their name may be and wherever they may be found. It is also a useful signpost for the many pilgrims seeking the way in a complex and, at times, troubling world.

ROGER CARDINAL ETCHEGARY
President, Committee for the Jubilee of the Year 2000
Vatican City

ARCHBISHOP'S FOREWORD

R ome is famous as the 'city of a thousand churches'. The author of the present volume has chosen that unique characteristic to illustrate 2,000 years of Christian history in Rome – from the ancient catacombs to the most recent churches raised, sometimes haphazardly, in the sprawling suburbs.

She has done this for the occasion of the Great Jubilee for the Year 2000, in response to Pope John Paul II's invitation, in his apostolic letter Tertio Millennio Adveniente, to give glory to God by recalling the beauty the Church has brought to the world during its two-millennial history.

Before the pilgrim's eyes, the author parades twenty centuries of history in the Eternal City. Descriptions of churches from many different eras evoke the 'historical–religious memory' of the world capital, where, after the fall of the Roman Empire, life centred around the Roman Church and, to a large extent, took place in Roman churches.

These sacred edifices were often the centre of family and social life for the Roman people. Their placement largely determined the city's physical aspect. The writer examines their historical origins, evolving religious and civic functions, and the roles the churches played in the daily lives of Roman citizens. The result is a broad panorama – enriched by events, personages, and some surprising new findings – of the influence Rome's churches had on everyday life.

In the course of this long and lively chronicle, the spiritual importance of Rome's churches becomes very clear. Centres of assembly and prayer, of ritual and liturgy and popular piety, the churches of Rome disseminated faith and practice throughout

the universal Church. I feel certain that upon opening the pages of this book the reader will discover a mine of historical information, fascinating stories and practical suggestions. In the course of an entertaining and informative itinerary, the pilgrim will come to understand how Rome's places of worship gave birth to that Christian civilization which now character-izes not only Rome, but much of the Western world as well.

FRANCESCO ARCHBISHOP MARCHISANO
President of the Pontifical Commission
for the Cultural Patrimony of the Church

ACKNOWLEDGEMENTS

I am deeply aware of how much I owe to His Eminence, Cardinal Roger Etchegaray and His Excellency Archbishop Francesco Marchisano. Their support provided the inspiration and stimulus for carrying through this project on the churches of Rome. Thanks also to Sister Marjorie Keenan for her help and enthusiasm.

I acknowledge with gratitude the assistance of several experts who read the draft texts and advised me with their knowledge of and love for Rome and its monuments: Father Leonard Boyle, eminent paleographer and medievalist at S. Clemente Monastery; Bert Treffers, Professor of seventeenth-century Devotional Art, Nimegen University, Holland; John Nicholson, Professor of History and Fine Arts, Loyola University, Rome; Jack Ullman, instructor of European and Islamic History, St Stephen's School, Rome; Mr Michael Brouse, teacher, guide and writer on imperial Rome; architect Nigel Ryan, and also Lucina Vattuone and Cristina Gennaccari at the Vatican Museum, who provided many helpful suggestions for contacts and background reading.

To my own dear family thanks and appreciation. Above all, Tariq, who first gathered my articles together, researched some chapters, critiqued others, and managed my office while I wrote the final text. Ashley, my faithful reader, tested the pilgrimage herself, chapter by chapter. Kristen has always found just the right words or provided the necessary insight in difficult times. And my husband Mike has been lovingly by my side from start to finish.

Kristen Jarratt was my first churches of Rome companion. Annarita, Rita, Sany and Michela taught me much about Italian art and culture during our museum and exhibit outings. Nelide Giammarco's counselling and guidance were indispensable at every step along the way, and Claire Hammond, owner of Trastevere's 'Corner Bookshop', could be called the 'midwife' of the entire project.

The basis for many of these chapters was a collection of articles first contributed to the monthly publication *Inside the Vatican*. Editor Robert Moynihan generously allowed me the use of the office and magazine resources to finish the manuscript. Without the staff of *Inside the Vatican*, particularly Giuseppe Sabatelli and Stefano Navarrini, this book would never have come about.

I am indebted to Asia Haleem for putting me in touch with Weidenfeld & Nicolson. Many thanks to my editors Caroline Knight, whose love of art and history launched the book, and Claire Wedderburn-Maxwell, whose competence and receptiveness saw us through the final stages.

JUNE HAGER

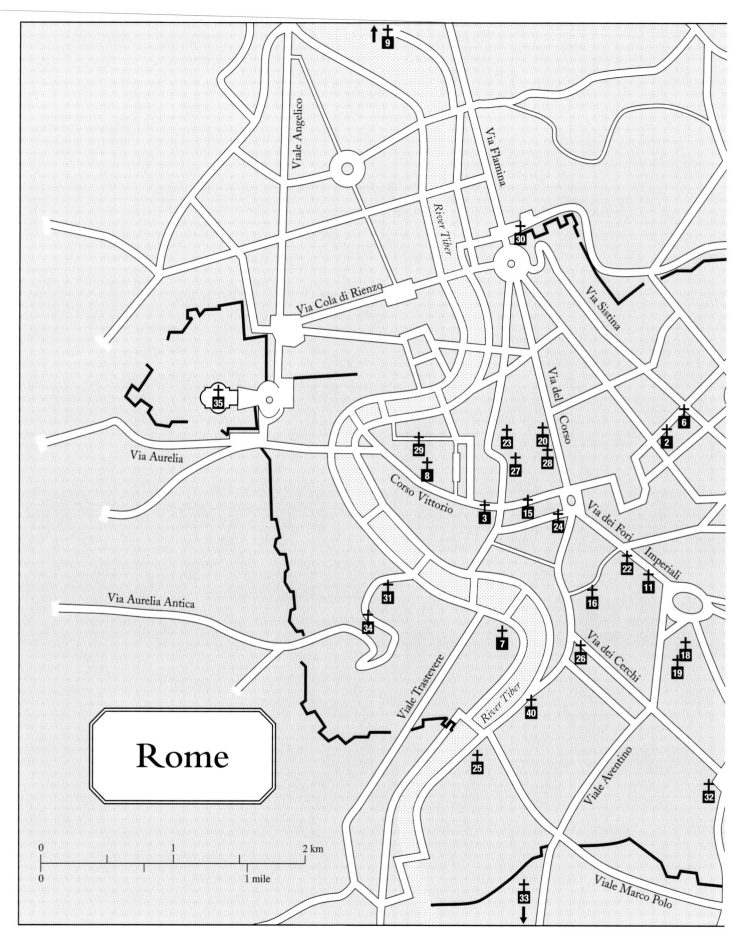

Rome

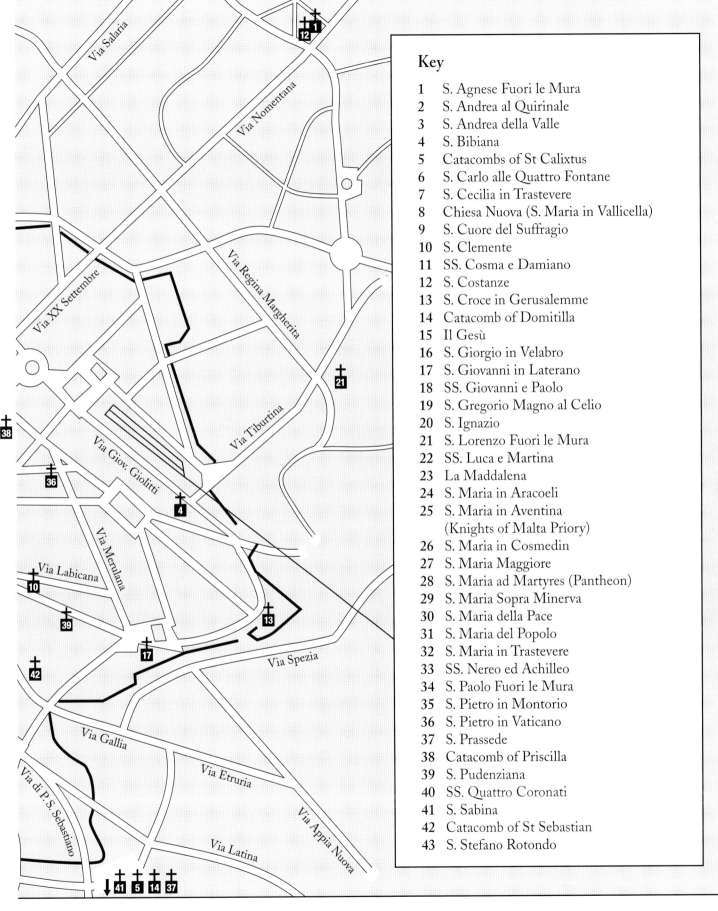

Key

1 S. Agnese Fuori le Mura
2 S. Andrea al Quirinale
3 S. Andrea della Valle
4 S. Bibiana
5 Catacombs of St Calixtus
6 S. Carlo alle Quattro Fontane
7 S. Cecilia in Trastevere
8 Chiesa Nuova (S. Maria in Vallicella)
9 S. Cuore del Suffragio
10 S. Clemente
11 SS. Cosma e Damiano
12 S. Costanze
13 S. Croce in Gerusalemme
14 Catacomb of Domitilla
15 Il Gesù
16 S. Giorgio in Velabro
17 S. Giovanni in Laterano
18 SS. Giovanni e Paolo
19 S. Gregorio Magno al Celio
20 S. Ignazio
21 S. Lorenzo Fuori le Mura
22 SS. Luca e Martina
23 La Maddalena
24 S. Maria in Aracoeli
25 S. Maria in Aventina
   (Knights of Malta Priory)
26 S. Maria in Cosmedin
27 S. Maria Maggiore
28 S. Maria ad Martyres (Pantheon)
29 S. Maria Sopra Minerva
30 S. Maria della Pace
31 S. Maria del Popolo
32 S. Maria in Trastevere
33 SS. Nereo ed Achilleo
34 S. Paolo Fuori le Mura
35 S. Pietro in Montorio
36 S. Pietro in Vaticano
37 S. Prassede
38 Catacomb of Priscilla
39 S. Pudenziana
40 SS. Quattro Coronati
41 S. Sabina
42 Catacomb of St Sebastian
43 S. Stefano Rotondo

ROME'S CHURCHES: A SPIRITUAL PALIMPSEST

Introduction: Capital of Christendom

Through the Holy Door and into the third millennium. A solemn procession during the night of Christmas Eve in the year 1999 knocks at the Jubilee Portal and passes into St Peter's Basilica, tomb of the First Apostle. Led by St Peter's successor, its sovereign Pontiff, the Roman Catholic Church celebrates the completion of 2,000 years of Christian history.

Indirectly, this is also a celebration for the whole of mankind. For almost all modern calculations of the passage of time begin with the birth of Jesus in Bethlehem 2,000 years ago. Christ's coming into history was a pivotal event, a starting point for the calendar most widely used throughout the world today. Of course, for much of the world the Nativity is not a central tenet of faith, and other religions use different beginnings for calculating the passing years. In Judaism, for example, 2000 will actually be the year 5760 (computed from the creation of man as described in Genesis); for Muslims the year 1421 (from the *hegira*, the Prophet's exodus from Mecca to Medina); and some Buddhists count time from the year of Buddha's birth, *c.*544BC.

Nevertheless, along with Christians, the entire world observes the end of the second millennium and the beginning of the third. There are special Jubilee observances for Jerusalem and other Holy Land sites, and to some extent in local churches throughout the world. But it is to Rome that millions – of different nationalities and even faiths – come for the Great Jubilee of the Year 2000, for Rome is the acknowledged capital of Western Christendom. How can that be when Christ's coming took place so many years ago in far-away Palestine?

Much of Christianity's history in Rome is shrouded by legend and the veils of time. With patience, however, many evanescent traces can be followed along the winding paths of tradition to some historical source. In Rome today pious pilgrims and curious tourists alike can see with their own eyes and touch with their own hands material evidence left by Rome's earliest Christian converts. This book follows a two-millennium journey – through the artistic and archaeological testimony in the churches of Rome – back to Christianity's very roots.

The cupola of St Peter's Basilica has become the symbol of Catholicism worldwide. This is the famous 'keyhole' view from the garden entrance to the Knights of Malta Priory on the Aventine Hill.

FROM PALESTINE TO ROME

Almost everything we know about Jesus's life and teachings comes down to us from the Gospels of Matthew, Mark, Luke and John. These 'glad tidings' of salvation were written several decades (c.65–100) after Christ's death, apparently for the needs of various early Christian communities. The dating and authorship of the Gospels have been studied and much debated. However, most historians agree that the Gospel of Mark was the first to be set down and that the work was composed in Rome for Roman Christians. According to Bishop Papias of Hierapolis (c.130), a late disciple of the Apostle John, Mark was Peter's interpreter and faithful companion and recorded first-hand the Apostle's words for posterity.

Mark's Gospel begins with Jesus's baptism by John in the River Jordan, his choosing of the Apostles with Peter as leader, and his prophetic ministry in the villages and towns of Galilee. Jesus's preaching, healing and exorcism of devils drew huge crowds in rural Palestine and even in Jerusalem. His words and activities became increasingly threatening to the Jewish authorities, who condemned him in their religious court and handed him over to Roman officials to be crucified as a religious heretic and political rebel. Mark's description of Christ's death on the cross of Golgotha – abandoned by his disciples and seemingly also by his Father in heaven – forgiving his howling mob of enemies below – is tremendously moving from a human point of view.

But afterwards, on the morning of the third day, something occurred that changed the course of world religious history. Jesus's followers reported that on that day their Lord arose from the dead, and that during the next forty days he appeared repeatedly to them, both in groups and individually. That was the true beginning of Christian faith. From that time Christians believed that Jesus's death was a redemptive sacrifice for man's sins, and that his Resurrection was a promise of their own immortality in the world to come.

The Acts of the Apostles, written by the author of the Third Gospel, St Luke, gives us a lively account of the Holy Spirit's Pentecostal descent upon the Apostles and their organization of the infant Church in Jerusalem. Soon, however, harassment and persecution by the Jewish authorities made Christians' life and work in Palestine almost unbearable. The early leaders had first tried to reclaim the 'lost sheep' of Israel (Matt. 5:17–19) inside the homeland. Then, following Christ's instructions to 'go into the whole world and preach the Gospel to every creature' (Mark 16: 15), they left to carry the Word throughout the Greco-Roman cities of the Mediterranean coast.

Jesus had called himself the Son of Man and the Son of the Living God. When he asked his disciples: 'Whom do men say I am?' Peter replied: 'You are the Christ' (Mark 7: 27–9). Thus Christ was not a part of Jesus's name, but rather his title, a translation into Greek of the Hebrew word for Messiah, the 'Anointed One', the fulfilment of Jewish Scriptures. Yet Christ's message had a universal resonance from the very beginning.

Apparently well versed in Jewish law and tradition, Jesus nevertheless preached a revolutionary ethic, insisting on the superiority of inward motivation over external rituals. His primary emphasis was on a personal love for God and respect for all other human beings. His teachings on peace, concern for the poor and oppressed, and the equality of all men and women before God, provided the bedrock of social values for modern Western civilization. He prophesied that his message, planted like a tiny grain of mustard seed, would grow into a great tree to house the birds of the entire world (Mark 4:31–2).

It was the intense and ever indefatigable Paul who became the energetic 'Apostle to the Gentiles' (Romans 9:13). By his own admission Paul, a former persecutor of Christians, experienced conversion during one of his journeys in pursuit of Christ's converts. Acts records Paul's missionary journeys all over the Near East. (Luke was also Paul's companion for most of these trips.)

Paul's Epistles of instruction to the first Christian communities of Asia Minor signal the growing realization of Christianity as a new faith, separate and supplanting the Law of Moses. It was Paul's vision of a universal Church for all men and all nations which eventually triumphed and changed the course of history. It was that mission which brought both St Paul and St Peter to Rome – capital of the world of their time.

THE APOSTOLIC CHURCH

Rome's status as the capital of Christianity is based upon the continuous tradition of the mission and martyrdom here of the two great Apostles: Peter, whom Christ himself had chosen to lead the Church; and Paul, who described himself as the Apostle to the Gentiles. What is really at the heart of the tradition that says Peter and Paul founded the Roman Church? For over 2,000 years the memory of the two Apostles has been preserved in legend and art, but actual written records of their Roman activities are extremely hard to come by.

For Paul the situation is fairly clear. In the very last chapter of Acts, the Evangelist Luke narrates Paul's arrival, 'in chains', on Italian soil – 'delivered (by the Jews) as a prisoner from Jerusalem into the hands of the Romans' (Acts 28:17). 'And so we came to Rome,' Luke announces dramatically, describing Paul's enthusiastic reception by Roman Christians, who travelled some sixty-five kilometres to the Forum of Apius (near Terracina) and down the Appian Way to greet the Apostle at the resting place called Three Taverns (Acts 18:16).

Luke ends Acts by informing us that Paul remained two entire years under guard in his own hired lodgings. 'And he received all that came to him, preaching the kingdom of God, and teaching the things that concern the Lord Jesus Christ, with all confidence, without prohibition' (Acts 28: 30–31). And then what happened? In one of his Epistles, the Apostle complains bitterly of abandonment during his first Roman trial (II Timothy 4:16). But he implies that he has been incarcerated again and calmly awaits his coming martyrdom. 'For I am even now ready to be sacrificed, and the time of my dissolution is at hand. I have fought a good fight; I have kept my course' (II Timothy 6–7).

As for Peter, his career after leaving Jerusalem is for the most part a lost chapter. As oblique proof of Peter's Roman sojourn we do have his First Epistle, which concludes: 'The Church that is in Babylon salutes you, and so does my son Mark.' It would not be far-fetched for the simple fisherman from Galilee to consider Roman imperial decadence as 'Babylonian'. Furthermore, as mentioned above, scholars affirm that Mark wrote down his Master's words in Rome as a Gospel for Christians there.

Some historians quote a document written by the theologian Tertullian in 198, which mentions Peter's baptizing of converts in the River Tiber. St Jerome (342–420) ascribes a Roman ministry of twenty-five years to the Galilean Apostle,

St Peter's Basilica was built over the tomb of Peter, the Galilean fisherman, whom Jesus Christ chose to lead his Church on earth.

apparently basing his assumptions on some earlier sources. As for the Apostles' martyrdoms in Rome, we have a continuous tradition threading its way back 2,000 years. During the Papacy of Zephyrinus (199–217), a certain churchman named Gaius defended the Apostles' memory against heretics. In a work called *The Dialogue* he wrote: 'If you go as far as the Vatican or the Ostian Way, you will find the mortal remains of those who founded this church.' Quoting that passage, the first great Church historian, Bishop Eusebius of Caesarea (260–339), confirmed the martyrdoms by adding that: 'The cemeteries are still called by their names' (II: 26,2).

Even today, each visitor to the churches of Rome will sense the Apostles' enduring presence – in magnificent basilicas built over early tombs, pious graffiti scratched on underground walls, and both rich and humble art treasures of every type and age.

ROME – THE ETERNAL CITY

It was only natural that Peter and Paul should come to Rome to spread the Gospel, for Rome in their time was the capital of the Empire and centre of the then-known world. With the Julio–Claudian Emperors (AD14–68) Rome had stretched its borders from the Hellenistic East to the edges of Gaul in the West. Under the protection of the Roman military, government and law, and a system of efficient roads and communications, peoples of different cultures, languages and faiths were brought together in a single state.

This unity made it easy for the Church to disseminate the Christian message. Did Peter and Paul have a premonition that the Popes would replace the Emperors and assure the survival of Roman civilization? That after the dissolution of the Empire in 476, the Papacy would use the Latin language and liturgy, and the Christian faith, to again forge the West into a unified whole?

The rapid spread of Christianity was also due to the profound appeal of its message. After its high-water point under the early Emperors, the Empire began to weaken internally and crumble at its borders. In a world of uncertainty and confusion, Christianity offered the comfort of a personal, loving God and the promise of immortality – elements which had been missing in Greco-Roman paganism and even in the Law of Moses. As Roman society became more corrupt and degenerate, the example of individual Christians' virtue and humility could not fail to make a strong impression. Even under tremendous stress, the Christian community proved itself to be amazingly fraternal, cohesive and disciplined.

The Conversion of St Paul on the Way to Damascus is depicted in this dramatic painting by Caravaggio (located in the Cerasi Chapel of the church of S. Maria de Popolo).

Several phenomena accelerated the final predominance of Roman Christianity. The fall of Jerusalem in AD70, amid great slaughter of Jews and the destruction of the Temple, left Christians without a point of reference in Palestine. In spite of the authority of such early Christian communities as Antioch or Alexandria, Rome, which had been especially honoured by the preaching and martyrdom of both Peter and Paul, easily took on the mantle of Mother Church.

Persecution and martyrdom may have actually hastened Christianity's triumph. Roman Christians were ferociously persecuted from the first to the early fourth centuries, as we will see in the following chapters. It is estimated that around 100,000 Christians died for their faith throughout the Roman Empire before Constantine ended the imperial persecutions in 313. Yet by their courageous and often serene martyrdoms, Christians proved that their faith was worth not only living, but also dying for. Each martyrdom seemed to produce a new conversion.

THE INSTITUTIONAL CHURCH

When Peter and Paul arrived in Rome they found a small but apparently well-organized Christian community. (Probably Christ's message had been brought to Rome by merchants from Palestine, or travellers from some of the early Christian centres in Asia Minor.) Paul had already written to Roman Christians expressing his desire to visit them, and praising them 'because your faith is spoken of in the entire world' (Romans I:7–10).

Although the official Jewish community was decidedly cool to Paul's evangelization (Acts 18:22), the Apostles did make conversions among the Jewish people. Their efforts found more fertile ground, however, among two other groups: Romans of every profession and class, who were thirsting for something more than the empty decadence of imperial Roman society; and expatriates from all over the Empire, especially slaves, freedmen and merchants, attracted by Christianity's message of equality and justice. (Converts' names mentioned in the Epistles give us an idea of the different groups.)

By the end of the second century, the Roman Church was already an institution with its own property (cemeteries and house churches), shared sacraments (particularly the Eucharist and Baptism) and liturgy (prayer, hymns and readings of the Scriptures). A hierarchy of presbyters (priests), deacons and bishops, ordained by the laying-on of hands (as described in both Paul's and Peter's Epistles), led the Christian community. At the beginning the bishops (from the secular Greek *episkopos*, meaning supervisor or overseer) seem to have governed the churches collectively, similarly to the elders in Jewish synagogues. But gradually one 'bishop' assumed control of the local congregation (*ecclesia*, or church).

The Bishops of Rome, or Popes, traced their line of succession back to the Apostle Peter, whom Jesus himself had chosen as leader of his Church. 'When the Blessed Apostles Peter and Paul had founded and built up their Church, they handed over the ministry of the Episcopate to Linus,' wrote Irenaeus, Bishop of Lyons (178–c.200), in his scholarly work *Against Heresies*. He then listed Peter's twelve successors in Rome, from Linus down to Eleutherus (175–89), insisting on Rome's 'apostolic' pre-eminence among the early Churches.

The imperial persecutions, which began under Nero in 64 and effectively ended with Diocletian's massacres of 303–5, only seemed to strengthen the Church and increase its membership. The Christian religion could not be suppressed and its numbers continued to grow. Christianity became the official religion in the Roman Empire in 394.

A PERSONAL NOTE

Rome, the Pope's home and Christianity's capital, is a city of churches. Hundreds of domes and bell-towers rise above the city roofs. Many of these mark sites of decisive moments in spiritual history. Even the smallest chapels contain inestimable treasures of art and architecture.

Deciding which churches to include in this Pilgrimage through Roman Christianity was extremely difficult. It was hard, for instance, to leave out the Aventine sanctuary of S. Prisca, built over the first-century home of St Peter's and St Paul's dearest friends. Or the church of S. Pietro in Vincoli, which hosts Michelangelo's monumental sculpture of Moses, Borromini's most beautiful church, S. Ivo, or a personal favourite – S. Crisogono with its wonderful chimes.

Furthermore, every Roman church is a veritable layer-cake of history and art. Disentangling the superimposed strata can be a bewildering – although always fascinating – task. The visitor should sit quietly in a dusky corner or peaceful cloister, with imagination travelling backwards in time to the countless stories that linger among all these ancient walls.

The second section of this volume is devoted to Rome's officially designated pilgrimage churches – the Jubilee basilicas. Visits to these pre-eminent sanctuaries of Western Christendom can offer a 'review' through the various epochs in Christian history to the very foundation of the churches of Rome.

THE CATACOMBS: UNDER-GROUND ARCHIVES OF THE PRIMITIVE CHURCH

Beneath the cypress and pine trees along the Appian Way and other roads leading out of ancient Rome extends a vast city of the dead. Here, in the first centuries AD, early Christians carved out labyrinths of dark tunnels, some on three or four levels, to host underground tombs and secret chapels.

The catacombs. No other word so vividly evokes the primitive Christian Church. Even today, the image of those maze-like underground passages, where Roman Christians reportedly hid from terrible persecutions and buried their early martyrs, awakens in us a sense of dreadful awe and reverence. Literature and cinema have fanned the flames of our imagination regarding these legendary asylums for early Christians. In fact, the catacombs were not used as secret refuges for Christians fleeing from persecution. The ancient Romans had great respect for the dead and Roman law protected their places of burial. From the fourth century BC, official statutes had dictated that graves be outside the city walls. All – even Christian – burial grounds were registered, and thus known to and safeguarded by the Roman authorities. For these reasons the catacombs were not appropriate as Christian hiding places. As very early Christian cemeteries, however, they do provide us with first-hand testimony of belief and customs in the primitive Roman Church.

The catacombs took their name from a particular site along the Appian Way, a well-known hollow, probably a deserted tufa quarry, about two miles from the city gate. Here, from the first to the fourth centuries, Christians developed an extensive underground cemetery known as *ad catacumbas*, or 'cemetery at the hollow place', later known as the Catacomb of St Sebastian.

Since St Sebastian was the only catacomb which was not covered up and forgotten in the Middle Ages, it became the synonym for all others rediscovered at a later date. Apparently the term 'catacomb' was not used until medieval times for the Christian graves of this area. Pagan Romans called their burial grounds by the Greek word 'necropoles', meaning 'cities of the dead'. In contrast, early Christians preferred the word 'cemetery', from the Greek word for 'to sleep', emphasizing that Christian dead were only sleeping, while awaiting their final resurrection.

The earliest Christians were often poor and buried their dead in the midst of open pagan cemeteries, along with other

The Good Shepherd, the most frequent subject of very early Christian art, is shown here in a wall fresco in the Catacomb of Domitilla.

common people. St Peter, for example, was entombed near Nero's Circus (now inside Vatican city state), where he was martyred. Afterwards, many Christians wished to be interred near the saint's grave, and a large cemetery grew up around his tomb. Later in the first century, Christianity spread to other classes, and Christians with private property buried their dead in family tombs, usually above-ground.

By the middle of the second century, many prosperous and patrician families had been converted to Christianity, and they extended their private cemeteries, excavated on villas and estates, to their Christian brethren. At that time, Christians began digging their graves below ground. Because of Rome's demographic surge and a gradual change in funeral rites from cremation to inhumation, land for burial was becoming scarce and expensive. Increasingly, Christians also needed to keep a low profile. During the era of persecutions, from the first to the fourth centuries, the number of Christian dead swelled massively, and so did the number of their graves.

When Constantine legalized Christianity in AD313, Christians continued to be buried in the catacombs out of devotion to the martyrs, and basilicas and monuments were built to mark the sites. The fourth-century Pope Damasus (366–84) was especially devoted to the early saints; he located martyrs' graves, composed verse inscriptions for their tombs, and transformed the catacombs into popular and venerated shrines.

Destruction by barbarian invaders, the 'translation' by ninth-century Popes of saints' and martyrs' relics to safer city churches, neglect, abandonment, and eventual oblivion characterized the catacombs' fate in later centuries. There was only intermittent rediscovery and attention to these monuments ('itineraries' written for pilgrims in the seventh century) until the consistent archaeological excavations of Giovanni Battista de Rossi in the pontificate of Pius IX (1846–78).

The catacombs have always been considered the cradle of the Christian Church. Those kilometre-long burial galleries, with their simple tomb inscriptions and brightly frescoed walls are our direct link with the threatened but steadfast first Christian community in Rome.

This underground gallery in the Catacomb of St Sebastian has hundreds of wall tombs for the burial of poorer Christians during the age of persecutions.

THE CATACOMB OF ST SEBASTIAN
The Apostles' Traces

Apart from its reputation as Rome's first Christian catacomb, St Sebastian offers the pilgrim two other important discoveries. It was the burial place and shrine of one of early Christianity's most popular martyrs. It also contains an archaeological mystery – traces of the Apostles Peter and Paul, whose presence here was venerated for only a short period in Christian history.

EVOKING EARLY CHRISTIANITY

St Sebastian is located at the corner of the Old Appian Way and Rome's ritual pilgrimage route, the road of Sette Chiese, or Seven Churches. Sometime during the first millennium, pious pilgrims began the custom of visiting Rome's four major basilicas, sometimes in a single day. Later, in the sixteenth century, three other basilicas were added to the itinerary, and the road which led from one basilica to another was called Sette Chiese. The last basilica was St Sebastian, built over the catacomb.

This sacred spot is ideal for beginning a pilgrimage through the churches of Rome. Few other Roman sites are as rich in early Christian memories. Poplars and umbrella pines, interspersed with ruined tombs and mausoleums, march along the ancient highway. The visitor can almost hear the tramping imperial legions, off to conquer outlying provinces.

A procession of Christians on the Appian Way around AD61, greeting the Apostle Paul upon his entrance into Rome, is described in the Acts of the Apostles 28: 14–15. Nearby,

according to legend, Christ appeared to St Peter as he fled from the Mamertine prison. A small chapel down the road marks the spot where the Apostle asked Jesus, 'Domine quo vadis?' (Lord, where are you going?) Jesus's reply, that he was entering Rome for a second crucifixion, convinced St Peter to return to his flock – and certain martyrdom. Early Christian families walked this route to bury their friends, relatives and martyred dead in underground graves outside the city walls. Many bought refreshments for a discreet banquet in honour of the deceased.

St Sebastian was considered the first catacomb, and gave its appellation to all the others. It is a confusing archaeological site and only a very limited section is open for visiting. But despite the uncertainty surrounding its history, the following chronology has been conjectured by scholars and archaeologists.

Perhaps as early as the first century, the Christian Catacomb of St Sebastian began in the galleries of the tufa pit on the Appian Way. Next to the depression stood two country villas and a series of impressive pagan tombs, suggesting that wealthy converts may have allowed the Christians to build on the land. By the third century, the Christians' underground cemetery was extensive and well known. The site became even more famous because of a much-frequented sanctuary (see below), and as the shrine of the martyr St Sebastian. In the fourth century a great basilica was constructed over the catacombs, perhaps by Constantine.

THE VISIT

St Sebastian is entered through an open courtyard, porch and a seventeenth-century façade. At this point visitors will undoubtedly be accompanied by a guide, who leads them along the dank tufa passages, on three different levels, where thousands of *loculi* (rectangular graves) were hollowed into the walls for common Christian burials. Family burial chambers (*cubicoli*) open out of the maze of tunnels; these have larger arched graves (*arcosoli*) for several family members, and are

Above: The façade of the basilica of S. Sebastiano. The original church, built by the Emperor Constantine above the Catacomb of St Sebastian in the fourth century, was completely restructured in the Baroque era.

Right: This finely worked sarcophagus (called the Sarcophagus of Lot) was made for a wealthy Christian couple and is now in the Catacomb of St Sebastian.

often decorated with frescoes or inscriptions. At several points, ancient shafts (*lucenari*) allow light and air into the tunnels.

In one chamber guides usually point out symbols of the dove, the fish, and the inscription for the child 'Libera', who died in AD360 at the age of three years and two days. A touching wall-drawing of a child appears below; she stands with tiny outstretched arms, between a lamb and a dove. In one of the galleries we find the elaborately carved 'Lot Sarcophagus', named for its description of the Old Testament episode. The sarcophagus came from one of the wealthier Christian tombs built near the later fourth-century basilica.

The catacomb's most venerated martyr was a Christian soldier in the Praetorian Guard of Diocletian (284–305). Sentenced to death and shot by archers of his own company, Sebastian was nursed back to health by the pious matron Irene. He recovered, only to be clubbed to death, and was buried by another devoted lady, Lucina, on the Appian Way. His former crypt on the lower level (his remains have been transferred to the basilica above) still contains its original sarcophagus and a marble bust, attributed to the Baroque sculptor Gianlorenzo Bernini, of Sebastian as an extremely handsome arrow-pierced youth.

Next is the surprising *piazzuola*, or subterranean piazza, with its three richly decorated second-century mausoleums. The first tomb, according to an inscription, belonged to Marcus Clodius Hermes, and has lovely Pompeii-style frescoes on the walls and ceilings. Some scholars interpret a few of these paintings as Christian symbols: the Good Shepherd with his flock; the multiplication of the loaves; grapevines and opulent vases of fruits as symbols of paradise. The two other tombs have magnificent, perfectly preserved stucco ceilings, which appear as fresh as if they were carved yesterday and are almost Baroque in style. In fact they have been here for nearly two millennia. Here archaeologists also found some Christian graffiti.

Apparently these large elegant tombs were covered by sand in the third century for construction of what was St Sebastian's most important, and most mysterious, monument, the Memoria Apostolorum.

REMEMBERING THE APOSTLES

One level above the *piazzuola* are some tablets with graffiti on the walls. This area is still underground, but archaeologists maintain that at one time it was an open-air trapezoidal terrace *(triclinium)* with covered loggias, benches along two sides and stairs leading to a well below – built on top of the sand-covered *piazzuola*. This must have been a type of open-air taverna with country views. In fact, Christian mourners burying or visiting their dead in the catacombs had to trek quite a way out of Rome, so they brought refreshments with them, and shared them here, as a sort of remembrance feast (*refrigerium*).

There are hundreds of graffiti references here to the Apostles Peter and Paul. And in fact, Roman historians know that around the middle of the third century, an intense cult to the memory of Peter and Paul began at some point along the Appian Way. But why here, when Peter was buried at the Vatican and Paul on the Via Ostiense? This is a mystery, but most scholars offer the following explanation.

In 257 Valerian (Emperor 253–9) began a rigorous persecution of Christians, forbidding them to celebrate the sacraments or assemble for burying their dead. Since the Apostles' tombs were strictly patrolled, the Christians may have secretly transferred their remains to this less-known cemetery (in 258).

This site, dating from the mid-third century, has always been known as the Memoria Apostolorum. Many of the graffiti inscriptions, in both Latin and Greek, are personal invocations to Peter and Paul ('Peter and Paul pray for Victor'; 'I, Thomas Caelius, have taken refreshment here in honour of Peter and Paul'). All this supports the assumption that the Apostles' relics were temporarily moved here during Valerian's raids.

LOOKING FORWARDS AND BACKWARDS

Soon after Constantine (306–37) legalized Christianity, the Apostles' remains were evidently returned to their former shrines. In the fourth century a great basilica was built, perhaps by Constantine himself, over the Memoria Apostolorum and called the Basilica Apostolorum, to recall the earlier sanctuary. By the Middle Ages, however, the basilica had changed its allegiance, and its name, to St Sebastian, powerful protector against the plague in medieval times.

The early Christian basilica was completely restructured by Cardinal Scipione Borghese (1576–1633) in 1609, and that dull and sterile seventeenth-century church, with its single hall-like white nave and shiny floors, is the one that survives today. There are things to see: an elaborate gilded wood ceiling; Annibale Carracci's painting, on the right of the entrance, of the medieval St Bridget of Sweden (1303–73), who frequently prayed here, as did the early Doctor of the Church, St Jerome (340–420), and Rome's male patron saint, the sixteenth-century St Philip Neri (1515–95), shown, respectively, opposite St Bridget and towards the front of the church; St Sebastian's altar (to the left of the entrance), with an overly ecstatic marble sculpture by Antonio Giorgetti (d. 1670).

Perhaps visitors can recover some of their earlier awe by visiting the 'chapel of the relics', to the right of the entrance. Here, between an arrow that presumably wounded St

Sebastian and the column to which he was bound, are the supposed imprints of Christ's feet, left, according to legend, when the Saviour met Peter fleeing Rome along the Appian Way. This stone (originally kept in the Quo Vadis chapel, mentioned earlier) has the carved outlines of two feet, and the measurements of the footprints correspond almost exactly with the one foot imprinted upon what tradition has held to be Christ's burial sheet, the Holy Shroud of Turin.

This Byzantine-style fresco of Christ Pantocrator (Omnipotent) dates from the ninth century and is found in the Crypt of St Cecilia, in the St Calixtus Catacombs.

converted Christian members allowed Christian burials on their land. Under Calixtus (third century) this subterranean graveyard, comprising at least five underground cemeteries, originally independent from one another, was organized and administered by the early Church. By the fourth century it was one of Rome's most extensive catacombs – eventually extending over an area of almost twenty kilometres, on four different levels of three to thirty metres in depth, and including approximately half a million tombs.

The St Calixtus Catacombs owe their creation, and later their rediscovery after long centuries of oblivion, to two remarkable individuals.

St Calixtus came from a family of Christian slaves in third-century Rome. His extraordinary talent for accounting and administration earned him his freedom and a position with a wealthy banker. Rumours of fraud and embezzlement or maybe simple envy caused Calixtus to be sent off to the Sardinian mines, but during a general amnesty the resilient young Christian appeared again in Rome, where he convinced the reigning Pope Zephyrinus (199–217) to appoint him chief deacon and administrator of the large underground cemetery which now bears his name.

After serving as the catacombs' guardian and administrator for almost twenty years, Calixtus himself became an important Pope (217–22). He established one of the first house churches (now the basilica of S. Maria in Trastevere), and was martyred by being thrown into a well near that same spot. Calixtus was not buried in his catacombs, but in the smaller cemetery of St Calepodius on the Via Aurelia.

Over the centuries the catacombs, except those of St Sebastian, were covered up and forgotten – barring some isolated discoveries in the fifteenth and sixteenth centuries. Then in 1849 an enterprising young archaeologist named Giovanni Battista de Rossi (c. 1822–94) tripped over a broken slab of marble in a vineyard on the Appian Way. Reading the inscription fragment 'NELIUS MARTYR', he guessed that the missing part named Pope Cornelius (251–3), who was known to have been martyred and buried in a catacomb nearby. With the help and encouragement of Pope Pius IX, de Rossi began digging in the open fields and eventually excavated this vast cemetery complex.

GALLERY TOMBS

Inside the catacombs a narrow staircase, originally built by Pope Damasus (366–84) in the fourth century, leads down to

THE CATACOMBS OF ST CALIXTUS
The First Official Catacomb

This pilgrimage to Christianity's earliest underground burial places began with a visit to the catacomb from which all others take their name. The next stop is the St Calixtus Complex, oldest official cemetery of the Roman Church.

PAST AND PRESENT

Not far from the St Sebastian Catacomb, slightly nearer the city walls, the Catacombs of St Calixtus are reached by a poplar-lined drive off the Appian Way. The St Calixtus Catacombs probably originated around AD150 as the private open-air burial ground of the noble Cecili family, whose

corridor a pile of these has been gathered behind a glass case. It is not hard to imagine the love and faith with which the early Christians buried their dead in these dark tunnels – humble relatives, nameless slaves, hundreds of persecuted and martyred faithful. The inconspicuous groups arrived from Rome along the Appian Way, accompanied by a revered priest or deacon, to officiate at a simple ceremony and say the final prayers.

THE CRYPT OF THE POPES

Around a corner, in one of the narrow passages, the visitor will come upon the Crypt of the Popes. Here, in 1854, de Rossi stumbled into a marble-pillared chamber filled with rubble and found, amid the debris, fragments of inscriptions suggesting the burial places of several early Popes.

Today the tombstones of five third-century, mostly martyred, Popes have been re-erected: St Pontian (d. 235), who died in the Sardinian mines; the Greek St Anterus (d. 235), who perished in prison: St Fabian (d. 250), who reorganized and strengthened the Church in a period of peace and was then martyred during the Decian persecutions; St Lucius I (d. 254), who spent part of his pontificate in exile; and St Eutychian (d. 283), who escaped persecution but struggled with early heresies. According to Pope Damasus' inscription in the crypt, Pope St Sixtus II (257–8) was beheaded and buried here along with four of his deacons. Some sources claim that the crypt earlier contained the remains of three other third-century Popes and eight bishops. Most of the inscriptions are in Greek, the official language of the early Church.

THE SHRINE OF ST CECILIA

Next to the Crypt of the Popes is the shrine of St Cecilia, one of the most popular early women martyrs. Cecilia's story will be told in a later chapter. In brief, she was of the patrician Cecili family, upon whose estates the Calixtus Complex was excavated, and was first buried in these catacombs and then moved to her former Trastevere house. The most wondrous aspect of St Cecilia's history is that when her grave was opened during St Clement VIII's pontificate (1592–1605), her body was found to be perfectly intact. The artist Stefano Maderno was there, and immediately made a beautiful marble statue. A

dark labyrinthine corridors winding in all directions. In the rough tufa rock walls, rectangular graves have been carved, honeycomb-style, on four different levels. These were the tombs of poorer Christians, whose bodies, wrapped in shrouds and sprinkled with lime, were placed in the shelf-like recesses. A tragic forty per cent of these nooks are very small, indicating the graves of children or babies. In fact, contemporary historians, Tertullian among others, recorded that early Christians collected newborns from refuse dumps and gave them decent burials here.

Tiles and marble slabs are plastered along the walls, some with simple names and dates in primitive Greek letters. These originally covered the tombs – now all open and empty – which were tightly sealed with cement or mortar. Small round slots between the graves were for oil lamps; at the end of one

Above: The Crypt of the Popes in the St Calixtus Catacombs, the burial place of at least five third-century Popes, was discovered in 1854 by archaeologist G. B. de Rossi.

Right: The Crypt of St Cecilia in the St Calixtus Catacombs. The statue shown here is a modern copy of Stefano Maderno's work, designed when the saint's body was rediscovered completely intact in the year 1599.

copy (the original is in the Trastevere church), funded by the twentieth-century American, Edith Cecilia McBride, now lies in the Calixtian Crypt. The shrine is also decorated with some interesting eighth- to ninth-century frescoes: a wide-eyed Christ with a huge Bible, and the famous *orante*, a female figure with outstretched arms, representing, according to Church historians, the beatific soul after death.

THE CHAMBERS OF THE SACRAMENTS

Here and there along the corridors are small chambers with several floor tombs, vault ceilings and delicate fresco decorations. These were family mausoleums, called 'crypts of the sacraments'. The third-century paintings convey a light and almost happy spirit, expressing a serene confidence that the families reunited here in death will enjoy peace together in heaven.

The scenes in these chambers often represent early Christianity's two main sacraments – Baptism and the Eucharist – or scenes from the Old and New Testaments. Everything is symbolic here: Holy Communion is prefigured by Christ's multiplication of the loaves; Jonah and the whale symbolize death and resurrection.

ARCHIVES OF FAITH

In these catacombs we find many secret Christian signs, known only to the faithful: the anchor as hope; a palm branch for martyrdom; fruit and flower baskets for paradise; a peacock for immortality; a ship as the Church. The most ubiquitous catacomb image is that of the Good Shepherd. Christ is referred to by a monogram composed of the first two letters of the Greek spelling for Jesus Christ, or by a fish (see page 28). Nowhere is he shown on the Cross.

EARLY CHRISTIAN SYMBOLS

The symbols used by the early Christian Church in Rome have an almost naive candour which appeals even today. Carved into the walls of underground cemeteries and gathering places in Christian homes, these signs are emblematic. The faithful were keeping a low profile in the age of persecutions, and the simple pictures refer only indirectly to Jesus and to Christian tenets of faith. The sign of the cross was not widely used until the sixth century. For identification, Christians often used the fish symbol, the explanation being that the first letters of the Greek words for 'Jesus Christ, Son of God, the Saviour,' formed the Greek word fish (*ichthys*). Symbols from nature such as the dove, the vine and grapes, sheep and shepherds suggest to us today the serene and almost 'happy' attitude with which believers regarded their life on earth and in the world to come.

 The Alpha and Omega, the first and last letters in the Greek alphabet, stand for Christ as the beginning and end of all things.

 The first two Greek letters for the name of Christ (*chi*=x; and *rho*=p).

 The peacock is a symbol of immortality.

 The dove, a sign of Christ's peace and reconciliation.

 The vine and grapes symbolize unity with Christ, who said: 'I am the vine; you are the branches.'

 The Good Shepherd, a frequent image of Christ.

 The anchor represents hope in Christ.

 The frond of the palm, a sign of victory, usually stood for any Christian martyrdom.

 The *orante* represents the resurrected soul.

 Sign of the Eucharist.

Designs by Stefano Navarrini, *Inside the Vatican.*

THE CATACOMBS OF DOMITILLA AND PRISCILLA
Courageous Roman Matrons

Excavated tombs in the Catacombs of Domitilla and Priscilla confirm a progressive Christianization of earlier pagan cemeteries. In these subterranean tunnels pilgrims can become eyewitnesses to the emergence of Christianity as part of Roman society.

DOMITILLA'S CATACOMB

Another road leading out of Rome, the Via Ardeatina, was lined with tombs and mausoleums slightly less imposing than those of the nearby Appian Way. Here the first-century patrician Roman matron, Flavia Domitilla, wife (or niece, according to some historians) of the martyred Christian Consul Flavius Clemens and niece of the Emperor Domitian (81–96), granted some of her personal property to her freed slaves for Christian burials. Four first-century inscriptions found on the property give evidence of Domitilla's ownership of the estate and of her generous donation.

In AD96, the Emperor Domitian exiled the openly Christian Domitilla (historians of the time reported she had been accused of 'Jewish practices') to the island of Ponza, where she died a slow, lonely death – she is thus sometimes considered a martyr.

Scholars tell us that around AD100 the small cemeteries, located at some distance from one another on Domitilla's property, sprouted underground galleries on several levels and developed, during the next three centuries, into the vast Catacomb of Domitilla. The Catacomb of Priscilla had a similar beginning.

One of early Christianity's greatest strengths was its appeal to all classes of Roman society. The downtrodden, slaves and soldiers, but also prosperous aristocrats, accepted the Christian message of redemption through Christ. The legal position of married Roman women, who could own and dispose of property in their own right, was a great boon for early Christianity.

IN THE PRESENCE OF SAINTS AND MARTYRS

Most catacombs were founded because of the generosity of wealthy Roman converts. Their amazing expansion was usually due to the presence of beloved saints and martyrs among the buried dead. Between the end of the third century and the beginning of the fourth, the bodies of two martyrs, Nereus and Achilleus, were placed in a crypt in the third level of Domitilla's cemetery. According to tradition, these two soldiers of the Praetorian Guard of Diocletian (284–305), accustomed to executing Christians, were themselves converted, martyred by decapitation, and buried in Domitilla's Catacomb.

Soon an intense cult developed in their honour and graves mushroomed around their tombs. Pope Damasus built an

Left: Many staircases in the catacombs' underground galleries were built after the legalization of Christianity by Pope Damasus (366–84).

Above: A brightly-painted *cubiculum* (chamber for family tombs) in the Catacomb of Domitilla.

underground basilica on the site, which was enlarged by Pope Siricius (384–99). Today, in the reconstructed basilica, we can see an apparently very early sculpture of Achilleus' decapitation; it graces a column which originally supported Damasus' altar, but now stands alone among sarcophagus fragments.

Another moving illustration of *retro sanctus* (behind the saints) burials may be seen in a crypt behind the basilica apse. Here, a vivid fourth-century wall fresco shows the deceased Veneranda being introduced into paradise by St Petronilla, whose tomb must have been located nearby. This Petronilla has caused much controversy and debate. Was she merely a pious woman, and not a saint at all, as some claim? Or was she, as popular legend holds, St Peter's daughter?

A tradition dating from a second-century copy of the apocryphal *Acts of Peter* relates that the Apostle had a paralysed daughter. Entreated by the crowds, St Peter healed the girl, but only temporarily; he let her walk around for a bit, then restored her paralysis as beneficial for her soul. We have sixth-century accounts of pilgrims visiting the Domitilla Catacomb to venerate the grave of Petronilla, Peter's daughter. They describe her sarcophagus, with her name and the inscription 'dearest daughter'.

In 757 Petronilla's remains were solemnly transported to St Peter's Basilica and placed in a rotunda next to the left transept. A twin rotunda on the right transept was dedicated to Peter's brother, St Andrew, so there seems to have been some family connection. Somehow Petronilla was adopted as the patroness of the Franks, and her mausoleum eventually became the French monarchy's official chapel in Rome (for which Michelangelo's *Pietà* was commissioned by a French ambassador). Today's visitor to St Peter's will not find Petronilla's shrine, however. In the splendid new Renaissance–Baroque structure, her rotunda disappeared without a trace; her sarcophagus was placed upside down on the floor of the Blessed Sacrament chapel. Petronilla now has her own small altar, to the right of the Papal Throne (and Clement X's

Left above: It was on the Appian Way leading out of Rome that many early Christians buried their dead in underground cemeteries we now call catacombs.

Left below: This funerary inscription in the Catacomb of Domitilla shows fish framing an anchor, signifying Christians' hope in Christ.

Above: A candlelit vigil held in the fourth-century underground basilica of the Catacomb of Domitilla.

memorial); above is a mosaic copy of a painting by Guercino (1591–1666), *The Glory of St Petronilla*.

CHRISTIANITY OVERTAKES PAGANISM

In Rome, Christians were only a small and persecuted sect in the years following Christ's death. Throughout the second and third centuries, the courage and devotion of Christian martyrs attracted more and more converts to the new faith. The Domitilla and Priscilla Catacombs attest to the amazingly rapid growth of the early Church.

Above ground on the Flavian estate, archaeologists have identified several first-century *columbaria* (tombs with cremation urns) and even a luxurious first-century pagan mausoleum. Under these, the first subterranean nucleus of second- to early third-century burial vaults is mostly pagan. Yet among the classical cavorting cupids we find grapevine decorations, which can be Paleo-Christian symbols, and Old Testament scenes with Daniel and Noah. Beyond this earliest nucleus, the Domitilla Catacomb – with 174,000 graves carved out along seventeen kilometres of galleries on four levels – appears to be entirely Christian.

In the increasingly decadent late Empire, Christianity brought a new message of faith, love and everlasting life. In place of a distant multitude of gods, it offered a personal Redeemer, the Son of God, who became human to save mankind. The most popular of all catacomb motifs is that of the Good Shepherd. The Catacomb of Domitilla has, perhaps, the most beautiful and varied renditions of this comforting theme – from Greek-style youths to wiser, bearded types – on basilica sarcophagi and frescoed ceilings. One chamber in this catacomb hosts the family tombs of a certain Diogenes, identified as a catacomb grave-digger (*fossore*) by both his inscription and his pictured tools. Christians believed all equal before God; even a humble worker could have a finely decorated tomb.

THE CATACOMB OF PRISCILLA

On the ancient Via Salaria, or Salt Road, leading out of Rome to the Adriatic Sea, archaeological excavations have uncovered the remains of a first-century villa with gardens and underground water cisterns about two kilometres from the city gates. This was the property of the wealthy Acilian family; one family member, the senator and former consul Acilius Glabrione, had been exiled by the Emperor Domitian (81–96) for practising Christianity. (According to the second-century Roman historian Suetonius, Acilius was deported 'for trying to introduce new things'.) Later, in the early second century, another family member, Priscilla, built a *hypogeum* (underground burial vault) on this spot, and set aside an adjacent area as a Christian cemetery.

Here, beneath the extensive villa, excavators found, in the so-called 'Acilian vaults', burial inscriptions with the titles 'most illustrious M. Acilius and Priscilla', indicating that persons of senatorial rank had occupied the tombs. Nearby, an *arenario*, or subterranean quarry area, had been used since the second century for poorer Christians' burials, with hundreds of narrow rectangular graves (*loculi*) carved into the tufa galleries. This area, along with the *cryptoporticus* mentioned below, became the nucleus of the Catacomb of Priscilla, which developed in the third and fourth centuries to become one of the largest Christian cemeteries in Rome.

As in Domitilla's Catacomb, the Catacomb of St Priscilla expanded primarily because of the saints and martyrs who were

Above: The *cryptoporticus*, probably the underground storage area of a Roman villa, was one of the earliest Christian sections in the Catacomb of Priscilla.

Right: Also in the Catacomb of Priscilla, this *orante* figure represented the resurrected soul.

particularly venerated here. These included: Pope Marcellinus (296–304), martyred in Diocletian's persecutions; Pope Marcellus (308–9), who perished under Maxentius; the martyrs Felix and Philip, Crescentianus, Prisca, Prudentiana and Praxedes, and a group of 365 other martyrs – all unidentified. The visitor should look out for the graves of these holy personages, located at different points throughout the catacombs.

Priscilla's oldest section (besides the areas discussed above) is probably the *cryptoporticus*, a pillared and vaulted hall which may have belonged to the cellars of the late first-century Acilian villa. This formed the main artery of the underground cemetery, with tomb chambers on each side, and galleries extending outward. The catacomb was vastly expanded and embellished in the fourth century, as fervent devotion drew the faithful to the martyrs' tombs.

Several interesting paintings throughout Priscilla's Catacomb give an idea of Christian religious practices. In one crypt, a deceased woman's exemplary life is portrayed in a series of simple frescoes: marriage (a priest blesses the bride, who holds the tablet of marriage duties, and the groom, who hands over the red-edged nuptial veil); maternity (a mother with a child on her knee); and blessed afterlife (an ecstatic standing *orante* figure as the resurrected soul).

In the Greek Chapel (so-called because of inscriptions found there), the central wall fresco shows a Eucharistic feast (seven persons, including a veiled woman, sit at a banquet table, with a wine chalice, and plates of fish and bread loaves, while the bearded celebrant prepares to break the bread). The stone benches along the chamber walls might well have been used for such a sacramental meal.

This burial chamber has many of the early Church's favourite story symbols: Hebrews in the fiery furnace (faith); Moses striking water from a rock (Baptism); Susanna and the Elders (the persecuted Church): the phoenix in the flames (resurrection of the body); Christ healing the sick (penitence). Of all the Bible scenes, those of Jonah and the whale and Daniel and the lions appear most frequently in the catacombs. The meaning is obvious: the example of salvation and the hope of eternal life.

Priscilla's Catacomb also contains what is perhaps the very earliest representation of the Virgin Mary. A gallery ceiling fresco (very difficult to see) shows the Virgin Mother presenting the Child Saviour to a prophet (Balaam? Isaiah?), who points to a star above their heads. Although images of the Adoration of the Magi occur in many catacombs, this Madonna is unique – and very significant. Prophecy and fulfilment are shown occurring at the same time, and Mary is exalted as the Mother of the Redeemer.

In the declining Roman Empire, the Christian community stood apart by its simple lifestyle and strong ethical basis. In these catacombs it is not difficult to sense the appeal Christianity must have had in a society thirsting for spiritual renewal.

ROME'S TITULAR CHURCHES:HOUSE CONGREGATIONS IN THE ERA OF PERSECUTIONS

Even today a visitor to the churches of Rome can step into rooms where, two millennia before our times, the first Christians professed their new faith and often awaited suffering and death.

Here, small clandestine congregations, composed mostly of Jewish tradesmen-converts, immigrant slaves and lower-class freedmen, gathered under the roofs of Roman patricians who had embraced the new religion. The early Christian assemblies may have listened to the Apostle Peter's first-hand descriptions of Christ's Crucifixion and Resurrection. They were encouraged by Paul's preaching, and later by circulating his letters, or other correspondence from abroad.

The faithful read the Scriptures, participated in the Eucharist and communal prayer, and welcomed and baptized new members. Often the congregations were raided by Roman authorities and, refusing to sacrifice to pagan gods, were hastened away for detention, torture and death.

House churches were mentioned in very early Christian writings. The Apostle Paul several times alluded to their existence in first-century Christian Rome. In Romans 16:3–5 he greeted his friends Prisca and Aquila 'and the church which is in their house'. We know that Paul led a congregation which met in his rented residence (Acts 28:30). In the second century, St Justin (100–165) records that Christians of his day met in private dwellings.

A private house, or parts of a house, used for early Christian worship came to be known as a *domus ecclesiae* (house church). Since the proprietor's name was generally inscribed on a marble slab or wooden plate, known as the *titulus* (title), above the entrance, the house churches came later to be referred to as *tituli*, and to be named after their owners or donors.

There were twenty-five *tituli* – Rome's original parish churches. The *Liber Pontificalis* (a collection of Papal biographies composed in the sixth century from earlier sources) relates that Pope Cletus (76–88), following St Peter's instructions, ordained twenty-five presbyters and that Pope Evaristus (97–105) assigned these senior priests to twenty-five titular churches. In the early fourth century the parish churches were confirmed by Pope Marcellus (308–9) as religious community

According to legend, the basilica of S. Clemente began as a Christian gathering place in the first-century villa of a Roman consul.

centres and seats of Church administration. All twenty-five were certified by the Church synods of 499 and 595.

Archaeological excavations reveal gradual remodelling of many early house churches. A good number of these became official Church property around the same time as the Roman Church gained ownership of the Calixtus Catacomb. By the third century, dividing walls in many house churches had been knocked down to provide hall-like rooms for expanding congregations, as well as areas for storage and neighbourhood distribution centres.

In the fourth century, with the triumph of Christianity over paganism, large basilicas were built over the earlier house churches for the liturgical purposes of the expanding Christian population. And by the sixth century all the *tituli* were named after saints (sometimes by simply 'sanctifying' the original owner).

The duties of titular priests soon included serving the Christian cemeteries, and later the major basilicas. Because they were thus 'incardinated' (or seconded) to different churches, the priests were known as Cardinal priests. Eventually many Cardinal priests became Papal assistants and the title took on increasing importance and prestige. Even today, each new Cardinal is assigned a titular church.

Amazingly, the sites of all twenty-five original titular churches still exist and can be visited by the pilgrim to Rome today. And despite transformations down through the ages, each one contains important archaeological or artistic traces of the first Christian gathering places.

S. MARIA IN TRASTEVERE
Serving Rome's Oldest Christian Community

A sanctuary originally built for Rome's first Christian community is the first stop on this pilgrimage to some of Rome's oldest titular churches. Located in the city's picturesque quarter 'across the Tiber' (Trastevere), the basilica of S. Maria in Trastevere had its origin – in the dark days of persecutions and catacombs – as a house church used by the first Roman converts from the Jewish faith.

ROME'S FIRST CHRISTIAN COMMUNITY

According to a census taken during the reign of the Emperor Augustus (29BC–AD14), the Trastevere district, across the river from the city proper (zone No. XIV, called *Trans Tyberim*), was the largest and most populous in the imperial capital. The quarter had always been inhabited by a large number of foreigners who came to service the Tiber's last dock before the busy seaport of Ostia. There were Greek craftsmen, sailors from Ravenna, Syrian and Egyptian traders. But the Jewish community was by far the largest – estimated at about 50,000 in the first century AD.

These humble Jewish families, merchants in wine, oil, grain, and sometimes marble, were in regular contact with their homeland; they certainly heard about Christ's teachings, and some must have been sympathetic. In fact, the Acts of the Apostles 2:10 reported that 'visitors from Rome' were present in Jerusalem on the day of Pentecost, and could have brought news of the event back to Rome.

Historical records suggest that Christians were a significant presence in the Jewish community at that time and that their beliefs were causing trouble in the synagogues. According to the Roman chronicler Suetonius, the Emperor Claudius (41–54) expelled a large number of Jews in AD49 for 'disputes concerning Chrestus', probably a misspelling of 'Christ'.

The Apostles were able to make their first converts among Trastevere's large Jewish population. According to tradition, St Peter came to Rome c.AD42, residing first in the home of the Senator Pudens, and then in the villa of Aquila and Prisca on the Aventine Hill. From the Aventine, Peter descended to preach to the numerous and receptive Jewish immigrants in Trastevere; many of these converted and joined together to form Rome's first Christian community.

St Paul's evangelization, c.AD61–5, also found fertile ground among the lower-class, culturally diverse Trasteverini. The Christian cult flourished and expanded here. It was in Trastevere that imperial guards hunted down most of their Christian victims for martyrdom in the Roman arenas. It was from Trastevere that most Christian families travelled secretly to bury their dead in catacombs along the Appian Way.

The beautiful mosaic in the apse of S. Maria in Trastevere is an example of a twelfth-century motif: the Virgin Mary enthroned on an equal footing beside her son, Jesus Christ.

DIVINE PROPHECIES
AND A MARTYRED POPE

Many Romans claim that S. Maria in Trastevere is their city's earliest church. Legend and history confer on it undeniable spiritual significance, and, not least, it is one of the loveliest spots in Rome.

Numerous historians assert that this ancient titulus was the first church in the world to be dedicated to the Virgin Mary. In fact, legends associate the site with the birth of Christ. Thirty-eight years before the Nativity, a jet of pure oil reportedly sprang from the spot where the church now stands, running all day long into the River Tiber nearby. Although modern scientists investigating the case have found that a small volcanic eruption could have caused the oil flow, St Jerome wrote in the fourth century that the Jewish community of that time had interpreted the event as a sign that God's grace would soon flow into the world.

There are many reasons to give credence to S. Maria in Trastevere's 'earliest church' claim. Trastevere's first Christian converts, recalling the miraculous fountain of oil as a prophecy of Christ's birth, established an early meeting place on the sacred spot (now marked by a sign and small window inside the church and by the name of an adjoining street).

The martyrdom of one of early Christianity's most important Popes gave the site even further prestige. According to tradition, the leader of the original church located where S. Maria in Trastevere now stands was no other than Pope Calixtus I (217–22), encountered earlier as the administrator of the catacomb which still bears his name. Calixtus was reportedly jailed, flogged and martyred by an angry pagan mob by being thrown from his house into a well near S. Maria, where a more recent church and piazza in his name now mark the spot.

Calixtus' original grave has been identified in the Aurelian

Way catacomb where Trastevere Christians buried their dead. He was loved and revered by Rome's earliest Christians, who, according to tradition, gathered in large numbers in the house church he founded. Later histories mention that in the third century the Emperor Alexander Severus (222–35) gave to Christians as a tolerated place of worship the *taverna meritoria*, a hospice for retired or wounded Roman soldiers, located on the site of the prophetic fountain of oil.

All this is a bit confusing. But it seems likely that, due to the importance of the Trastevere Christian community, imperial authorities permitted Calixtus' congregation to expand into the adjacent veterans' home (there could have been Christians among the soldiers). In any case, from then on the edifice was referred to as the *Titulus Calisti*, and could well have been the first place for public Christian worship in Rome.

By the fourth century legend and tradition give way to historical fact in descriptions of S. Maria in Trastevere. We have records for the construction of a large church dedicated to the Virgin Mary (denoted therein as the first of its kind) by Pope Julius I (337–52), and the building appeared in the list of titular churches compiled by the Council of 499. Even this comparatively late record would grant S. Maria in Trastevere the status of one of the oldest churches in Rome.

A MAGICAL SETTING

The piazza of S. Maria in Trastevere is always a magical scene. As in imperial days, the square is a gathering place for people from different countries – artists, writers and tourists who read their foreign newspapers in the sunny cafés across from the church. The Trasteverini, who pride themselves on being one of Rome's earliest and most '*popolare*' (in the sense of simple and down to earth) neighbourhood communities, meet to gossip after Mass and to watch their children chase balloons around the central fountain. On Sundays, weddings, first communions and local military concerts draw the local residents in bustling crowds to the ancient square.

Above the lively piazza, sparkling thirteenth-century mosaics parade lamp-bearing virgins in jewelled and golden robes across the church's medieval façade. And over the Neo-classical portal, built by Carlo Fontana in 1702, four Baroque statues of S. Maria's favoured saints, Calixtus, Cornelius, Pope

Julius and Calepodius (their relics are beneath the main altar inside), gesticulate gracefully in flowing robes.

S. Maria in Trastevere is a palimpsest of the spiritual and artistic history the church has experienced over the last 2,000 years. The front doors have stone cornices dating from the imperial age, and the granite pillars of the nave were taken from the Baths of Caracalla. Close inspection of the columns reveals the heads of several pagan female deities peering from their classical capitals.

Under the portal there are sarcophagi from the third and fourth centuries and some architectural decoration from the eighth and ninth centuries, when the church was first restored. The Medici coat-of-arms in a side chapel honours one of Italy's most powerful Renaissance families, while the Altemps Chapel, built by Martino Longhi the Elder in 1584–5, commemorates the Council of Trent, which ushered in the Catholic Counter-Reformation. The gilded ceiling dates from the seventeenth century, and the paintings of saints on the nave walls were done in the nineteenth century under Pope Pius IX (1846–78).

MARY'S CHURCH

The monument's prevailing character, however, is medieval. The church was almost completely rebuilt by Pope Innocent II (1130–43) around 1140. (He came from Trastevere's powerful Papareschi family and is buried in the left aisle of the church.) The profound spirituality of the twelfth-century world is evoked by the basilican interior (three aisles divided by twenty-one massive pillars supporting a flat wooden roof), the Romanesque campanile, the handsome mosaic pavement (redone in the nineteenth century), the sombre tomb of Trastevere's pre-eminent medieval Cardinal, Pietro Stefaneschi (d. 1417) – and, above all, the splendid mosaics over the altar.

It was in the twelfth century that the cult of Mary spread throughout Europe, as churches and cathedrals were built in her honour, and S. Maria's mosaics have a special place in the history of Marian worship. They are considered the first example of the 'glorification' of the Virgin, in which Mary is shown as a youthful and queenly spouse – rather than as a Madonna with Child – enthroned and on an equal footing with Christ the King. On Mary's right are St Calixtus, St

S. Maria in Trastevere, which had its origins as a house church built by the martyr Pope St Calixtus (217–22), is reportedly the first church dedicated to the Virgin Mary.

Lawrence, and Pope Innocent II, holding a model of his church; to Christ's left are St Peter, St Cornelius, Pope Julius I, and St Calepodius. Around the apse the thirteenth-century master Pietro Cavallini added another series of famous mosaics (*c.*1290) on the life of the Virgin. Over the main nave, in the centre of the coffered ceiling, is Domenichino's *Assumption of the Virgin*, painted in 1617.

A SENSE OF COMMUNITY

The sense of community which must have characterized St Calixtus' early Christian congregation is still evident in the parish of S. Maria in Trastevere today. The neighbourhood is one of the few in Rome to celebrate its own festival. During the *Festa di Noiantri* (meaning 'we others'), a large doll-like statue of the Madonna, dressed in a new gown every year, is paraded through the quarter's crowded streets. When the church's precious sixth- (or seventh-, no one is quite sure) century icon of the Madonna came 'home' in May 1993, after many years of restoration, the entire piazza was covered by a floral decoration representing the image. The painting was paraded with appropriate pomp and fanfare and displayed on a warm spring night in front of the illuminated basilica, before returning to its own chapel to the left of the main altar.

As in the days of early Christianity, the Trastevere parish is devoted to service to the city's poor. It is said that Rome's female patron saint, Frances of Rome (1384–1440), came to the basilica to pray for strength to assist the needy. Now the Community of Sant' Egidio, with its headquarters around the corner from the basilica's back door, is well known for its charitable activities among the city's hungry and homeless. The community runs a soup kitchen, feeding about 1,600 a day, and a centre for abandoned children – as well as a weekly communal prayer and Scripture reading service – where Rome's first Christian congregation would have felt quite at home.

S. PUDENZIANA AND S. PRASSEDE
Two Sister-martyrs Gather Peter's Converts
S. Maria in Trastevere has two rivals for the honour of 'oldest church in Rome'. For years, the churches of S. Pudenziana and S. Prassede were believed to be the sites of Rome's earliest centres of Christian worship. This is not surprising, since tradition holds that St Peter himself lived and taught in the original house congregations located here. In fact, the domestic churches were the *tituli* of two of the Apostle's first converts.

FEARLESSNESS AND FIDELITY
Around the year AD50, the Christian religion was outlawed and its followers were often martyred after the most atrocious tortures. In those days, Senator Pudens, an early convert to Christianity, had his residence in Rome's Vicus Patricius on the Esquiline Hill. Here, according to tradition, Pudens had given shelter to St Peter himself for seven years. After Pudens' martyrdom, Christians continued to gather here, ever more frequently and numerously, under the supervision of Pudens' faithful daughter Pudenziana.

This courageous Roman matron had a secret task. Together with her pious sister Prassede (Praxedes), she crept to spots where Christians had been martyred to collect their remains and sponge up their blood. The two women then deposited these in wells on Pudens' estate. Legend tells us that Prassede witnessed the slaughter of twenty-three Christian faithful in her own home, and that she and Pudenziana were both martyred soon after.

As usual, modern guidebooks point out that the above-related story has little historical basis. Or, at least, that archaeology and research cast doubt on any relationship between the legend and the site of churches now dedicated to the sister-saints. However, the force of tradition is still strong in this church.

The original *tituli* were named *Pudentianae* and *Praxedis*. In the Catacomb of Priscilla a plaque commemorates the burial of the Senator Pudens, who was mentioned by St Paul in his second letter to Timothy.

S. PUDENZIANA
The Apostle's Memory
The church of S. Pudenziana is located on the Esquiline Hill, on what was the Vicus Patricius (now Via Urbana), a street of patrician residences in classical times. The church is now below street level, and the first approach is often disappointing. From the outside only the Romanesque door-frame and bell-tower suggest the building's ancient origins. Over the main entrance, a charming sculptured frieze depicts St Pastor, Senator Pudens, Pudenziana and Prassede. From their eleventh-century lunettes, the wide-eyed sister-saints exhibit their collecting urns.

Inside the church, at the end of the left nave, is a chapel dedicated to St Peter. There is a marble inscription on the left wall which informs us that: 'This house was the first to give hospitality to St Peter.' Part of a wooden altar, where St Peter allegedly celebrated the Eucharist under Pudens' roof, is now

enclosed in the chapel's marble altar. An unbroken tradition links this chapel to an oratory, long since disappeared, built in the fifth century in Peter's memory.

In S. Pudenziana there is still much to remind the visitor of the First Apostle's presence – and of the courage and faith of Pudens and his family. Over the altar in St Peter's chapel, Giovanni Battista della Porta has sculpted the scene of *Christ Giving the Keys to St Peter* (1596). From here, a side door leads to the so-called Marian Oratory, where faded eleventh-century frescoes of Paul preaching, the baptism of Pudenziana's brothers Novatus and Timothy, and Pudenziana with Prassede and the Virgin are faintly visible.

On the church's back walls, unknown sixteenth-century artists have portrayed St Peter baptizing Pudens, and Pudens welcoming Sts Peter and Paul. Dome frescoes, executed by Cristoforo Roncalli in 1588, show Sts Peter, Paul, Pudens, Pudenziana, Prassede, Timothy and Novatus.

Finally, towards the front of the left aisle is the well into which, tradition claims, Sts Pudenziana and Prassede placed the remains of Christian martyrs. The sisters are also depicted in a chapel towards the back, painted by an anonymous sixteenth-century Tuscan artist: Prassede is shown gathering the martyrs' blood, as Pudenziana places a severed head in the well.

A CHURCH FOR ALL AGES
Tradition holds that Pope Pius I (*c*.142–*c*.155) made the

The apse mosaic in the church of S. Pudenziana is a stunning example of the classical style of art, which early Christians inherited from imperial Rome.

Pudens residence into a small church. Seventy years after Constantine's Edict of Milan (313) ended the persecution of Christians, the *Titulus Pudentianae* was transformed into an imposing Christian basilica. Dedicatory inscriptions found in the church revealed that construction was financed by 'Illiceus, Leopardus and the Presbyter Maximus', in the reign of Pope Siricius (384–99); decorations were completed during the Papacy of Pope St Innocent I (401–17).

Excavations have revealed that in the second century thermal baths were built above St Pudenziana's original first-century Roman residence, and that it was into this structure that the fourth-century church was built. Although this discovery has been used to refute the church's legendary origins, perhaps the Roman administration hoped to wipe out all traces of the early Christian cult by building a thermal institution over the site.

S. Pudenziana was rebuilt many times in the course of the centuries, and two of the most important medieval Popes contributed enduring elements. It is to Gregory VII (1073–85) that we owe the medieval door-frame (although some historians claim it was commissioned by Hadrian I in the eighth century), and Innocent III (1198–1216) contributed the Romanesque bell-tower.

In 1589 a drastic restoration was conducted upon the instructions of Cardinal Enrico Caetani, who ordered the medieval choir removed and imparted an overall late Renaissance aspect to the interior. The last touches of remodelling were carried out in 1870 by Cardinal Luciano Bonaparte, who is buried in the church.

CLASSICAL GARB

The true glory of S. Pudenziana is its astonishing early fifth- (or perhaps late fourth-) century apsidal mosaic. There is nothing comparable to be seen in all of Rome. Tourists to Rome are accustomed to Byzantine-style mosaics – with their hieratic compositions against solid gold backgrounds – which dominated early Church art. But S. Pudenziana's apse antedates the Byzantine influence, and offers a window into the Roman world through which Christianity entered.

Here is a scene out of pagan imperial Rome. The Saviour, dressed in golden Roman robes, sits upon a throne in the midst of his Apostles, who are dressed in the togas of Roman senators. Against a background of imperial buildings, the patrician matrons Pudenziana and Prassede crown Peter and Paul with Hellenistic laurel wreaths. (Many art historians claim that the female figures represent the 'Church of the

Circumcision', i.e. Jewish converts, and the 'Church of the Gentiles', rather than the sister-saints.)

The figures are highly individualized, the buildings are modelled with shadows and perspective, and the colours seem to be awash with the light and delicate tones of a huge watercolour painting. The ox representing the Evangelist Luke is so lifelike he could lean down and bite. This is the last gasp of naturalistic Roman art: nothing similar – in terms of perspective, colouring and portraiture – will be seen in Rome until the early Renaissance, which, of course, took its inspiration from classical art.

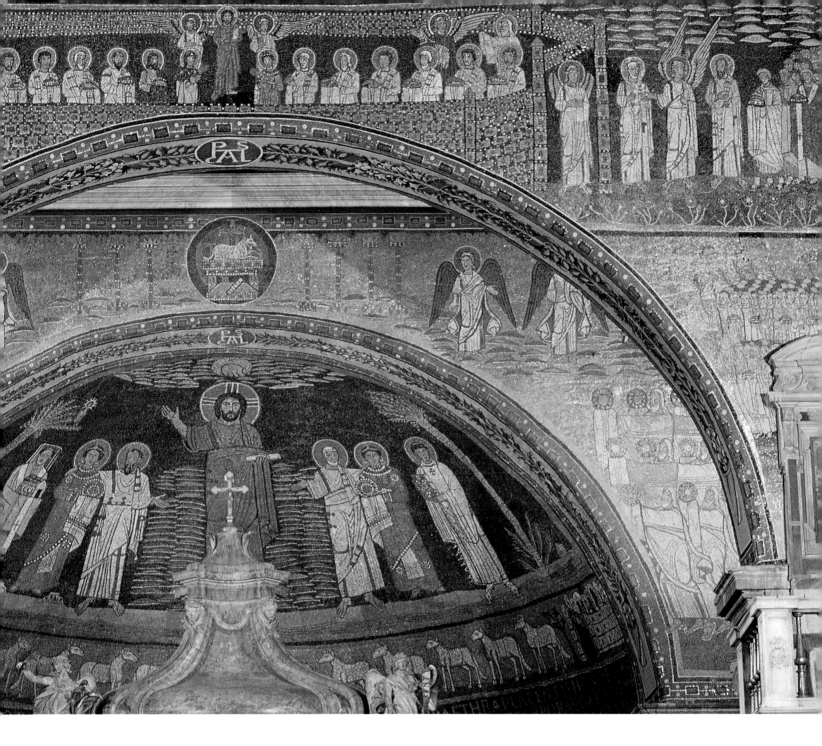

S. PRASSEDE
Courage and Conversion

Just as the *Titulus Pudentianae* marked the site of Pudens' and Pudenziana's early centre for clandestine Christian worship, the nearby *Titulus Praxedis* identified another place where Pudenziana and Prassede collected the remains of Christian martyrs in the secret well.

The church is located on a small street (Via S. Prassede) on the right side (approaching from S. Pudenziana) of the great basilica of S. Maria Maggiore. Entering S. Prassede through an inconspicuous side door, the pilgrim finds many references to the courageous sister-martyrs. In the centre of the nave, a porphyry disc marks the site of the martyrs' well, while the sisters' relics, together with one of the famous sponges, are preserved in an early Christian sarcophagus in the crypt below

Very different in spirit from the mosaic in S. Pudenziana, the ninth-century apse mosaic in S. Prassede is characteristic of a Byzantine style prevalent in Rome for most of the Middle Ages.

the high altar. To the right of the main entrance, fixed into the wall, is a slab of marble upon which St Prassede allegedly slept, with a statue of the saint in front.

Sts Pudenziana and Prassede appear in the crypt (a ninth-century fresco), while a large oil painting behind the main altar by Domenico Muratori (1730) portrays *St Prassede Gathering the Blood of the Martyrs*. In the apse and triumphal arch mosaics, and in those above the door and inside the chapel of Zeno, the Roman matron-saints have been transformed into Byzantine princesses in jewelled robes.

BYZANTINE SPLENDOUR

As in the case of S. Pudenziana, it was Pope Siricius (384–99) who commissioned a Christian basilica to be constructed over St Prassede's house church. The structure was renovated by Pope Hadrian I (772–95), and Pope Paschal I (817–24) rebuilt the church, apparently orienting it in a different direction, as seen today, with its three naves separated by ancient columns, and the profusion of mosaics covering the apse, triumphal arch, and right-aisle chapel.

S. Prassede's chapel of Zeno was called 'the Garden of Paradise' because of the sparkling beauty of its ninth-century mosaics.

And nothing could be more unlike the early Christian apse of S. Pudenziana than S. Prassede's ninth-century mosaics – often described as the most important Byzantine monument in Rome. Here the figures are frontal and one-dimensional, the composition rigidly hieratic, and the background flat, with stylized palm trees and wavy clouds. But what a wonderful moment in the Roman school of Byzantine art! In the apse, on each side of Christ the Redemptor, Sts Pudenziana and Prassede, dressed in Oriental robes, are being presented by Sts Peter and Paul, while Paschal I (his square halo indicates he was still alive at the time and destined for sainthood) holds up the model of his beloved church. In the triumphal arch, among an opulence of saints, Apostles, martyrs and angels, all proceeding to the heavenly Jerusalem, St Prassede and St Peter (with Pudenziana and Paul on the other side) stand side by side. On the apsidal arch, the twenty-four elders of the Apocalypse offer crowns to the Lamb of God above.

The chapel of Zeno, commissioned by Paschal I as a tomb for his mother Theodora but named after a Roman martyr whose relics Paschal had placed here, is even more splendid. In fact, throughout the Middle Ages the sanctuary was referred to as 'the Garden of Paradise' by native Romans and foreign pilgrims alike. All the walls, vaults and ceilings are covered with bright and lively mosaics, glittering and glowing in the intermittently illuminated spaces. There is a dazzling profusion of attenuated bodies of angels and saints, liturgical symbols, and in every free space, charming flowers and animals. One of the most appealing mosaics, in a lunette to the left of the entrance, shows heads of the Virgin, the bejewelled and crowned Sts Pudenziana and Prassede, and Theodora with her square halo.

OTHER TREASURES

S. Prassede was substantially renovated by its titular Cardinals St Charles Borromeo (1564–84) and Ludovico Pico della Mirandola (1728–31) and contains many treasures from different periods, among these a very early sculpture by Gianlorenzo Bernini (1598–1680), a funerary bust of G. B. Santoni, executed in 1615 when the artist was only seventeen, and another moving funerary monument by Arnolfo di Cambio (1245–1303) for Cardinal Anchier de Troyes, a titular Cardinal of S. Prassede assassinated inside the church in 1286 during a popular uprising.

A stone tablet on one of the right-nave piers commemorates the remains of about 2,300 martyrs which Pope Paschal I had brought from catacombs outside Rome. The relics now repose in the crypt, in four sculpted sarcophagi. (The sarcophagus on the lower right contains the bodies of Sts Pudenziana and Prassede.) In a niche to the back of the chapel of Zeno is displayed a marble column, to which, according to tradition, Christ was tied for scourging. The column was brought to Rome in 1223 by Giovanni Colonna, Papal legate to Constantinople and titular Cardinal of the church.

The nave frescoes depicting angels and scenes from Christ's Passion were made between 1594 and 1600 by artists from the Roman Mannerist school: Paris Nogari, Baldassare Croce and Giovanni Balducci. More frescoes, by Cavalier d'Arpino, decorate the middle left-nave chapel, and in the chapel to the left of the presbytery is a *Scourging of Christ* attributed to Giulio Romano.

S. CLEMENTE
Three Churches in One
S. Clemente is not one church but three, constructed one above the other, resting on the remains of even earlier Roman habitations. In fact, it is an ideal example of how titular churches evolved in early Christianity.

ROME BURNS
S. Clemente's complicated journey backwards in time begins at the lowest point of the basilica complex. Two levels below the present church, the visitor enters a musty tufa-walled corridor and peers through an iron grille into a dark tunnel five metres below. The sound of rushing water is constant and disquieting.

When in AD64 a great fire engulfed the narrow streets and crowded apartment buildings between Rome's Coelian and Oppian Hills, the first stratum of S. Clemente was reduced to smouldering rubble. Through the grille can be seen a section of orange brick wall and a piece of brick pavement (discovered during the construction in 1912–14 of a tunnel to drain a lake located under the basilica), identified as the charred remains of houses destroyed by the fire. The ruins of these gutted dwellings were filled in and used as the foundations for a later residential area. It was the new Flavian dynasty, in an attempt to gain the people's goodwill after Nero's misdeeds, who acquired the land here and began an ambitious building programme, including the Colosseum, or Flavian Amphitheatre (built in approximately AD70–75), about 300 metres away.

CLANDESTINE CHRISTIAN MEETINGS

The first corridor leads into a labyrinth of dark and mouldy chambers, tunnels and niches. Thick tufa walls alternate with brick surfaces in diamond patterns (the Roman *opus reticulatum*), and the floors are composed of herringbone tiles. Here, still two floors below street level, are the foundations of two buildings separated from one another by a narrow passageway: on one side a brick *insula* or apartment complex, and on the other the ground-floor rooms of a first-century mansion, or perhaps a warehouse, surrounding an open courtyard.

Most historians infer, from both tradition and ancient records, that the large building raised on the ravages of the great fire belonged to the consul-martyr Titus Flavius Clemens. (Some recent scholars claim instead that it was the Roman Mint.) According to the Roman historians Suetonius and Dio Cassius, Clemens was executed by Domitian in AD95, for 'godlessness' and 'following Jewish practices' – obviously Christian worship and disrespect for Roman deities. It was Clemens' wife, Flavia Domitilla, or her niece of the same name, who started the Catacomb of Domitilla. The open interior courtyard of the Flavian villa (or warehouse) would have been ideal for Christian gatherings. The church built here centuries later was identified as the *Titulus Clementis*, and later named after Pope St Clement (88–97) who, according to tradition, had served as a slave in the first-century household.

SECRET PAGAN RITUALS

Across the passageway dividing the Clementine mansion from the Roman apartment complex on the other side, still deep beneath the pavements of the modern city, emerge the shadowy images of Corinthian columns, Roman bas-reliefs and the fragments of large granite pots. There are the remains of a small Mithraic temple, dated to the end of the second or early third century AD, which was built into the first-century

Above: Beneath the basilica of S. Clemente, this third-century Mithraic temple (the cult banquet hall is shown here) had been built in a Roman apartment complex next to a Christian villa.

Right: In S. Clemente's fourth-century church (now underground), a wall fresco contains one of the first examples of an inscription in the Italian vernacular.

insula. The visitor first comes upon the temple antechamber, with stone seating for the initiated, thick pilasters supporting the vestibule arches, and a stucco ceiling with geometric and floral patterns. On the other side, the *triclinium*, or banquet hall, is an artificial cave with stone benches on two sides. What was probably the altar, a marble block between the benches, has a classical bas-relief portraying Mithras in his Phrygian cap, plunging his dagger into a bull. At the end of a corridor leading from the *triclinium* and vestibule, another room has been identified as the probable instruction room. There are seven niches here (taken to represent the seven-stage Mithraic initiation), a black and white mosaic floor, and a faded wall portrait of a bearded and scarlet-cloaked Roman.

In Mithraic dogma, the god Mithras was born of a rock to be the bearer of life and fertility to the world. At Apollo's command, Mithras slew the bull from whose blood all good forms of life emerged, evil ensuing from a scorpion's sly theft of some of the blood. Cult members celebrated a ritual banquet commemorating Mithras' victory feast with Apollo, before the two ascended into heaven in the sun god's chariot. Introduced to Rome during the time of Pompey (67BC), Mithraism became popular among the Roman legions in Asia Minor and spread rapidly throughout the Empire. The cult reached its peak in the late second century, when even the Emperor Commodus (180–92) converted, and was finally outlawed in the late fourth century.

A FOURTH-CENTURY CHURCH

On the second level of S. Clemente the air is less dank and the sound of water fainter, but an atmosphere of mystery still prevails. For this is a fourth-century church, which was filled in, abandoned and forgotten for eight long centuries until an amateur nineteenth-century archaeologist dug his way through hundreds of years of rubble and refuse.

Four long, shadowy hallways of varying widths are separated by thick walls and square pilasters supporting the more recent basilica above. Here and there wide-eyed Byzantine figures peer out from the crumbling frescoed walls. The visitor is, in fact, looking at the nave, narthex, and north and south aisles of the early Christian church, with a modern altar on the spot of the ancient presbytery.

With Constantine's victory and the Edict of Milan in 313 the Christian Church in Rome could expand confidently. In the pontificate of Pope Siricius (384–99) the clergy attached to

47

the small titular church of the Clemens family acquired the adjoining apartment complexes. They filled in the rooms and courtyards, constructed a central nave over the large area of early Christian worship, and extended an apse over the former Mithraic temple. The new church, mentioned by St Jerome as early as 392, was dedicated to Pope St Clement, a contemporary of the Roman Consul Clemens.

As the centuries passed S. Clemente became one of Rome's best loved and most adorned churches. In the sixth century, Justinian's wife, the Byzantine Empress Theodora (d. 548) had her portrait painted in a niche in the north aisle. (In the ninth century a throne and infant were added, converting the portrait into a Madonna and Child.)

In the eleventh century large areas of the city were laid to waste by the Normans under Robert Guiscard, and many churches were burned to the ground. S. Clemente may have been among these. At any rate, several years later the gutted rooms were filled with rubble to provide foundations for a new building, and the original structure lay utterly forgotten for eight centuries.

Now, wandering through the rows of squat supports for the basilica above, we can imagine the wonder that Father Joseph Mullooly, S. Clemente's Irish Dominican Prior, must have felt in 1857. Acting on intuition, and armed with little more than pick and shovel, he broke through tons of rubble to discover the abandoned fourth-century church below – and eventually the Roman house church and Mithraeum as well. Mullooly found many long-forgotten treasures: a Roman pagan sarcophagus later used for Christian burial, the tomb of the ninth-century Slav missionary St Cyril, and some charming frescoes depicting the life of St Clement, as well as the Byzantine mosaics of the ninth century.

A LEGENDARY SAINT

The St Clement frescoes in the fourth-century basilica have links to the church's first-century origins. The historical Pope St Clement, to whom the church is dedicated, was the third successor of St Peter as Bishop of Rome. According to legend, St Clement was banished by Trajan (98–117) to the Crimean

S. Clemente's bright and joyful twelfth-century apse mosaic shows the Cross as the Tree of Life, with charming scenes of medieval life entwined in the foliage.

mines, where he converted so many soldiers and fellow prisoners that the Romans tied an anchor to his neck and threw him into the Black Sea. Rescued by angels and conveyed to an underwater tomb, the saint was revealed to believers once every year by a miraculous ebbing of the tides. A delightful fresco (commissioned by a local family named de Rapiza in the eleventh century) in the narthex of the fourth-century church shows how, on one of these occasions, a small child was whisked away by the waves, to be recovered safe and sound at the next year's ebbing.

Across from this, another fresco shows the Slavic missionaries, Sts Cyril (826–69) and Methodius (815–85), who supposedly recovered St Clement's body from the Crimean Sea, solemnly escorting the saint's remains to be interred in Rome in the church of his name. When St Cyril died in Rome some years later, he was also buried in S. Clemente, where his tomb became a place of pilgrimage for many Slavic Catholics.

Another – humorous – fresco located in the nave of the fourth-century church tells the story of a jealous husband, complaining of his wife's constant attendance at St Clement's Masses, and making a fool of himself by mistaking a ponderous column for the saintly Pope. His surprising expletive ('*Fili dele pute*') is the earliest known writing in the Italian vernacular.

Pope St Clement was also the author of a famous document which marked a turning point in the life of the Roman Church. In his letter to the Corinthians (AD96), known as 'First Clement', he appealed to the Corinthian Church to reinstate a group of deposed presbyters. Speaking in the name of the Roman Church, he insisted on the principles of order, discipline and respect for authority. Clement's ideas prevailed, resulting by the late second century in a solidly organized Roman Church, with a Pope (Bishop of Rome) in Apostolic succession, a hierarchical clergy and official Church property.

AFTER THE NORMANS

S. Clemente's top – and present – level was for centuries considered by worshippers and scholars alike to be the church St Jerome visited in 392 and described as 'preserving the name of Clement in Rome'. In fact, this is the 'new' basilica, constructed under Pope Paschal II in around 1100, and replicating, on a slightly smaller scale, the fourth-century structure that may have been destroyed by the Normans.

Here, inside an eighteenth-century restoration, we find a typical medieval church, central nave and two side aisles divided by marble and granite columns, a beautiful mosaic

pavement, and a white marble choir enclosure. After the dark mysteries of S. Clemente's lower levels, the brilliant gold and jewel-like colours of the basilica's apsidal mosaic are almost overwhelming. The central crucifixion, represented as a graceful 'tree of life', sprouts from a leafy base, with bright blue streams flowing below. Deer, peacock and geese cavort by the water, while curling vines, flowers, and charming scenes from everyday medieval life unfurl against the sparkling background.

The basilica has other treasures to offer: the white marble choir donated by Pope John II (533–5) to the earlier basilica and transferred above; two high marble pulpits and a mosaic-encrusted Paschal candlestick; the *confessio*, or martyr's tomb, below the altar, containing the relics of St Clement and St Ignatius (the first-century Bishop of Antioch and author of seven authoritative letters written on his way to martyrdom in Rome).

Above all, the early fifteenth-century frescoes in the chapel of St Catherine of Alexandria have been recently restored and are wonderful. Delicate yet colourful scenes show the young Alexandrian disputing with learned doctors, her conversion of the Emperor Maxentius' wife, her miraculous escape from torture on the spiked wheel and eventual decapitation, and the angels' transfer of her body to Mt Sinai. Art historians are still debating the authorship of these paintings. Were they done by Masolino da Panicale (1383–1447) or by Masaccio (1401–1429)? Or did they represent a harmonious collaboration between two early Renaissance artists?

RECENT RAVAGES AND DOMINICAN CARE

On one wall of St Clemente's outside courtyard a wall plaque signed by Pope Clement XI (1700–1715) exults: 'This ancient church has withstood the ravages of the centuries' – a curious reminder that at that time the twelfth-century structure was assumed to have been the same one described by St Jerome in 392. Clement XI then inflicted his own ravages on S. Clemente: his eighteenth-century restorations, including an ugly façade, ponderous gilded ceiling and large rectangular windows over the nave, were carried out by the currently fashionable architect Carlo Fontana – but somehow spoil the overall medieval ambiance of the basilica complex.

S. Clemente has been under the care of the Irish Dominicans since 1677, when the English outlawed the Irish Catholic Church and expelled the entire clergy. At that time the Order was given refuge at S. Clemente, where they still maintain a monastery for priests studying and teaching in Rome.

MARTYRS' SHRINES: THE BEGINNINGS OF POPULAR DEVOTION

On a summer evening in the year AD64 a great conflagration spread throughout Rome, quickly destroying most of the city. Many, including the historian Tacitus, hinted that the Emperor was himself to blame. But scapegoats were needed, and for these Nero (54–68) chose a proscribed but growing new sect, the Christians. A great spectacle was made of their suffering and death. Some Christians were dipped in pitch and burned as human lanterns to illuminate the imperial gardens, others were thrown to wild beasts in the arenas for the sport of Roman crowds.

Nero's was the first of the Christian persecutions, but other Emperors followed his example: Domitian (81–96), Marcus Aurelius (161–80), Decius (249–51), Valerian (253–60). Throughout the second and third centuries Christian deaths became one of the most exciting entertainments for the Roman populace. Christians were thrown to the lions, torn apart by wild dogs, boiled in pots of oil, dismembered by wild-running horses, skinned, hacked and roasted. Perhaps the most fierce persecution was under Diocletian (284–305) *c.* 303–5, when 3–4,000 Christian martyrs may have given their lives.

How many martyrs perished up until the time of Constantine? Scholars, consulting early Christian writings, burial grounds and other archaeological evidence, have come up with an estimate of 100,000. Yet the Christians' courage and steadfastness could not help but impress the Romans, and each martyr seemed to produce another convert.

By the early fourth century the Christian community had grown to around 5 or 6 million, and one of the next Emperors, Constantine (306–37), legalized Christianity and even embraced it himself. It was indeed, as the early Christian theologian Tertullian (160–230) wrote in his *Apologetics,* the blood of the martyrs which watered the seed of the early Church ('*Sanguis martyrum – semen christianorum*').

Martyrs' shrines soon became stations of worship for the persecuted Christian community. The martyrs' example inspired constancy among the faithful and gave them the strength to face torment and death. We have seen in the catacombs how many Christians sought interment near the martyrs' graves. Many of the faithful, both rich and poor, arranged to be buried near the martyrs' tombs, and these shrines soon became some of the most visited sites of the early Church.

The church of S. Stefano Rotondo probably contained a relic (now lost) of Christianity's first martyr, St Stephen. It was modelled on the church of the Holy Sepulchre in Jerusalem.

After Christianity's legalization, churches and magnificent basilicas were built over the tombs of the martyrs and pilgrims came from far and wide to pray at the holy shrines. Soon there was a proliferation of martyrs' and saints' sanctuaries, each claiming to possess if not the martyr's body then at least an important relic. Legends concerning the martyrs' lives and the circumstances of their deaths grew quickly, multiplied and were written up in popular martyrologies. (The most important of these were the sixth-century devotional texts called *passiones*, or martyrs' passions.)

Invasion, pillage and abandonment of the Roman country-side led to the so-called 'translation' of saints' and martyrs' relics from the catacombs into more secure city sanctuaries. Starting in the seventh century, but especially throughout the eighth and ninth, many churches hosted martyrs' relics and changed their names and dedications in honour of these early Christian witnesses.

In early Christianity, a church built over a martyr's shrine was called a *martyrium*; if the sanctuary contained the saint's actual body, it was referred to as *ad corpus martyrium*. The most important of all *martyria* are the shrines of the Apostles Peter and Paul, executed according to tradition in Nero's persecution, and that of the Roman deacon St Lawrence, martyred under Valerian. These are described later in the Jubilee basilicas itinerary in Part II.

SS. GIOVANNI E PAOLO
Two Martyred Brothers

The tomb of SS. Giovanni e Paolo (John and Paul) was unique in early Christianity. For in spite of ancient Roman laws requiring all burials to be outside the city gates (hence the catacombs), it was located in one of the imperial city's most exclusive residential districts. Moreover, the grave was erected not in a Christian cemetery, but upon the site of the martyrs' execution – in their own home.

TIME STANDS STILL

High on the Coelian Hill, hidden by greenery, surrounded by country gardens and orchards, mossy walls and the untidy ruins of aqueducts and classical arches, the basilica of SS. Giovanni e Paolo seems to be isolated in time and space. The ancient complex rises above a cobblestone piazza, far from tourists and traffic, and fortuitously preserved from modern 'improvements' – a place to sit and savour the spirit of another age.

The church spreads its broad portico across one entire side of the square. Eight dignified classical columns support the twelfth-century porch, above which soars the triangular summit of the basilica's original façade. On the other side, one of Rome's loveliest Romanesque belfries towers above a medieval monastery. The twelfth-century campanile is decorated with coloured ceramic tiles; its base is formed by travertine blocks taken from the nearby Temple of Claudius (41–54).

Before entering the basilica, the visitor should go round to the back of the church. After descending a narrow road which still bears its Roman name, Clivus Scauri, and passing under a series of medieval arches, there is an evocative view of the graceful arcaded apse, and across the hill to the ruins of the Palatine. On one side of the church a tablet tells us that this is the house (discovered in 1887) of two early Christian martyrs.

MARTYRS' TESTIMONY

The earliest record of Sts John and Paul, to whom this church is dedicated, comes from the sixth-century *passio* which describes their life and martyrdom. Probably brothers, they had been officers in the service of Constantine (306–37) and guardians of his daughter Constantia. During a particularly fierce military campaign, they revealed themselves as Christians to their superior officer, Gallicano, and by their prayers won a decisive victory for his beleaguered legion. After Constantine's death in 337 they were allowed to retire in wealth and renown to their luxurious home on the Coelian Hill.

With the accession of the Emperor Julian the Apostate (361–3), who returned to paganism and to the persecution of Christians, John and Paul were called back to military action. Refusing to serve the 'idolatrous' court, the brothers were beheaded in their home on 26 June 362 and were secretly buried by other pious Christians. A later addition to the *passio* states that the priest Crispus, the cleric Crispinian and the matron Benedicta were later found praying at the brothers' tomb; they were beheaded, and buried on the same spot.

Modern scholars often disparage the *passio* as fervent fantasy. However, the fact that the brother-martyrs' grave almost immediately became a sanctuary of devotion and pilgrimage,

that other tombs were built nearby, and that an imposing basilica was raised here not long after their death, seems to vindicate tradition. If that were not enough, the discovery in 1887 of a richly decorated Roman house and an early Christian oratory under the church, and consistent findings from then until 1958, appear to confirm that these are the rooms of two venerated early Christian martyrs.

Excavations below the basilica of SS. Giovanni e Paolo have revealed a complex of Roman structures from the Republican to the imperial age (first to third centuries), including shops (facing the Clivus Scauri), a thermal establishment and a rich villa (or several villas) of at least twenty rooms. With

Left: The basilica of SS. Giovanni e Paolo, built over the home of two fourth-century Christian soldier-martyrs, is located in a quiet medieval square on the Coelian Hill.

Above: Excavated rooms, believed to be the Roman villa where Sts John and Paul (Giovanni e Paolo) were martyred in the persecutions of Julian the Apostate (361–3).

permission from the sacristan, visitors can descend to this ancient subterranean world from the right transept inside the church.

Grilled bridges with railings lead over dizzying arches and rooms on at least three levels to the *nympheum*, an indoor water-garden with a fountain, a fine mosaic floor, and a truly beautiful pagan marine fresco from the second century. The adjacent *triclinium*, or dining-room, is also pagan in spirit, with its second- or third-century border of handsome youths, cavorting cupids, and realistically observed birds, ducks and peacocks. In a corner of the *tablinum*, or reception room, is an obviously Christian symbol: a third-century *orante*, a tunic-clad figure with arms outstretched in prayer.

A short staircase leads to the oratory, the assumed burial place of the brother-martyrs John and Paul. This tiny room contains fourth-century frescoes showing, on the upper left wall, the arrest by soldiers and, on the upper right wall, the beheading of two men and a woman. It is believed that these represent Crispus, Crispinian and Benedicta, and that the main portrayal of John and Paul's martyrdom has been destroyed or lost. On the lower left and right walls are painted two unidentified males and two unidentified females. Single figures depicted on the shrine's front wall are assumed to be Sts John and Paul, and another figure worshipped by bowing figures may be Christ.

Several bodies were found in the oratory area, and in another section of the Roman home more tombs were discovered. The martyrs' sanctuary was connected to the church above by a shaft-like structure. In 1558 the saints' relics were brought to the upper church, and in 1726 they were placed in a porphyry urn under the main altar.

Relics of another fourth-century Roman martyr, Saturnius, are located in a chapel to the right of the entrance. The chapel to the left of the entrance contains the remains of eleven Christians (men and women) from Scillium in North Africa, martyred in Carthage in 180 for refusing to hand over one of St Paul's letters.

THE TITULAR CHURCH

It seems that soon after the saints' martyrdom their villa was used as a house church. This explains the frescoes and the care taken with the burial site. According to our earliest records, this became the *Titulus Byzantiis*, named after the subsequent owner, the Roman Senator Byzantius, who donated the edifice to Christians for their worship.

Around 398 Byzantius' son, Pammachius, built a large basilica on the site of his father's church, and this was for some time thereafter known as the *Titulus Pammachii* (synod listing of 499). The granite columns in the nave and the upper part of the façade are leftover elements of the fourth-century basilica. (Viewing the high tympanum from outside, the visitor will have an idea of Pammachius' basilica's amazing size).

Pammachius' correspondence with St Jerome, a personal friend, shows that after many years of public service as a Roman senator, he (Pammachius) gave his money to the poor and retired to a life of seclusion and prayer. A fifth-century

inscription found in the church also indicated Pammachius as the founder.

Some ancient inventories list the original *Titulus Byzantiis* as the earliest of Rome's titular churches. By the sixth century most Roman *tituli* had taken the name of the saints whose memory they honoured. In fact, in the synod listing of 595 this church already appeared as the basilica of SS. Johanis e Pauli.

The basilica had a rough start – sacked by Alaric and the Visigoths in 410, and damaged by an earthquake in 442. Evidence of these disasters survives in the gashes running across the upper portion of the original façade. The basilica was reconstructed by Pope Leo I (440–61), but was again sacked in 1084, this time by the Normans under Robert Guiscard. Pope Paschal II (1099–1118) began renovations and construction of the monastery and belfry, and these were completed by Cardinal Giovanni Conti of Sutri (*c*.1150), who honoured himself with a large inscription on the portico architrave.

This Byzantine-style fresco of Christ, dated 1255, was recently discovered in a cubicle off the main altar of the church of SS. Giovanni e Paolo.

The interior of SS. Giovanni e Paolo today bears little resemblance to Pammachius' fourth-century basilica or Paschal's medieval reconstruction. Gutted and remodelled in the early eighteenth century (under Cardinal Fabrizio Paolucci, from 1715 to 1718), the church now has a late Baroque style and spirit.

The Passionist Congregation has served the church since the late eighteenth century. The huge domed chapel off the right aisle, built in 1867, is dedicated to their founder, St John of the Cross (1694–1775). Cardinal Francis Spellman, titular of the church from 1946 to 1967, with the help of American millionaire Joseph Kennedy, restored the façade to its medieval state and underwrote excavations of the underground villa.

DAZZLING DISCOVERIES

The basilica of SS. Giovanni e Paolo is still very beautiful, both inside and out. Sunlight streams past the Romanesque lions guarding the entrance portal, between two original fourth-century columns, and across the thirteenth-century mosaic pavement. If the sacristan agrees to turn on the lights, as if by magic an ethereal blue-white illumination will gradually fill the interior, from what seem like hundreds of crystal chandeliers (actually only thirty-five).

The illumination seems to transform into pastel rainbows Pomarancio's apsidal vault fresco of *The Trinity in Glory* (1588), as well as otherwise mediocre eighteenth-century paintings below: in the middle, Giacomo Triga's *Sts John and Paul Decapitated*; to the left and right, G.D. Piastrini's *Sts John and Paul Give Their Goods to the Poor* and *The Conversion of Terentianus* (the imperial official who supervised the brothers' execution and then converted when the saints' intervention healed his son).

The pilgrim should not miss two further treasures: Antoniazzo Romano's 1455 picture of the *Madonna and Child with Sts John and Paul*, located in the sacristy; and a 'secret' Byzantine fresco (in an almost inaccessible closet-like room behind the altar), *Christ with Apostles*, datable to 1255 – a period represented very rarely in Roman art.

Although surrounded by an eighteenth-century shell, visitors will find much to remind them that Pammachius' ancient titular church, honouring an early martyrs' sanctuary, is not forgotten. To the right of the central nave, a walled-in section of the pavement informs us that we are directly above the *locus martyrii*, 'the place of martyrdom of John and Paul in their own house'.

S. STEFANO ROTONDO
The Sphinx on the Coelian Hill

The church of S. Stefano Rotondo is not actually a martyr's tomb. However, it was built to honour Christianity's very first martyr and has close and mysterious associations with Christ's own tomb in Jerusalem. It also has an extensive – and terrifyingly realistic – series of frescoes of early Christian martyrdoms.

HOLY LAND BEGINNINGS

Just a short walk away from the basilica of SS. Giovanni e Paolo is the circular church of S. Stefano Rotondo, affectionately nicknamed the 'sphinx of the Coelian Hill'. S. Stefano gained this appellation because of its mysterious origins, unusual architecture and occult symbolism. The fact that the church was closed (off and on) to visitors for almost twenty years has added to its inscrutability.

S. Stefano Rotondo's round brick drum and red-tiled roof rises above a curve of crumbling walls and tufts of pines. This circular form, so unusual among Rome's predominantly hall-like basilicas, suggests a singular attribute: its unusually intimate connection with the Holy Land, where Christianity was born.

There is every reason to believe that the shrine of S. Stefano Rotondo was built as a replica of the Holy Sepulchre in Jerusalem. Although no contemporary historical chronicle attests to that fact, it cannot be just coincidence that the circumference and diameter of the church differ from those of the Jerusalem sanctuary by only a fraction of an inch.

S. Stefano was originally constructed in three concentric ambulatories (one is now walled up), separated by rings of antique columns and intersected by four arms in a Greek cross.

In Jerusalem the concentric design facilitated maximum circulation of pilgrims around the sanctuary over Christ's grave. The purpose of S. Stefano's circular design is still a puzzle. What was in the middle? Tradition suggests that the sanctuary hosted a very important relic.

From the beginning the church was dedicated to the proto-martyr St Stephen, and this reveals another link to the shrine's Palestinian roots. For St Stephen was one of the seven deacons appointed by the Apostles to help look after the poor in the Holy Land and to assist in preaching the faith. The first martyr was stoned to death in Jerusalem, for blasphemy against Judaism, even before Peter and Paul began evangelizing in Rome. (Paul, before his conversion, in fact witnessed and consented to Stephen's death.)

The discovery of St Stephen's remains at Kafr Gamala in 415 provided a strong impetus for spreading the saint's cult from the Holy Land throughout the Mediterranean world, and especially to Rome. It is very probable that at least some relic of St Stephen was buried in this church on the Coelian Hill.

The church definitely preserves the remains of two other early Christian martyrs, Sts Primus and Felician, executed at Nomentum outside Rome around 300 (in the persecutions of Diocletian and Maximian). Their story is quite touching. Tradition says they were patrician brothers who became Christians and visited the faithful awaiting death in Roman prisons. They underwent atrocious tortures, and Felician was told that his eighty-year-old brother had recanted. The brothers held fast, however, faced the hungry lions together, were miraculously saved, and finally died by decapitation.

Inside the church, the S. Primus and Felician Chapel to the left of the entrance has wall frescoes depicting their martyrdom and burial, as well as a highly-prized seventh-century mosaic. In this mosaic, the two saints stand on either side of a jewelled cross surmounted by a bust of Christ. Most art historians consider this to be a reproduction of the large cross Constantine had set up on the summit of Golgotha in the early fourth century.

The S. Primus and Felician Chapel in S. Stefano was commissioned by Pope Theodore I (642–9). Since Theodore's

Left: The circular church of S. Stefano Rotondo is located among the green and quiet gardens of the Coelian Hill.

Right: In the sixteenth century, S. Stefano Rotondo's walls were frescoed with frightening scenes of early Christian martyrdom.

family were Greek residents in Jerusalem, the Pope had undoubtedly seen Constantine's famous cross before it was carried off by Chosroes during the Persians' Sack of Jerusalem in 614. Pope Theodore had the martyrs' remains brought from their Nomentana cemetery (the first instance of translation of martyrs' relics within the city walls), built the chapel and buried his father (a Greek bishop in Palestine) there. But that was in the seventh century, and the church's story begins much earlier.

IMPERIAL HEIR

S. Stefano Rotondo was built and consecrated during the pontificate of Pope St Simplicius (468–83), at the very moment when the Roman Empire was breathing its dying gasp. Early in the fifth century the city had suffered barbarian incursions, and in 476 the last Roman Emperor, Romulus Augustulus, lost his throne to the German warrior Odoacer.

During this time the moral and political leadership of the Papacy increased remarkably. To assert the Papacy's assumption of Rome's spiritual and temporal leadership, Simplicius built S. Stefano Rotondo both as a reflection of Jerusalem's Holy Sepulchre, and as a mirror of such centralized classical structures as the Pantheon and Hadrian's tomb.

S. Stefano Rotondo's origins are a mystery; it does not appear among the lists of Rome's first titular churches (like, for instance, the basilica of SS. Giovanni e Paolo just up the street). Perhaps the shrine was financed by the noble Valerian family, whose large estates covered the Coelian Hill; one family member, St Melanie, was a frequent pilgrim to Jerusalem and eventually died there.

To make room for the church, part of a vast army barracks, the *Castra Peregrinorum*, was demolished, including an adjacent sanctuary to the Persian god Mithras. During excavations under S. Stefano, the gold-covered head of a Mithraic statue was in fact unearthed from rubble beneath the church. Building over pagan shrines or temples was another way the Church signalled its triumph over the pagan Empire (as in San Clemente).

MEDIEVAL MARVELS AND RENAISSANCE REVIVAL

In the sixth century, Pope John I (523–6) and Pope Felix IV (526–30) embellished S. Stefano's interior with mosaics, marble and other costly materials, including porphyry, serpentine and mother of pearl. Pope St Gregory (590–604) preached a much-quoted sermon here around 580; his marble episcopal throne (minus arms and back) can be seen to the left of the church entrance.

The chapel of S. Primus and Felician was built by Pope Theodore I in the seventh century. Seventh-century art is extremely rare in Rome, and this chapel's mosaic should be enjoyed at length. (Another example can be found in the St John Lateran Baptistery not far away.) The medieval Pope Innocent II (1130–43) introduced a serious of transverse arches on classical columns to support the arched roof.

In the later Middle Ages Rome became the battleground of warring noble families, and anarchy reigned throughout the city. The round church on the Coelian Hill participated in the general decline, as its rich decorations faded or disappeared and its walls mouldered away.

Pope Nicholas V (1447–55), early Renaissance scholar a nd arts patron, restored many churches to their former splendour, among these S. Stefano Rotondo. For the centre of the church the Pope commissioned a Florentine artist, Bernardo Rossellino, to construct a marble altar in early Renaissance style. Unfortunately, Nicholas had the outermost concentric ambulatories demolished and the space between the colonnades filled in with masonry; three arms of the Greek cross disappeared as well. These changes considerably reduced the size of the church and obviously changed its original impact.

RETURN OF THE EARLY MARTYRS

In 1583 Pope Gregory XIII (1572–85) asked the artist Nicolo Circignano (1530–92, better known as Pomarancio) to paint S. Stefano's walls with scenes of early Christian martyrdom. The result – twenty-four large frescoes with explanatory titles, Bible citations, and the names of the Roman Emperors who ordered the tortures – are some of the most terrifying representations the pilgrim to Roman churches will ever see.

To the sides of the entrance are frescoes of the Crucifixion and the stoning of St Stephen. Next are depictions of the Apostles' deaths and those of other well-known early Christian martyrs. In harsh detail we see: St Thekla tied to the legs of two bulls and torn apart; Christians dressed in animal skins and chased by wild dogs; Gervasius and Protasius nailed to trees; St Ignatius thrown to the lions in the Colosseum; St John cooked in boiling oil, while St Eustachius is roasted inside a bronze bull and St Calpodius is dragged by horses and thrown into the Tiber.

Other martyrs are depicted chopped to pieces, crushed between heavy slabs of stone, grilled, beheaded, drowned, suffocated. The saints' expressions range from shocked disbelief to calm acceptance; from fear and pain to religious ecstasy. The tormentors are portrayed in varying states of sadistic cruelty, shamed compassion, and even imminent conversion. This grisly cycle was meant to involve the spectator totally in the martyrs' torments. The Pope and his artist had a definite objective in mind.

When S. Stefano Rotondo was built around 480, the Church had just emerged triumphant over paganism and recalled its first martyr, St Stephen. By the time Gregory XIII commissioned Pomarancio in 1583, Catholicism was combating another enemy – Protestantism in Europe. S. Stefano's martyrdom scenes were meant to inspire sixteenth-century Catholics with the militancy of the early martyrs' courage and faith.

Furthermore, in 1580 Pope Gregory XIII had entrusted S. Stefano to one of the Counter-Reformation's new militant orders – the Jesuits. They soon became the Church's foremost missionaries. Pomarancio's frescoes would prepare Jesuit seminarians for the trials of faith they could confront in far-away lands.

ARCHITECTURAL SYMBOLISM

The church of S. Stefano Rotondo provides convincing evidence of the early Roman Church's deep ties to its Holy Land roots and its victory over imperial paganism. But the

shrine also suggests a spiritual significance which can only be guessed at today.

Shorn of its sparkling marbles and other decorations, the church now seems bare and empty. It is missing one of its circular ambulatories, one of its rings of antique columns, its original eight entrances and upper windows. Its early structure must have provided an almost mystical play of light and shade among the columns and circular spaces.

Scholars have suggested the Apocalypse and other biblical passages as the basis for S. Stefano's design. It is true that in antiquity round temples signified both the earthly planet and the universe. In S. Stefano, the scholars surmise, a Greek cross could have been architecturally imposed upon the symbolic 'All', as the sign of Christ's redemption of all mankind

The exit from S. Stefano Rotondo is by a gate through high stone walls, past the well-tended garden of the next-door convent. The area remains much as it was in early Christian times, with its vineyards, monasteries and atmosphere of secluded peace.

SS. NEREO E ACHILLEO
The Fisherman Was Also Here

SS. Nereo e Achilleo, one of Rome's earliest and most venerated titular churches, is a tribute to the First Apostle, two soldier-martyrs and early Christian spirituality.

MARTYRS AND MATRONS

At the base of the Coelian Hill a busy intersection orients roads outwards to Roman suburbs. Here, hiding behind a fringe of pine and cypress, dominated by the colossal ruins of the Baths of Caracalla, is the tiny church of SS. Nereo e Achilleo, often bypassed by Rome's tourists. This is a shame, for it is one of the city's oldest and most evocative Christian memorials.

In the Catacombs of Domitilla, about a mile and a half away, were buried two soldier-martyrs, Nereus and Achilleus, whose cult in early Christianity was particularly intense throughout this area on the city's edge. Domitilla's cemetery, and its underground basilica Pope Damasus dedicated to the saints,

Originally built in the Romanesque style, the church of SS. Nereo e Achilleo was restored in the 1500s.

have been described earlier. This equally ancient church first had a different name and dedication, as we will see below. It was referred to as the *Titulus SS. Nerei e Achillei* as early as the Roman Church Council of 595, although Nereus' and Achilleus' relics, along with those of Domitilla, were not transferred to the church until the ninth century (during the Saracen invasions).

Damasus' inscription in Domitilla's Catacomb notes that Nereus and Achilleus were members of the imperial Praetorian Guard (most historians assume the Emperor was Diocletian,

The episcopal throne in the church of SS. Nereo e Achilleo dates from the twelfth or the thirteenth century.

who ruled 284–305). After putting to death many Christians, the two executioners themselves converted to the new religion. 'Throwing away their swords, shields and medals,' the inscription states, 'they confessed their faith and made ready to enjoy triumph with Christ.' Martyred by decapitation, the soldiers were first buried in a crypt on the cemetery's third level, and their grave soon became a site of fervent devotion and pilgrimage.

Sts Nereus and Achilleus are almost always associated with St Flavia Domitilla, the wealthy Roman matron who donated her property for the catacomb which now bears her name. (One legend claims that the saints were brothers and her personal eunuchs.) She may have been the same Domitilla whose house church later became the *titulus* of S. Clemente. (In that case, the persecuting Emperor would have been Domitian, who reigned from 81 to 96, rather than Diocletian.) The story of the three saints is told in large frescoes by Pomerancio along both sides of the main nave. Behind the apse and over the inside entrance, other frescoes show the saints (among other martyrs) glorified in heaven. Three side altars also have paintings representing Domitilla, Nereus and Achilleus.

IN ST PETER'S STEPS

At the beginning the church had a different title. It was not named after Nereus and Achilleus, or even identified by the original owners' name like most *tituli*, but was called the *Titulus de fasciolae* ('of the bandage'). This designation stemmed from an ancient tradition concerning the Apostle Peter.

As recounted earlier, when St Peter escaped from the Mamertine prison and was fleeing out of Rome along the Appian Way, he encountered Christ, who told the Apostle that he did not wish his people to be abandoned and was returning to Rome to be crucified a second time.

Peter felt ashamed, and turned back to his Roman flock – and thus to certain martyrdom. As the Apostle hurried along, the bandage covering his ankle, wounded by his prison chains, fell by the wayside. It was on that particular spot, where the bandage fell and was found by a pious neighbourhood matron, that the church was then constructed.

The tradition of St Peter's flight and the loss of his leg-bandage can be traced to the sixth-century *Acts of Sts Processus and Martinianus* (Peter's converted prison guards) and to the second-century 'Pseudo Linus' account of the *Martyrdom of St Peter*.

Modern historians are fond of disparaging such pious stories, but the different layers of legend relating to the *de fasciolae* parish probably cover a nucleus of historical truth. An un-interrupted oral tradition affirms that this ancient church – built at the very beginning of the Via Appia, a few hundred metres from the spot (now marked by the small 'Quo Vadis' shrine) where Peter is said to have encountered Christ – has always been known for its special devotion to the Apostle Peter.

Carved inscriptions attest to the fact that the church already boasted an established clergy in the early fourth century. An epitaph, dated 377 and found in the basilica of S. Paolo Fuori le Mura, identifies a deceased man, Cinnamius, as a '*lector*' in the '*Titulus de fasciolae*'. Other grave markings discovered in the Catacomb of Domitilla name members of the '*de fasciolae basilica*' clergy who were also responsible for administration of the Domitilla cemetery (one was the '*lector*' Pascentius, whose dates are given as 389–404). A Church Council of 499 refers to a '*Titulus de fasciolae*' as having five presbyters.

EARLY SPIRITUALITY

Besides tradition and historical evidence, the atmosphere of this ancient sanctuary speaks for itself. Standing beneath the enormous ruins of the Baths of Caracalla (completed in 217), the modest structure seems to emerge from imperial Rome's pagan shadows. In fact, excavations outside the apse have revealed a thick curving wall about three yards below, which some archaeologists identify as part of a temple to Isis.

The interior of the church also seems to partake of two worlds. A medieval pulpit stands on an enormous porphyry urn recovered from the Caracalla Baths. At the back of the presbytery, a stone frieze, perhaps taken from some nearby Roman theatre, has strange mask-like faces emerging from classical foliage. Behind the main altar, two sacrificial blocks from pagan temples sport graceful winged spirits (very much resembling Renaissance angels).

What caused the church to change its name – and its dedication – around 595? Sixth-century Popes, and particularly Pope St Gregory I (590–604), attempting to purify and deepen popular devotion, had insisted on replacing the *tituli* names of former proprietors with those of early martyr-saints. Just as the *Titulus Pammachii* on the Coelian Hill was renamed after Sts John and Paul; the *Titulus de fasciolae* underwent a similar process. In any case, in the present-day church, the legend of St Peter's bandage has been almost totally eclipsed by remembrances of Sts Nereus, Achilleus and Domitilla.

MEDIEVAL MOSAICS

The present church of SS. Nereo e Achilleo was built (slightly to one side and on a higher elevation) in the early ninth century by Pope Leo III (795–816), probably to house the saints' relics removed for safety from Domitilla's Catacomb. From Pope Leo's building there remains a wonderful mosaic on the triumphal arch. The centre representation of *Christ Transfigured* is said to be rare, if not unique; on the sides are scenes of the *Madonna and Child* and *The Annunciation*, where the Virgin is shown spinning (an iconography typical of the very early Middle Ages).

The interior has a typical basilican form (a nave, two aisles and a wooden roof), but is small and intimate and full of medieval atmosphere. The medieval spirit is enhanced by the choir's inlaid marble floor, glittering mosaic decorations on the altar, and a typical twelfth- or thirteenth-century mosaic pulpit.

One of the church's most evocative features is the ancient marble throne behind the altar. The episcopal seat is guarded by two weathered lions (perhaps they were originally on the church exterior), and its back is inscribed with a homily by Pope Gregory I. (It was long assumed that St Gregory preached here; an apse fresco shows him doing so. But it is now thought that the sermon must have been delivered in the 'other' basilica of SS. Nereo e Achilleo in Domitilla's Catacomb.)

A DISCREET RESTORATION

The church was extensively rebuilt by Pope Sixtus IV (1471–84), and the octagonal columns in the nave are undoubtedly from that period. But it is to the titular Cardinal Cesare Baronius (1596–7), the famous scholar and art historian, that we owe the judicious renovation we now see. From Pope Clement VIII (1592–1605), Cardinal Baronius requested the title of SS. Nereo e Achilleo for his religious Order, the Oratorians, and the church has remained in their care to this day.

Baronius restored the church to a semblance of Romanesque–Renaissance purity. Following his wishes, the building has been spared the intrusive redecorations suffered by many other Roman churches. Baronius also commissioned Pomarancio to fresco the side aisles with terrifying scenes of the Apostles' martyrdoms. In gruesome detail, like Pomarancio's other martyrdom frescoes in S. Stefano Rotondo, the paintings show how each of the Apostles was tortured and martyred.

VIRGIN MARTYRS: ROME'S MOST BELOVED SAINTS

Christianity's rapid expansion and victory over paganism in imperial Rome was largely due to the sacrifices of the early martyrs. The sufferings and martyrdom of several young Christian girls particularly touched the hearts of the early Christian community. Perhaps because of their youth, purity and alleged beauty, perhaps because they came from the upper classes, or perhaps because of the type of martyrdom they endured, these Roman virgins impressed members of the pagan community as well as their early Christian brethren. The stories of their lives and deaths are credited with playing an important role in the final conversion of Rome.

During the centuries of Christian persecution, the Roman Caesars seemed to be at the height of their glory. But in fact the Empire was fraying at the edges, strained by its immense size and threatened by restless conquered peoples at its every border. Moreover, the imperial world seemed to have lost its soul. The traditional rites were now empty habits; the official gods (including some of the degenerate 'divinized' Emperors themselves) seemed fatuous and ludicrous. Although Romans relentlessly dedicated themselves to worldly pleasures and cruel spectacles in the amphitheatres, mysterious Oriental cults, such as that of Mithras, also began to flourish. Many Romans were searching for deeper answers to the questions of life and death.

For many, Christianity could provide those answers. From the beginning, the Christian community showed uncompromising fidelity to its spiritual and moral ideals. Christians placed their God above all, even the Emperor and the Empire, which is why they were perceived as a threat and fiercely persecuted by the imperial authorities.

Along with their courageous martyrdoms, it was also the Christians' exemplary lives which led to the conversion of so many Romans. Charity and honesty towards their friends and enemies alike, a serene outlook on life and death, chastity in a decadent society – these were qualities the virgin martyrs so luminously displayed.

Even today, many of Rome's most appealing churches are dedicated to early virgin martyrs. Many of these have been built over houses where the Roman maidens lived and died for their faith. Here, almost immediately after the virgins' deaths, Christian congregations began to pray together, aware that they could soon face a similar fate. The virgins' cults achieved great popularity. After Christianity's legalization, large basilicas were built over the original house churches, and in later centuries Popes and Cardinals vied with one another to restore, rebuild and embellish the sanctuaries.

This monument to the virgin martyr St Agnes, in the church of her name, portrays the saint as a Byzantine princess in the seventh-century apse mosaic. Beneath the altar *baldachin*, an ancient Oriental statue of Isis was provided with a new head to represent the girl-martyr.

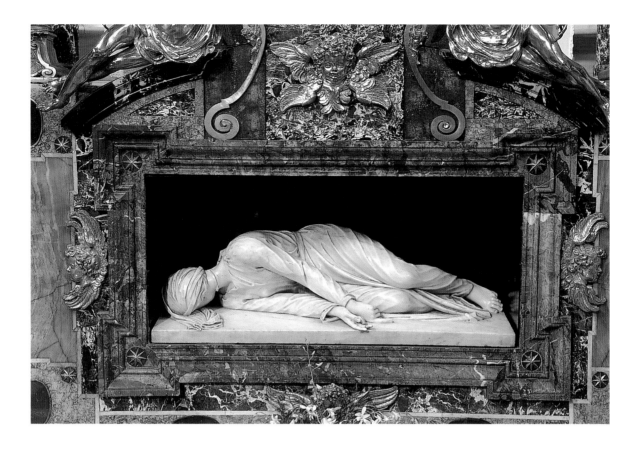

S. CECILIA IN TRASTEVERE

Patroness of Music

A tour of virgin martyrs' shrines often begins at the church of S. Cecilia in Trastevere, a place rich in memories of its maiden patron saint.

A BELOVED YOUNG MARTYR

The imposing church of S. Cecilia towers over Trastevere rooftops. It was built upon the foundations of a Roman villa belonging to a young Roman patrician – Valerian, fiancé of the beautiful and virtuous Cecilia.

According to many guidebooks Cecilia's story has little historical basis. She is not mentioned in the earliest martyrologies or Church calendars, or in the fourth-century hagiographies of Sts Jerome, Augustine, Ambrose and Damasus. Her widespread veneration can first be traced officially to her *passio* of the sixth century. Of course, the lack of written evidence does not at all disprove that the faithful honoured her in earlier centuries.

Fortunately, there is now a modern translation (from Latin to Italian) of Cecilia's *passio* (the booklet is available from the Trastevere church). In the twenty-five pages of this lively account, full of colourful descriptions and witty dialogue, there emerges a convincing portrait of the young saint: fresh and loving, learned and headstrong, and ultimately resolute and courageous.

Valerian and Cecilia were one of imperial Rome's most popular young couples – rich, attractive, and from the very best of families (Cecilia's was the ancient and aristocratic Cecilii lineage). Cecilia was particularly noted for her fine golden gowns. Little did her companions know that underneath, next to her delicate skin, she wore a rough sackcloth, to remind her of her calling to Christ.

On the night of her wedding, Cecilia forbade Valerian the richly decorated *talamo* (bridal couch), informing him of the guardian angel who protected her virginity. Valerian's disappointment was eventually allayed by promises, upon certain conditions, of an introduction to the angel. He was dispatched to the Appian Way, where the holy Pope Urban dwelt among the poor. Here the young patrician was instructed and baptized, and upon his return he saw Cecilia's angel waiting for him with a crown of heavenly flowers.

The couple lived in secret chastity and blessed happiness. But Valerian greatly desired the conversion of his beloved brother Tiburtius. One evening Tiburtius found the young couple at supper, 'engaged in saintly discourses', and, remarking on 'the divine perfumes of roses and lilies', he was told of the angels and holy garlands. Throughout the night Cecilia offered her sceptical brother-in-law Christian arguments worthy of the most learned Doctors of the Church. By morning the noble youth was on his way to Pope Urban for his Christian baptism. The pious brothers then began to dispense their riches to the poor and to bury Christian martyrs, and thus came to the attention of the authorities. They refused to sacrifice to pagan gods and were martyred by decapitation. On their way to execution they converted their guard Maximus, his entire family, and many of his fellow soldiers.

Next Cecilia was called before the wicked Prefect Almachus. She defended herself with great self-confidence and wit, but was finally condemned to suffocation by steam in her own overheated baths. After a day and night she emerged, allegedly singing hymns to the glory of God, only to suffer three attempts by soldiers to decapitate her. The holy maiden lingered on for three days, during which time she managed to convert a great number of Romans. When she finally expired, Cecilia was buried in the St Calixtus Catacombs on the Appian Way. Pope Urban immediately consecrated her house as a church, 'with orders that it remain as such for ever'.

There is much confusion as to the dates of these events, attributed to the reigns of various Emperors. If the St Urban mentioned in Cecilia's *passio* was Pope Urban I (222–30), Cecilia must have perished around 230. On the other hand, the reigning Emperor of that time, Alexander Severus (222–35), was known to be tolerant of Christians. Thus some historians claim that the Urban of Cecilia's *passio* was not the Pope, but rather an important bishop. We have no record of the first church built here, but by the time of the Roman Synod of 499 S. Cecilia was already numbered among Rome's most important titular churches (*Titulus Caeciliae*).

Cecilia's remains, along with those of Valerian, Tiburtius, Maximus, Pope Urban and Pope Lucius I (253–4), were brought to her Trastevere church in the ninth century, and when her tomb was opened in 1599, her body was found to be miraculously intact. Eye-witnesses commented on her golden robes, as well as on the brotherly resemblance of Tiburtius' and Valerian's severed heads, and on Maximus' gladiatorial physique.

A *caldarium* (hot bath), now a chapel off a small corridor in the present church's right aisle, has been identified, by its terracotta pipes and complicated heating system, as the possible place of the first attempt to martyr Cecilia. This room contains scenes from the saint's life by Pomarancio and two important paintings by Guido Reni: *The Angel's Coronation of Sts Cecilia and Valerian* (1600) and *The Beheading of St Cecilia* (1601). Excavations beneath the church (not to be missed) have revealed the foundations of several Roman houses with storerooms and mosaic pavements.

TRIBUTES TO THE VIRGIN SAINT

In early Christianity and later during the Middle Ages devotion to St Cecilia spread far and wide. Today she is most famous as the patroness of music. This title mainly results from legends of her joyous hymn-singing during her martyrdom and death. Some think the connection between St Cecilia and music comes from a possible misunderstanding of one verse in her *passio*. This recorded that 'while the organs were playing on her wedding day, Cecilia sang in her heart only to God'. An early misreading of this text led devotees to think that Cecilia was playing the organ, and that became her symbol. (She can also be portrayed with a violin, viola, lute, etc.)

The church of S. Cecilia in Trastevere has organs on every other nave pilaster, in the vault fresco, and in the seventeenth-century frescoes of the narthex and side aisles. When the Academy of Music was established in Rome in 1584, Cecilia was chosen as its patron saint, and she continues as such today.

By the beginning of the ninth century, the church was in ruins. Luckily the same Pope Paschal (817–24) who so lovingly reconstructed the church of S. Prassede came to S. Cecilia's rescue as well. According to his own first-person account (also translated in the above-mentioned booklet), Paschal had already commenced rebuilding the church when St Cecilia appeared to him in a dream, 'accompanied by a heavenly

Opposite: Stefano Maderno's statue of St Cecilia, carved when the saint's intact body was rediscovered in 1599, is now in front of the main altar in the church of S. Cecilia.

harmony of sounds'. She scolded the Pope for believing rumours that King Astolfo the Lombard had taken away her remains, and led him to her grave and to those of Valerian, Tiburtius, Maximus, and Popes Urban I and Lucius I (253–4). Paschal placed these in three sarcophagi beneath the main altar of the Trastevere church and established a monastery next door, 'for singing day and night' the praises of God and the saints.

To celebrate the discovery and reburial of the saints' relics, Paschal commissioned a magnificent mosaic, which even today spreads its jewel-like colours across S. Cecilia's central apse. At the base, golden letters against a lapis-blue background describe Paschal's donation. Above, the wide-eyed Saviour, standing on brightly coloured clouds, is flanked by Sts Peter, Valerian and Agatha on his left, and Sts Paul, Cecilia and Pope Paschal on his right. Cecilia has her arm around the youthful Pope (with his square halo designating a living person destined for sainthood), as he presents a model of the church.

One century later, Pietro Cavallini (1293) executed a fresco of the *Last Judgement* to cover S. Cecilia's back wall (above the entrance). This world-famous work disappeared from view for several centuries, until it was rediscovered, in 1900, behind the panelling of the nuns' choir in the next-door convent. Even today Cavallini's work is partially covered by plaster and wood-work. A pity, for it is the only remaining painting attributed to this exceptional artist. (His mosaics decorate the church of S. Maria in Trastevere). No pilgrim should miss Cavallini's masterpiece, with its Byzantine-robed Christ, Virgin, saints and Apostles, and a rainbow of delicately-coloured angels' wings.

Around the same time (1283), Arnolfo di Cambio fashioned and signed the marble canopy over S. Cecilia's main altar, with its Gothic arches, gilded spires, and charming little sculptures. After this brief flowering of medieval art, S. Cecilia awaited the Renaissance for worthy artistic recognition of its patron saint.

In the late Renaissance year of 1599, the church of S. Cecilia in Trastevere witnessed a sensational event. During his remodelling of the church, Cardinal Paolo Sfondrati (titular of the church from 1591 to 1618 – his 1618 tomb by Carlo Maderno is in the outside porch) rediscovered the martyr-saints' sarcophagi which 'had been hidden for 800 years'.

Another eye-witness description, by the sixteenth-century archaeologist Antonio Bosio, of Sfondrati's official recognition of the saints' remains is given in the booklet already mentioned.

When the tombs were opened, Bosio reported seeing St Cecilia's body, seemingly intact, dressed in blood-stained golden robes over a rough haircloth, and wrapped in a dark silk veil, with rolled-up blood-stained rags at her feet. Her remains, along with those of the other saints, were exposed for the Roman faithful's veneration for a month and resealed by Pope Clement VIII (1592–1605).

The sculptor Stefano Maderno (1576–1636) was present during Cecilia's exhumation and made an on-the-spot sketch. He later sculpted the white marble statue which today is kept in a glass case beneath the main altar. Cecilia is shown just as Maderno saw her, lying on her side with her knees slightly bent as if in sleep. The saint's head is turned away from the viewer, and we perceive the sword wounds on her neck.

TODAY'S CHURCH

Fortunately we can still enjoy the beauty of Paschal I's mosaic and of Stefano Maderno's statue. Otherwise, the church of S. Cecilia today is, as many visitors agree, somewhat disappointing – a monument to the huge egos of later restorers. The entrance and façade were done by Ferdinando Fuga in 1725, on commission by Cardinal Francesco Acquaviva d'Aragona. Titular Cardinal from 1709 to 1724, Acquaviva prominently displayed his coat-of-arms on entrance, portico and gilded ceiling, near Sebastian Conca's *St Cecilia in Glory* (1721–4).

Cardinal Giorgio Doria (titular 1818–37) was responsible for S. Cecilia's nineteenth-century interior; his family symbol, the dove with olive branch, decorates several pilasters. The enormously wide nave has its former columns enclosed in massive piers and a shiny white floor. Cardinal Mariano Rampolla del Tindaro (titular 1887–1913) had the crypt redone (1899–1901) by Giovanni Battista Giovanale. The thirty-five slender forest-like columns and fine mosaics glimmer in the mysterious underground light. Rampolla's overblown tomb (by Enrico Quattrini, 1929) is in a chapel off the right aisle.

The church is entered under a Romanesque campanile and through a sunny garden-courtyard with a huge classical vase in

This large vase in the courtyard of the church of S. Cecilia may have decorated the home of the Roman virgin martyr.

the centre. Some surmise that this *cantharus* may even have graced Cecilia's and Valerian's Roman atrium.

To the left and right are buildings of the medieval convent. S. Cecilia in Trastevere is cared for by a Benedictine Order of cloistered nuns, who have been here since Pope Clement VII (1523–34) granted them Paschal I's former monastery. These nuns have a special task. In January they accept, from the nuns of S. Agnese Fuori le Mura, two lambs, decked with ribbons and flowers and blessed by the Pope. The S. Cecilia sisters tend the lambs until Easter, when their wool, woven into long sheets and kept for a while in an urn beneath St Peter's main altar, is used to make the *palliums* (neckpieces) which the Pope bestows on new patriarchs and archbishops. Each Sunday the nuns also sing Mass and Vespers in Gregorian Chant in tribute to their patroness Cecilia.

S. BIBIANA
A Forgotten Jewel

Few pilgrims discover this next sanctuary, a treasure which evades most guidebooks to the churches of Rome.

A FORGOTTEN MARTYR

Hidden among the massive outbuildings of Rome's central railway station, soiled by an adjacent smokestack, shaken to its delicate foundations by tunnel, overpass and tramline traffic, the tiny church of S. Bibiana hides behind a veil of soot and grime. This little-frequented church is, however, one of Rome's most artistically and spiritually significant monuments.

The first church of S. Bibiana was a shrine built to honour one of early Christianity's most appealing virgin martyrs. In the fourth century, the site of the present church was an area of meadows, cultivated fields and vineyards known as the *Horti*

Licinii, or Licini Gardens (after Emperor Licinius Ignatius Gallienus, whose family had owned the property since the third century). Even today, amid the squalor and unsightly cement, an occasional aqueduct remnant, or section of Aurelian wall, recalls the quarter's imperial past.

Here, around AD300, numerous suburban Roman villas sprang up in the country setting, amid small temples and *nymphea*. According to a later tradition (now disproved), one of the shrines was dedicated to the goddess of medicine, Minerva Medica, who allegedly worked her wonders down through the ages.

In one of these villas lived the young virgin Bibiana (or Viviana) with her father, Flavian, her mother, Dafrosa, and her sister, Demetria. Hagiographies dating from the fifth to ninth centuries state that Bibiana was born in 347, martyred in 362, and that her father was a noble Roman prefect. A Christian, Flavian was forced to retire from public service during the persecutions carried out under Julian the Apostate (361–3). The new Prefect, Apronian, a fierce opponent of Christians and his predecessor's personal rival, managed to have Flavian branded as a slave, exiled and martyred in a deserted area far from Rome.

The vicious Apronian then ordered Dafrosa, Demetria and Bibiana to be locked in their house and condemned to death by starvation. When, after twelve days, the three brave women were still alive, the prefect dragged them before a public tribunal to sacrifice to the pagan gods. When they refused, Dafrosa was beheaded, Demetria expired in fright, and Bibiana was tied to a marble column and scourged to death with iron-spiked whips. Her body was left outside the city gates to be eaten by wild dogs.

And here the miracles begin. When a devoted Flavian relative, the Roman matron Olimpina, came to collect Bibiana's body, the virgin's body was found to be miraculously intact. She was buried with her mother and sister beneath the family home. During the reign of the Christian Emperor Flavian Jovian (363–4), Olimpina had a small church built on the site of the martyred women's burial.

Curiously, from the beginning, the sanctuary was dedicated to Bibiana alone. Something about the young saint obviously

inspired special piety – and models and inspiration were certainly needed in the Church's early years of persecution and consolidation. In fact, popular veneration of St Bibiana spread so rapidly that only a century later, Pope Simplicius (468–83) consecrated the sanctuary as an official pilgrimage shrine.

Throughout the Middle Ages St Bibiana accumulated more and more miraculous qualities. She became protectress of the insane, of epileptics and of drunkards. The grass which grew around the church, the water from its well, scrapings from the sacred column (tradition has it that Olimpina moved the column where Bibiana was martyred to the saint's later shrine) – all took on almost magical medicinal properties (an interesting devotional 'transference' from the supposed pagan cult to Minerva Medica).

In recognition of Bibiana's expanding veneration, Pope Honorius III restored the church in 1224 and built an adjoining convent, later disbanded due to the notoriously hedonistic behaviour of the resident nuns. Plaques from earlier floor tombs of several medieval abbesses – Viviana, Lucia and Maria – can still be seen on the inside walls of the church.

Left: S. Bibiana, completely restored by the Baroque architect-sculptor Gianlorenzo Bernini in 1625.
His statue of the saint is behind the main altar.

Above: The fresco on the right wall of the nave in S. Bibiana (by A. Ciampelli c.1625) recounts a miraculous episode:
St Bibiana's body was thrown to the dogs and the next day recovered intact.

In 1624 the relics of Bibiana, Dafrosa and Demetria were found under the main altar of the decaying church. A piece of metal interred with the bodies bore the saints' names and confirmed their identification.

A BAROQUE CHURCH

To understand the story of the church of S. Bibiana, it is necessary to go forward in time to a much later period in Catholic Church history. Under the seventeenth-century Barberini Papacy, Rome was enjoying the fruits of the Catholic Counter-Reformation of the previous century. The church of S. Bibiana was in ruins, and one year from the triumphant Jubilee of 1625, Pope Urban VIII (1623–44) seized the opportunity to reassert the inspiration of a beloved martyr. The Barberini Pontiff commissioned Domenico Fedini to write a comprehensive life of St Bibiana – and hired the twenty-six-year-old Gianlorenzo Bernini to restore and decorate the virgin's ancient sanctuary. This was the renowned Baroque artist's very first architectural project.

Bernini barely touched the church's interior structure – divided into three naves by antique columns from earlier monuments. Each column is different – but red and smooth, or fluted grey, with Corinthian, Oriental or composite capitals, they all march in a solemn classical procession to the sanctuary's focal point, the artist's statue of St Bibiana. This stands within a classical altar, which is in perfect harmony with the early church: twin Corinthian columns, beside twin Corinthian pilasters, below a simple tympanum. But the statue itself is pure Bernini Baroque! An indirect light source from high on the left illuminates the figure with a theatrical chiaroscuro, playing on her draperies and hands. The saint's face is tipped backwards with eyes partly closed – an expression of ecstasy in a moment of vision. Her important iconographic signs – the pillar of flagellation, the palm frond for martyrdom, and the miraculous grass beneath her feet – are all present.

Two fresco cycles on the walls of the central nave depict events from the saint's life. On the left (facing the altar): as Demetria expires, Bibiana is condemned to death by the prefect Apronian; she refuses to sacrifice to the pagan gods; she is bound to the sacred pillar and scourged. On the right: Bibiana's body, left to the dogs, is recovered intact; the presbyter John buries Bibiana, Demetria and Dafrosa; and finally, matron Olimpina supervises the construction of the saint's first church.

The right-wall fresco cycle is by Agostino Ciampelli (1565–1630), a Mannerist painter then at the height of his

career. The artist responsible for the left-wall cycle, the still relatively unknown Pietro da Cortona (1596–1669), was described by Ciampelli as 'a little bean, easy to gobble down'. The older artist soon had a case of indigestion, however, as he witnessed his rival overtaking him in skill and fame.

The two artists evidently overcame their competitive ill-will for an impeccable professional collaboration. The frescoes exhibit a surprising stylistic and thematic unity, and even the painted figures between the main scenes (Demetria, Dafrosa, Olimpina, etc.) appear in classical niches similar to the altar-niche behind Bernini's central statue.

The martyrs' motifs are repeated throughout the church, in other paintings by Ciampelli and da Cortona, and in a gruesome still-life of torture instruments behind the entrance

The apse mosaic in S. Agnese Fuori le Mura shows St Agnes between Popes Symmachus (498–514) and Honorius (625–38), who were responsible for building and restoring her church.

S. AGNESE FUORI LE MURA AND S. COSTANZA

Three Early Christian Women

The churches of S. Agnese and S. Costanza hide behind high walls in a green oasis of palm trees along the Via Nomentana, slightly outside Rome. Shadowy centuries of tradition and legend have obscured the origins of the early saints to whom the churches are dedicated.

ST AGNES, ROMAN VIRGIN

Below the churches extend the ancient Catacombs of St Agnes. Here, in the early centuries of Christianity, the virgin martyr Agnes was buried. Her cult quickly achieved great popularity in Rome, and by the first half of the fourth century her burial site had become an important centre of pilgrimage. So many other early Christians desired entombment near St Agnes that her catacombs soon extended as dark, long galleries on both sides of the Via Nomentana.

After studying various anti-Christian imperial edicts, scholars have concluded that Agnes, a child of only twelve or thirteen, was killed during the Emperor Diocletian's persecutions of 303–5. According to Pope Damasus I (366–84), Agnes' parents were the first to tell her story. A young Roman prefect, struck by her beauty, importuned her constantly. Agnes, however, refused marriage because of her dedication to Christ. Spontaneously presenting herself to the authorities as a Christian, she announced her preference for death over any violation of her consecrated virginity.

At this point the accounts become quite startling. She was consigned to a squalid brothel near Domitian's Stadium, and when her nakedness was exposed to the crowds, her hair grew miraculously to cover her body. Then she was set on fire, but the fire left her to engulf her persecutors. Finally she was beheaded. During a vigil at her tomb outside the city walls, Agnes' parents saw her in a vision, accompanied by a procession of gold-robed virgins, and with a snow-white lamb at her right side.

The Depositio Martyrum, or early Church calendar, recorded that by 366 the Pope and the Christian community were celebrating St Agnes' martyrdom every year on 21 January. St Ambrose (334–97) and the Christian poet Prudentius (348–405) wrote her praises. After Agnes' death, one shrine, containing the martyr's head, was erected over the site of her martyrdom (now the Baroque church of S. Agnese in Agone; *in agone*, Latin for 'the place of public games', referred

door. To the right of the entrance, visitors can see the column where Bibiana was reportedly bound during her scourging. After centuries of chipping and rubbing (powder from the stone was thought to cure epilepsy in the Middle Ages), the relic now resembles a smooth brown tree trunk rather than a marble pillar. The column and the urn containing Bibiana's, Dafrosa's and Demetria's remains are behind elegant iron grilles, designed by Bernini himself to harmonize with the overall decor.

Most Roman churches are layer cakes of history and art. S. Bibiana is highly unusual in presenting us with only two eras of Church history – early Christianity and the seventeenth-century Baroque. The medieval restorations somehow disappeared along the way.

Gianlorenzo Bernini's first architectural initiative, executed according to strict instructions from Pope Urban VIII (whose heraldic bees are ubiquitous throughout the church), emphasized S. Bibiana's Paleo-Christian and classical heritage. The Baroque Pontiff and his architect wished to conduct seventeenth-century Catholics back to their early Christian roots.

to Domitian's Stadium, the present Piazza Navona). Another sanctuary was constructed on the site of her grave, and, less than fifty years later, transformed into the imposing basilica of S. Agnese Fuori le Mura (St Agnes Outside the Walls).

Beside the stairs leading down to the basilica of S. Agnese Pope Damasus' ten-line inscription tells of the virgin's miraculous growth of hair. (This was rediscovered in 1728, after having been embedded upside down in the church flooring for more than a millennium.) A few steps before this is a bas-relief of Agnes, childlike in a tunic and sandals, which supposedly decorated her fourth-century altar. Her present statue on the main altar, adapted from a Roman statue of Isis, was made in 1600 by Nicolas Cordier, with the addition of gilded head and hands (another symbolic example of Christianity's victory over Roman paganism).

By the time St Agnes was portrayed in the sparkling seventh-century mosaic in the basilica's apse, she had become, in keeping with the times, a Byzantine princess, robed, crowned and bejewelled; the symbols of her martyrdom, the flames and sword, are placed beside her tiny feet. A nineteenth-century fresco over the triumphal arch (by Pietro Gagliardi, 1856) depicts her in a grand classical setting, about to be beheaded before a pagan temple. Her symbol, the lamb (*agnus* in Latin, a reference to both her name, and her sacrifice, or martyrdom), occurs throughout the church.

A SISTERLY MARTYR

In the seventeenth century, Popes and Cardinals began to insist on 'confirmation' of martyrs' relics in Rome's major churches. When St Agnes' shrine was exhumed around 1600, her remains were found to be accompanied by those of another young female martyr. This was St Emerenziana, St Agnes' sister, or foster-sister. It is sad that so little is known about St Emerenziana, for she must have been a brave young woman. According to tradition, this second Christian virgin helped bury her sister-saint and was stoned to death when found praying at Agnes' tomb. She was buried near St Agnes in the Nomentana catacombs, and her feast-day was celebrated two days after that of her sister, that is, on 23 January.

In the basilica of S. Agnese, St Emerenziana has her own chapel, across from the altar off the right aisle. In the glittering Art Nouveau altar mosaic, she is depicted holding the palm of martyrdom in one hand and a large stone in the other. The rather sentimentalized paintings on the side (1856, by Eugenio Cisterna) show Emerenziana preparing Agnes for burial and praying at her tomb. St Emerenziana's relics rest along with those of St Agnes in a single silver urn (provided by Pope Paul V in 1605) beneath the main altar.

A PIOUS PRINCESS

The basilica in honour of St Agnes was erected by the daughter of the Roman Emperor, Constantine the Great (306–37). Tradition holds that the Princess Costanza (or perhaps Constantia or Constantina) came to the saint's tomb in hopes of a cure for a disfiguring skin ailment. During the night, Agnes appeared to the Princess in a dream, entreating her to become a Christian. The next morning, finding her skin smooth and clear, Costanza ordered a grand basilica built (342) over the saint's burial site. Adjacent to S. Agnese, Costanza built her own mausoleum (between 337 and 54), now known as the church of S. Costanza.

Knowledge of Costanza is very sketchy. She was married to two members of the imperial family, first Annibalianus (335), and upon his death Gallus (350), her sister Helena's husband. (Helena is also buried in the mausoleum.) Costanza died in Antioch in 354 and, in keeping with her last wishes, her body was returned to Rome to lie near that of her favourite saint. A contemporary historian, the Antiochian Ammianus Marcellinus, described Costanza and Gallus as especially cruel and bloodthirsty. That account is dubious, however, since Marcellinus was known to have been a political adversary of Gallus and was constantly plotting his downfall.

For centuries, Costanza's mausoleum was used as a baptistery for the S. Agnese basilica. It was first referred to as the church of S. Costanza in 865, during Pope Nicholas I's reinstatement of the unjustly deposed Bishop Rotardus. In 1256 Pope Alexander IV added two more virgin saints, Attica and Artemia, to the church dedication. In fact, most scholars doubt that the St Costanza of the church title was actually the Princess Costanza. There is no precise information that Costanza was even baptized as a Christian.

S. Costanza's ambulatory vault is completely covered with fourth-century mosaics – some of the earliest and most beautiful in all Rome. The tone of this decor is light and personal. Ten pairs of matched panels present (against a white background typical of Roman mosaic pavements) geometric patterns; playful cupids and graceful dancing girls; dazzling, gold-sprinkled birds, ducks, geese, foxes and other animals – amazingly realistic; mirrors, pots and pans, and everyday household furnishings. Medallions frame tiny bust-portraits of

Roman matrons and gentlemen, dressed and coiffured in the latest styles, and looking astonished to be there. Larger busts portray Costanza and her first husband, Annabalianus. A very similar portrait of Costanza can be seen on her porphyry sarcophagus (a copy, that is; the real one is in the Vatican Museum) at the back of the church.

S. Costanza abounds in mosaics of vine tendrils and vintage scenes, peacocks and sheep. Many pagan symbols were gradually taken over by Christian iconography (peacocks for eternal life; sheep for Christ's faithful flock; grapes for the harvest of souls). Niche mosaics are from a later period – the fifth to seventh centuries; yet even here, Christ and the Apostles have the appearance of Roman senators in their traditional togas. In the early fourth century Christian iconography had barely been developed. Even in the catacombs the imagery, except for a few Bible stories, was still taken from classical painting.

VISITS TO THE CHURCHES OF S. AGNESE AND S. COSTANZA

The basilica of S. Agnese, built by Pope Honorius I (625–38) over Costanza's crumbling edifice, is as Greek–Byzantine in character as S. Costanza is Roman classical. Ancient Roman columns support a double row of dim galleries (the top was the *matronea*, or women's section), while the apse mosaic dazzles with its solid gold background and courtly figures: St Agnes, Pope Honorius I, and Pope Symmachus (498–514), who undertook an earlier restoration.

All around the nave are paintings (by Domenico Tojetti, *c.*1850) of other virgin saints: Victoria, Lucia, Agatha, Barbara, Cecilia, Martina, Bibiana, Rufina, Colomba, Julia, Apollonia, Flora, Caterina, Susanna, and Candida. The basilica also has a pleasant marble altarpiece by Andrea Bregno (1418–1503), representing two other early Christian martyrs, the deacons Sts Stephen and Lawrence.

The exterior of the church of S. Costanza still reveals its origins as a classical fourth-century mausoleum.

Each year on St Agnes' day (21 January) two lambs are blessed here before the main altar, and then taken to St Cecilia's Convent in Trastevere, as described earlier. To further emphasize the link between St Agnes and St Cecilia, both of them appear with the Virgin on the basilica's gilded ceiling – a gift of the same Cardinal Sfondrati who (between 1599 and 1614) 'rediscovered' and reburied the remains of both these virgin martyrs.

The church of S. Costanza is entered via a shady pathway and a quiet courtyard. The monument is similar to other circular classical tombs, such as Hadrian's Mausoleum, now the Castel Sant'Angelo. The ambulatory, with its famed classical mosaics, has twelve double Corinthian columns linked by arcades. In the fourth century, the now-unpainted cupola was also covered with mosaics. Sketches made of the mosaics in the seventeenth century (they were destroyed in 1620) showed waterside villas in leafy forests, populated by mythological figures. The sketchbooks are preserved in the Escorial Palace in Spain.

Left: The vault mosaics of the church of S. Costanza show the very early transition between pagan and Christian symbolism.

Above: A harvest scene, light and pagan in tone, is meant to have clear biblical allusions.

VICTORY OF THE CROSS: THE CHURCH AS HEIR TO IMPERIAL ROME

Christianity's swift advance – from small forbidden sect to the recognized religion of the vast Roman Empire – was astounding. In fact, the Emperor Constantine's legalization of the Christian faith in AD313 came less than one decade after Diocletian's bloody persecutions (303–5), which had sent so many martyrs to their deaths. Today's visitors can trace signs of this amazing progress in the multiple layers of some of Rome's oldest churches.

Constantine (306–37), son of the army ruler of Gaul and the saintly Christian convert Helena, became sole Emperor of the West in a battle he won near Rome under the insignia of the Cross. During his reign he favoured Christianity's progress in both the East and the West. This important personage will be more fully described in Part II of this book, on the fourth-century pilgrimage basilicas he built as monuments to the 'victory of the cross'. Today these Constantinian churches are some of the world's most important Christian shrines.

Christianity's march forward was confident and rapid. In 394 the Emperor Theodosius I (d. 395) declared the new confession the Roman Empire's official religion, and a few years later the Senate abolished paganism in all its forms. The Roman Church signalled its success with a flurry of building throughout the city. No longer hidden by their modest size and by their location beyond the city walls, the new churches were raised as conspicuous and impressive witnesses to the advance of Christ's faith. Yet as the Roman Church asserted itself, the Caesars' imperial capital was sliding into decline.

Restless barbarian hordes were thundering at Rome's doors, and for the next few centuries would ravage the Italian countryside and the imperial city. To protect his Eastern borders, Constantine had founded a new capital in Byzantium, called Constantinople, and the court and army followed in his wake.

Left behind to protect the Western capital, the Popes began to consider themselves as the Emperors' spiritual and temporal successors. They treasured their classical heritage and identified with Rome's historical past. The religious buildings which now sprang up in Rome developed in the framework of

The Pantheon, the imperial Roman temple to 'all the gods', which was converted into a Christian church during the seventh-century papacy of Boniface IV.

classical Roman civilization. In the mausoleum built by Constantine's own daughter, the transformation from pagan to Christian iconography was just beginning.

Churches were first built acording to the layout of the Roman home, where for centuries the faithful had secretly gathered in inner courtyards or private rooms. But larger structures were soon needed for the mushrooming Christian community. The Church was not reluctant to build proudly near or over the sites of pagan temples, but Christianity soon required a new architectural language of its own. Besides, pagan temples were designed to contain only the gods' statues or symbols and a few initiated priests; they could not accommodate large and growing Christian congregations.

It seems to have been Constantine who conceived of the secular Roman basilica, a great hall of justice and a public meeting place, as an ideal structure for Christian worship. Here was a grand edifice, public in nature, impressive in size and form, and resplendent in material. (The ruins of one of the last significant secular models, the immense Maxentius and Constantine basilica, can still be seen in the Roman Forum.) The Roman basilica adapted for Christian services was a long oblong hall – a nave flanked by aisles – terminating in a semi-circular apse. Classical columns (often recycled from pagan religious or secular buildings), pediments, reliefs and mosaics were important classical features of the basilica's decor.

S. SABINA
The Aventine's Classical Citadel

Viewed from the banks of the Tiber, the basilica and priory of S. Sabina rise as a stalwart fortress commanding one of Rome's seven hills. Three sister churches join forces with S. Sabina to march their ochre walls – occasionally broken by a Romanesque campanile or gently bulging apse – in a stony palisade around the Aventine summit. It is no accident that the Aventine churches display a military front, for it was here, after the devastation and trauma of Rome's first barbarian invasion in the fifth century, that Roman Christianity took its confident new stand.

TWO MARTYRS

In the fourth century, the proletarian Aventine had become the setting for luxurious patrician villas and wealthy merchants' homes. Both pagan and Christian cult centres sprang up on the wooded slopes. After Constantine's legalization of Christianity in 313, churches such as S. Clemente, S. Prassede and S. Pudenziana were built upon the *tituli* of early martyrs' homes, and following the banning of pagan religions in 394, began to spread out over former pagan properties. The basilica of S. Sabina had similar origins.

Twentieth-century excavations have revealed the foundations of a large marble-tiled (third- or fourth-century) Roman mansion upon the site now occupied by S. Sabina's vestibule and nave (one of the columns can be seen in the right aisle), and, in particular, a room which seems to have been used for religious purposes. Here, according to tradition, the saintly Marcella created an anchorite cell modelled on those of Eastern desert monks and gave hospitality to Sts Athanasius and Jerome in the fourth century. And here Marcella and her group of pious Roman ladies kept and venerated the relics of the original St Sabina.

A prayer card distributed in the basilica says: 'St Sabina was a noble pagan, wife of the Senator Valentine; she was converted by her Greek serving maid Seraphia and suffered martyrdom on 29 August 125, under the Emperor Hadrian.' In fact, the *Acta* (stories of saints) written in the sixth century relate that Sabina and Seraphia were martyred and buried in

Built as a conspicuous witness to the resurgence of Christianity after the Sack of Rome in 410, the church of S. Sabina has a fortress-like exterior (above) and an interior modelled on the secular basilicas of imperial Rome (right).

Vindena, Umbria. Apparently, due to the threat of barbarian invasions, their relics were moved to the Aventine in Rome in the fourth century, where they became the focus for a Christian cult centre. The remains of Roman baths and several pagan sanctuaries under the present basilica suggest a Christian expansion similar to that in S. Clemente and S. Pudenziana. But S. Sabina was to undergo a different fate.

THE SACK OF ROME AND CHRISTIAN RESURGENCE

During the night of 24 August 410, Alaric's Visigoths broke their long siege and poured into Rome. According to contemporary historians, a lightning storm of extreme ferocity accompanied the invaders' cries and flashing swords. The Aventine's luxury and wealth made it vulnerable to the most complete destruction, and after three days of pillage, violence and finally a devastating fire, almost nothing remained of the imperial quarter. In fact, the event seemed to herald the end of the Roman world.

But it was not the end of Christian Rome. With Rome's pagan temples still smouldering, Roman Christians, as if hearkening to St Augustine's teachings in *The City of God*, began a frenzy of church building. New and more imposing basilicas rose like phoenixes from the ashes of smaller churches. Extensive convents and monasteries presented their thick walls against further barbarian incursions. It was during this period that work commenced on the basilica of S. Sabina.

The basilicas built after the Sack of Rome were increasingly massive and classical. They were intended not only as bastions against the Northern threat, but as direct heirs of imperial *aulae*, such as those of Maxentius and Constantine mentioned above.

A CLASSICAL CHURCH FOR THE FIFTH CENTURY

S. Sabina's dedication mosaic covers the rear wall above the basilica's entrance. In metric Latin – golden letters on a bright blue background – the inscription says that during the pontificate of Pope Celestine (422–32), a wealthy Roman priest, Peter, originally from Illyria, donated his entire personal wealth ('rich for the poor, poor for himself') to the construction of the church. (Peter may have chosen the Aventine for his project because of the presence of so many devotees to his fellow Illyrian, St Jerome, including the Christian women who harboured the relics of Sts Sabina and Seraphia.)

Construction started in 422 and was completed in the pontificate of Pope Sixtus III (432–40), who consecrated the basilica in 432. Two female figures flanking the inscription are identified as the Churches of the Circumcision and of the Gentiles, that is, the body of Christians converted from Judaism and from other religions. Volumes have been written on the church's perfect classical proportions and disposition of light. Logical balance and harmonious simplicity characterize

S. Sabina's wooden entrance doors were carved in the fifth century and have the very first representation of Christ on the Cross.

its basilican form: a high nave, approached through a narthex (porch), flanked by aisles and terminating in a semi-circular apse. Little decoration interferes with the purity of design.

Twenty-four white marble columns parade their Corinthian capitals along the nave to the main altar. Early historians claimed these were taken from a nearby temple to Juno, but now it is agreed that they were designed specially for the basilica. Where could so many perfect columns be found intact, especially after the Visigoths had put the Aventine to the torch? This is the first example in Rome of columns supporting arches without an architrave – an arcade design apparently imported from Illyria. A recent theory explains the strange coloured marbles above the arcades as insignia of Illyrian cavalry companies, a reference to the source of Peter's wealth (his father sold horses to the Roman legions).

One of the basilica's most famous treasures, the great cypress-wood door at the church entrance, still has most of its original fifth-century carved panels. These depict scenes from both the Old and New Testament; the panel in the top left corner showing Christ on the Cross between the two thieves is considered to be the earliest representation of the Crucifixion. It is a miracle that these wooden carvings have survived from the fifth century.

LATER ADDITIONS

After the fifth century, the most important additions to S. Sabina were made in the 800s. In 824 Pope Eugenius II (824–7) added the *schola cantorum* (choir), in the middle of the nave, and the *ambones* (pulpits). He also transported the relics of three other saints, Pope St Alexander I, St Theodulus and St Eventius, contemporaries of Sts Sabina and Seraphia, and interred them in the same sarcophagus under the high altar.

The apse fresco, painted by Taddeo Zuccari and his assistants in 1560, is believed to reproduce the theme of the original fifth-century apsidal painting: Christ, enthroned with the Apostles, salutes Sts Dominic, Sabina, Seraphia, Alexander, Theodulus and Eventius. In the late 1500s Taddeo and his brother Federico also frescoed the St Hyacinth Chapel (Hyacinth was a thirteenth-century Polish Dominican) off the right nave. The chapel's altar painting, specially commissioned by the Cardinal-Prior of the day, was executed by Lavinia Fontana (1552–1614), one of the few women painters of the late sixteenth century. In the same aisle is a pleasant fifteenth-century stone tomb by the school of Andrea Bregna.

The Baroque Chapel of St Catherine of Siena (1347–80),

off the left-hand aisle, contains a painting by Sassoferrato (1605–85) of *Our Lady of the Rosary with Sts Dominic and Catherine.* Apparently in 1902 the painting was stolen for several months, and was later recovered by a clever Roman policeman who posed as a rich collector of stolen art. St Catherine was a Dominican Tertiary, and the church contains many tributes to the Dominican Order, who have been serving the church since the thirteenth century.

Most guidebooks mention the mosaic floor tomb of an early Dominican Superior General, Munoz de Zamora, who died in S. Sabina in 1300. But there are two even more interesting funerary memorials. One medieval matron was so generous in her hospitality to wandering Dominicans that she was buried in S. Sabina in 1313 with the honorary rank of 'Hostess General of the Dominican Order'. Cardinal Vincent Maculano, a Dominican theologian–astrologer, defended Galileo's astronomical theories and was buried with full honours in the basilica in 1667.

S. Sabina today can be enjoyed in its almost pristine fifth-century state. This is because restorations this century (particularly under Professor Antonio Munoz who became Rome's Superintendent of Monuments in the 1930s) have stripped away most of the later additions, reopened the ancient clerestory windows, and replaced the ceiling with something similar to what would have been seen on the original structure. The portico (fifteenth-century) and vestibule have columns and sarcophagi from classical Rome.

THE DOMINICAN MONASTERY

Adjoining the basilica is a peaceful monastery, founded by St Dominic (1170–1221) himself in 1220, which has housed the Dominican Order of Preachers for over 700 years. Pope Honorius III (1216–27) confirmed the donation of S. Sabina to the Dominicans in 1222, and since 1936 the Priory has been the Dominican world headquarters, or Curia seat. Both St Dominic and St Thomas Aquinas (1225–74) lived and studied here.

The pilgrim must ring the monastery bell to visit the Romanesque cloister and the cell where St Dominic is said to have consulted with St Francis of Assisi and Angelus the Carmelite. A painting depicts a vision the saint had in this cell: the Virgin Mary protecting the future members of the Dominican Order under her mantle. Another discovery is the musty museum above the basilica, in the original friars' dormitory (St Thomas Aquinas resided and worked here for some time), with works of art from every historical period.

A secret window in the museum offers a bird's-eye view of the basilica below. From here the Dominicans watched one night as the devil hurled a stone (now on display at the back of the church) at St Dominic in prayer at the altar, smashing the tablet over the reliquary sarcophagus.

S. Sabina is often described – by writers and pilgrims alike – as the most perfect example of an early Christian basilica. Its grandeur, serenity and classical proportions are witness to the confidence of the early post-Constantine Church.

SS. COSMA E DAMIANO
Pagan Temples for Two Christian Martyrs

The sixth-century church of SS. Cosma e Damiano was constructed from two important monuments of the classical era, another example of the Roman Church asserting its conquest of paganism and its inheritance of the imperial past.

IMPERIAL BEGINNINGS

The basilica has unusual origins. Who would guess from the uninteresting façade (or even the interior, for that matter) that it was constructed from two important imperial pagan monuments? In fact, in 527 Pope St Felix (526–30) expropriated, with permission from the Byzantine Queen Amalasunta (d. 535), the library in Vespasian's Forum of Peace (73–4) and Emperor Maxentius' Temple of Romulus (309), in order to make a shrine for the two fourth-century martyrs Cosmas and Damian. This is certainly not the first or last time we find pagan sanctuaries converted to Christian churches. But why these saints and why this site?

Cosmas and Damian were two physician-brothers who worked in Cilicia (now Syria) until their martyrdom in 303, in one of Diocletian's last persecutions. They were famous for working miraculous cures – and for offering their services free of charge. By the fifth century their cult had spread from Syria to Rome and found a fervent devotee in Pope Felix himself.

Felix remembered that in imperial times Vespasian's Library had been used for lectures on medicine and science, and most physicians' offices were still located in that area. Furthermore, the temple of the twin-brother gods, Castor and Pollux, stood nearby, and had been particularly revered by ancient Romans. The Pope thus found it appropriate to substitute two Christian doctor-brothers for the pagan twins and at the same time 'convert' the practice of medicine.

To gain a feeling for the shrine's classical roots, the pilgrim should walk round the back of the church into the Roman Forum, where part of Romulus' temple, with its heavy bronze doors, can still be seen. In imperial times the edifice was located on Rome's sacred processional route, the ancient Via Sacra.

The Barberini Pope Urban VIII (1623–44) radically transformed the church in 1632 (according to plans by Luigi Arrigucci), giving it its present-day appearance. Unfortunately, the gilded wooden ceiling (with the Pope's family emblem, the Barberini bees, prominently displayed), Baroque altar, and wide nave with pilasters and side chapels have diminished the mystical atmosphere of the sixth-century church. But most visitors do not even notice.

CHRIST IN GLORY

Anyone who enters the basilica of SS. Cosma e Damiano is immediately struck by the magnificent sixth-century mosaic which spreads its brilliant colours across the wide apse behind the altar. Against a deep blue sky, Christ, in glittering gold robes, descends a staircase of fiery clouds. To the right and left, Sts Peter and Paul, dressed as ancient Romans in white togas and thonged sandals, present the martyr-saints Cosmas and Damian. The brothers are dressed in identical brown robes and have similar olive-skinned countenances (as befits their Syrian origins and blood relationship).

On the far left, Pope Felix presents a model of his church, and on the far right, Theodore, in a jewelled Byzantine cape, holds the martyrs' crown. (This figure is identified as St Theodore by an inscription above his head, but some scholars have conjectured that it might represent the Emperor Theodoric (d. 526), who ruled from Constantinople through his Ravenna exarch, and nudged along Felix's election to the Papal throne.) Below, twelve sheep (representing the Apostles) march solemnly towards the Lamb of God.

The mosaic dates from 527–30. The late fourth- (or early fifth-) century mosaic in the apse of S. Pudenziana was described in an earlier chapter as 'the last gasp of naturalistic Roman art', but perhaps this was a premature judgement. The most astonishing aspect of this later work is its naturalness and realism (in contrast to the more stylized Byzantine style which characterized Roman churches from the fifth to the fifteenth centuries). It is true that the Cosmas and Damian mosaic has the frontal, wide-eyed look of Byzantine figures, but here the faces are modelled as true portraits, the draperies have real weight, and the saints' feet are firmly placed upon the ground.

The flowers and rocks below look almost tangible, and each sheep has an individual, slightly amazed expression.

The mosaic was restored under Urban VIII; the figure of Felix and the three sheep below him clearly reveal a mediocre Baroque hand. Urban had his tell-tale Barberini bees painted on to the flowers in the left corner. On the triumphal arch above the apse, the less brilliant palette and more hieratic style of the mosaics date them to the seventh century. These are also very beautiful. A total of seven candlesticks and four angels are on either side of the Lamb of God. There are symbols for only two Evangelists, John and Matthew; those for Mark and Luke were covered up in later restorations. The odd objects on both lower ends of the arch are actually the draped hands of the twenty-four Elders of the Apocalypse, also covered over, offering crowns to the Saviour.

In the 1500s the basilica's titular Cardinal, Alessandro Farnese, later to be Pope Paul III from 1534 to 49, consigned the church to the Franciscans of the Third Order Regular, and it has remained in their care to this day. Seventeenth-century portraits of Franciscan saints and blesseds are painted in a row of medallions below the apse mosaic, and images of the Third Order patron saint, St Louis of France, appear throughout the church.

In the side altars there are art works from different periods. A series of frescoes around the nave, attributed to the seventeenth-century artist Marco Tullio Montagna, along with the vault painting, depicts scenes from the lives of Sts Cosmas and Damian. The crypt below has part of the original mosaic floor and a Paleo-Christian altar.

The main treasure of SS. Cosma e Damiano is this splendid sixth-century apsidal mosaic in the classical style.

THE INFANT JESUS IN A RARE SETTING

There is not very much in this church to occupy the visitor's time and attention, except, that is, the immense and delightful Neapolitan crib scene (sixteen metres long, nine metres high and seven metres deep) to the right of the inside entrance. Fashioned in the 1700s for Charles III, the Bourbon King of Naples, with the collaboration of many gifted artisans, it was donated to the church in 1939 by the Roman family Cataldo-Perricelli, and put on permanent display.

Anyone unfamiliar with this type of Christmas crèche is missing a rare treat. For centuries, Neapolitan artisans have lovingly and skilfully surrounded scenes of the Nativity with figures and activities from their everyday life. Everything is patiently hand-made. Farmhouses and taverns have real straw floors; on far-away hills, welcoming lights twinkle from medieval villages. Figurines in typical seventeenth-century costumes go about their daily chores: women wash and hang out clothes, a fishmonger noisily hawks his wares, guests eat outside a tavern, while girls with tambourines dance under grape-arbours. Above all this, swirling porcelain angels fly about like pastel-coloured birds. A procession of the Magi, with pearly turbans and rearing Arabian stallions, winds through the streets.

The centre of attention is, of course, the Holy Family. But here the Nativity grotto has been transferred to a classical pagan temple. Two lonely, beautifully rendered Corinthian columns and a broken marble pediment frame the Nativity manger, symbolizing paganism in ruins after the coming of the Saviour and the triumph of Christianity.

The crèche is a fitting addition to this early Christian church, which now covers – and hides – two of imperial Rome's most famous structures.

SS. Cosma e Damiano also contains an elaborate eighteenth-century Neapolitan Christmas crib, showing the Nativity in a classical Roman setting.

S. MARIA AD MARTYRES
The Pantheon Becomes a Christian Church

A significant moment in the 'victory of the cross' came when the most illustrious pagan monument in all of ancient Rome was transformed into a Christian church.

THE ONE GOD OVERCOMES

The Pantheon. Even in imperial times this building was considered one of the marvels of the ancient world. Admired throughout antiquity because of its immense size, advanced engineering and aesthetic effect, the monument became a symbol of classical Rome and of the Emperors' supremacy. Moreover, as its name indicated, the Pantheon was a temple dedicated to 'all the gods', protectors of the imperial city and its widespread territories.

In the end, however, neither the Roman Emperors nor their pagan gods proved to be invincible. In the year 608 the Pantheon was ceded to Pope Boniface IV (608–15) as a church for Christian worship. The transfer was granted by Phocas, Emperor of Byzantium and at that time overlord of Rome. By then, overcome by internal decay and external invasions, both the Roman Caesars and their Western Empire had bowed off the historical stage.

Boniface rededicated the Roman divinities' temple to 'St Mary and all the saints and martyrs'. To make his point, tradition holds, the Pope brought twenty-eight cartloads of martyrs' remains from the catacombs and reburied them in the formerly pagan sanctuary. A more fitting gesture for the triumph of Christianity over pagan civilization can scarcely be imagined.

As far back as Romans could remember, this had been a sacred site. According to tradition, a tumulus had existed here, in the far-away days of Etruscan kings and Republican tribunes, to mark the spot where Rome's mythical founder was taken off into heaven by the god Mars. Around 27BC the Emperor Augustus' son-in-law Agrippa built a large temple in his newly landscaped area of baths and public gardens.

Ravaged by several fires in succeeding centuries, Agrippa's temple was rebuilt from the ground up in AD120–125 by the Emperor Hadrian (117–38). Hadrian was an energetic and effective ruler, an outstanding patron of the arts, and an architect of rare skill. Some Christians were, however, executed during his reign (the pious Sabina, for instance), and it seems appropriate that many martyrs were later interred under the Emperor's justly renowned cupola.

The Roman Church, for both practical and ideological reasons, preferred to build great new churches rather than use pagan religious buildings. The Pantheon's design, however, was quite atypical, and much better suited for Christian services. Nevertheless, Rome's temple to all the gods had to wait for its Christian conversion until two centuries after S. Sabina was constructed on the model of a secular basilica, and another full century after Pope Felix incorporated two pagan buildings in the Forum into his SS. Cosma and Damiano church.

CLASSICAL CULTURE
AND CHRISTIAN CULTS

A first view of the Pantheon, from across the busy Piazza della Rotonda, already makes a tremendous impression. There are few other buildings in the world which stand so solidly rooted in both the past and present, impervious to the passing of centuries and the march of history. Hadrian was wise to leave Agrippa's stony façade and bold inscription ('Marcus Agrippa, son of Lucius, Consul for the third time, built this') across the entablature. The sense of permanence and solidity increases with the pedimented porch, supported by eighteen massive columns, and the huge (original) bronze doors.

The full interior effect is best enjoyed in the early morning, before the rush of tourists, when the light floods in from the cupola's large *oculus* to fill the vast spherical space. Most Roman temples had massive and imposing exteriors and shallow narrow interiors (the *cellae*), intended only for the initiated few. But in its huge circular hall the Pantheon can gather thousands under what was, until the beginning of this century, the largest dome in the world (43.30 metres in diameter).

Books and pamphlets on sale within the Pantheon will explain the perfection of the monument's proportions (the diameter of the dome is equal to the height of the building); its astronomical significance (light through the dome-opening is a super-precise sundial); the intricacy of its engineering (relieving arches built into the masonry); and its advanced construction techniques (concrete and brass rings). Structurally, the building remains much as it was in Hadrian's time: the floor laid in precious marbles (restored by Pius IX in 1873); great structural pillars and fluted columns; the lower wall articulation of niches and tabernacles; the upper storey with windows for statues and reliefs; the vast cupola itself.

In Hadrian's day, the dome exterior was covered by sheets of gilded bronze. Inside, the coffered ceiling symbolized the abode of the gods in heaven, and the wall recesses were filled with golden, silver and painted statues of gods and goddesses. Although the Pantheon's name indicates a temple to all the gods, historians now believe it was initially dedicated to the seven planetary divinities: Mars, Venus, Jupiter, the Moon, the Sun and Saturn, whose images stood in the seven major niches. Zeus, father of the gods, gazed down upon all through the *oculus* void.

Now, with most of the classical splendour stripped away, all attention is riveted on the great dome *oculus*, the all-seeing eye of heaven. Christianity's response to the idolatry and polytheism of the ancient world was just that: the light and grace which spread throughout the world emanate from one eternal and omniscient source. Hadrian had designed his rotunda to stress the theme of unity – of the gods and state, the eternal Empire and the everlasting revolutions of the planetary system. In the church of St Mary and the Martyrs, this unity came to represent the One God's one and universal Church on earth.

THE CHURCH OF ST MARY
AND THE MARTYRS

The Pantheon's magnificent simplicity might lead us to overlook its troubled and complicated history. In 663 the Byzantine Emperor Constans II stripped the roof of its gilded bronze tiles. Pope Gregory III (731–41) replaced these with lead sheeting – a great loss to the monument's aesthetics. Later the Barberini Pope Urban VIII (1623–44) spirited away bronze from the beams in the portico to use for the *Baldacchino* in St Peter's and for the Castel Sant'Angelo cannons (provoking a famous pun of the times: 'What the barbarians didn't do, the Barberinis did.') The Barberini Pope did commission two bell-towers for the façade from his favourite Baroque artist, Gianlorenzo Bernini (1598–1680).

In general it is true that the Christian art of later centuries has done little to enhance the Pantheon's classical setting. However, the delicate *Annunciation* by Melozzo da Forli (1438–94) is a lovely tribute to fifteenth-century art, as is the *Madonna of Mercy with Sts Francis and John the Baptist* by an anonymous Umbrian painter.

The Pantheon contains the tombs of two Italian kings, Vittorio Emanuele II and Umberto I, and the remains of some famous artists. Most important of these was Raphael (1483–1520), who requested that the name of his long-term fiancée, Maria Bibiena, be inscribed on a plaque to the right of his tomb.

The great painter had put off his marriage to Maria because of an infatuation with the beautiful 'Fornarina', and only repented of this, it is said, on his deathbed. Other famous Italian artists entombed in the Pantheon include Baldassare Peruzzi, Taddeo Zuccari, and Annibale Carracci, as well as Raphael's pupils, Perin del Vaga and Giovanni da Udine.

A LIVELY SETTING

On leaving the Pantheon a visitor may notice some unseemly holes in the portico columns: these were used to secure wooden poles for the support stands of an odoriferous and disorderly poultry market which took place here throughout much of the Middle Ages. In the early Renaissance, Pope Eugene IV (1431–47) made the cleaning out of the Pantheon portico one of his first priorities. A raucous fish market persisted in the piazza until 1847. Later, in the sixteenth and seventeenth centuries, the Pantheon porch was used as an exhibition hall for members of the artists' guild known as the 'Pantheon *Virtuosi*', which still exists today.

To this day the Pantheon's piazza continues to be a lively gathering place: for beggars and backpackers, visitors from every nation, and even the most aristocratic, after-theatre Romans, who still consider this their city's most important landmark.

An Egyptian obelisk, set on top of the late Renaissance fountain in the centre of the piazza in the eighteenth century by Pope Clement XI (1700–21), but dating from the dynasty of Ramses II (1292–1167 BC), looks down upon the scene with a four-millennial historical perspective.

**The Pantheon, begun by Augustus's son-in-law Agrippa in 27BC,
reconstructed by the Emperor Hadrian in AD120–125, and in the seventh century converted into
the Christian church of S. Maria ad Martyres.**

CHAPTER

BETWEEN TWO EMPIRES: POPES TAKE ON IMPERIAL FUNCTIONS AND ART

As the Papacy was consolidating its authority and building churches in Rome, beyond the city walls the Western Empire was rapidly expiring. During the fifth century, successive waves of barbarians – Goths, Huns, Vandals and Ostrogoths – swept down upon Italy and Rome. In 476 the last Roman Emperor, young Romulus Augustulus, lost his throne to the German warrior Odoacer, and the Empire of the West disappeared off the historical screen.

ut Rome did not die. The barbarian invasions had sent the city into deep emotional shock, and the Roman people turned to the Papacy for moral and political leadership. From the beginning, the Church had patterned its hierarchy and organization on imperial structures. Now, with the Emperor's desertion of Rome for the East, the Papacy was poised to take over the tasks of civic administration, law and order, food distribution and social services for the poor. The Church, proclaiming a kingdom not of this world, occupied the place abdicated by the Emperor of the West. In the words of one of early Christianity's greatest Popes, St Leo I (440–61): 'Rome remains the head of the world through the See of Peter.'

Two Popes in particular (both afterwards granted the title 'Great' by the Catholic Church) were responsible for the tremendous growth of Papal authority and prestige in the early Church. In 452 Pope St Leo I travelled north to deter Attila's Huns from sacking Rome; in 455 he restrained the Vandals under Gaiseric from razing the city to its foundations. (The Vandals managed to do enough damage, however, to give us their name as an English word for destruction.)

A century and a half later, Pope St Gregory I (590–604) restored and reorganized Rome after other invaders, the Lombards this time, had wreaked devastation on the city and its countryside. Gregory's accomplishments were many, (see page 90).

After the fall of the Western Empire, the Byzantine, or former Eastern Roman, Empire continued to exist and flourish. Byzantium was technically Rome's overlord, with its exarch, or Governor, stationed in Ravenna. But in fact, the

In the early Middle Ages, S. Maria in Cosmedin was established as a diaconia, or Church charity centre, to take over food distribution services after the fall of the Roman Empire.

Papacy increasingly asserted its spiritual and political independence. Eventually the two realms – constantly bickering and threatening one another – went their separate ways.

In the eighth and ninth centuries, as a result of Arab conquests and conflicts in Byzantium, skilled craftsmen and artists fled to Rome from the East. For a while the Western capital even became an important centre of Byzantine art and culture.

Finally, when the scion of a former barbarian dynasty, the Frankish king Charlemagne, became Holy Roman Emperor in St Peter's Basilica in 800, he accepted his crown from Pope Leo III (795–816), thus restoring the Western Empire and at the same time recognizing the superior authority of the Papacy.

S. GREGORIO MAGNO AL CELIO
Rome's 'Consul' and His Church
Pope St Gregory I restored Rome after the barbarian invasions – and established the Papacy as a spiritual and temporal power on the world stage.

A GREAT MOMENT
Pope St Gregory I's epitaph in St Peter's Basilica acclaimed him as 'Consul of God'. A consul in ancient Rome was elected to look after the people's interests and the title is a fitting tribute to Gregory's services to the Roman populace – and his link with the city's classical past.

As the sixth century drew to a close, Rome, like most of Italy, was in a state of degradation and decay. The fifth century had witnessed successive barbarian invasions and the disintegration of the Roman Empire. During the next century, battles raged between Byzantine forces and Rome's Germanic conquerors throughout the peninsula and even within the city walls, followed by further invasions. Fires, floods, famine and disease took over where siege and warfare had left off.

Against this desolate background, there came to the Papacy in the year 590 one of the worthiest occupants the throne of St Peter has ever known, Pope Gregory I (590–604), later referred to as Pope St Gregory the Great. Upon his election, Gregory found his city crumbling and corrupt, the countryside abandoned, and his people suffering from famine and outbreaks of the plague. By the end of his pontificate, the Pontiff had relieved social distress and confirmed the Papacy as a spiritual and temporal authority. He is viewed by historians as a noble (and much more saintly) successor to Roman Emperors, and as the creator of what would later become the powerful medieval Papacy.

A GREAT POPE
Roman-born in AD540 of an ancient patrician family, Gregory enjoyed every advantage of wealth and education. His lineage had already provided two Popes (Felix III and Agapitus I); his father, the Senator Gordianus, owned an immense estate on the Coelian Hill; his mother, Sylvia, had retired in her later years to a nun-like existence of prayer and meditation on the Aventine. The young Gregory advanced rapidly to one of Rome's highest civil positions, Prefect of the City, before renouncing all for the monastic life c.574. He converted his luxurious family villa into the Monastery of St Andrew and there embarked on what he expected to be a lifelong career of austere but peaceful monasticism.

Fortunately for the history of the Roman Church, that was not to be. Called into service as Papal Nuncio to Constantinople in 579, Gregory was recalled to Rome to be Pope Pelagius II's confidential adviser, and, upon that Pope's death in 590, was elected Pope in his stead. Pope Gregory's personal correspondence proves that he was sincerely unhappy to be taken away from monastic life. Eventually he accepted his promotion as being the will of God, and set about improving the lot of his flock, his city, his territories and his office.

The list of Pope Gregory's accomplishments is very long. In recognition of his saintly qualities, he was canonized by popular demand soon after his death. For his voluminous and important writings, Pope St Gregory was acclaimed one of the first four Doctors of the Church (along with St Augustine, St Jerome and St Ambrose). He contributed to liturgical reform and is credited with introducing the type of Church music we now call Gregorian Chant. He was also one of the foremost evangelizing Popes, dispatching missionaries not only to Germanic tribes, but even to the far reaches of then-pagan England.

Gregory devoted himself to the needs of the poor, the sick and increasing hordes of pilgrims. Since there was no central government in Rome at the time, he reorganized municipal food distribution and established new hospices and relief centres, known as diaconiae. Finally, he insisted on Papal primacy over both the Western and Eastern Churches, and in the absence of any real temporal leadership pacified the countryside and governed as *de facto* ruler of Italy. In this way, Pope Gregory launched the Papacy as the predominant spiritual, cultural and even political force in the West, a position it inherited from the Roman Empire, and which it later exerted throughout most of the Middle Ages.

GREGORY'S CHURCH

The church of S. Gregorio Magno (St Gregory the Great) is located across from the Palatine on one slope of the Coelian Hill (hence its other name, S. Gregorio al Celio). A towering Baroque façade rises at the top of a broad flight of stairs, and the exterior gives little evidence of the complex's ancient origins. In fact, even inside the church it is not easy to discover any remnants of St Gregory and of the spirit of his times.

The Coelian Hill was an area of opulent Roman villas and estates, and of these, the *Domus Gordianusi,* named after Pope Gregory's father, was one of the most splendid. Here, on his family's grounds, Gregory established the Oratory and Monastery of St Andrew *c.*574–5, incorporating the famous library of his great-great-grandfather, Pope Agapitus (535–6) into a study centre for the monks. (The foundations of the library can still be seen today.)

Later Pope Gregory II (715–31) built a church for his namesake on the monastery site. This church was completely transformed first in the seventeenth century and again later in 1734. From 1573 the church has been administered by the white-robed Camaldolese Order, a branch of the Benedictines founded by St Romuald of Ravenna (950–1027). Within the rather decrepit gardens beside S. Gregorio al Celio, Mother Teresa's Sisters of Charity also run a centre for the young homeless.

Once past the seventeenth-century façade, and through the open atrium built at approximately the same time, the visitor should head straight to the front of the church, to the little room on the far right of the main altar. According to tradition, this chapel was Gregory's own cell. It preserves the stone upon which he supposedly slept, and, most importantly, his well-worn, but still exquisite white marble episcopal throne. The seat is elegantly carved with what seem to be very Oriental motifs, perhaps a reminder of Gregory's posting to Byzantium before he became Pope.

The slightly larger chapel to the left of the cell (also called St Gregory's Chapel) was apparently part of Gregory's monastery. There are carved scenes from Gregory's life on the altar (Luigi Capponi, fifteenth-century), and above, a lovely painted

One of the oratories in S. Gregorio Magno al Celio, with a statue of Pope St Gregory the Great (590–604) and the table where he allegedly fed the poor of Rome.

predella (lower altarpiece) attributed to the early Renaissance schools of Signorelli or Pinturicchio. Through a door on the left of the church is the Salviati Chapel (*c*.1600, designed by F. da Volterra and Carlo Maderno, with paintings by G. B. Ricci), with its very old image of the Virgin, which is said to have spoken to St Gregory.

A visitor should appreciate the mosaic pavement and sixteen ancient columns from the earlier church. But the main impression is of an eighteenth-century structure (the church was radically restored by the architect F. Ferrari in 1734), with its vault fresco of *SS. Gregory and Romuald in Glory* by Placido Costanzi (1727) and other eighteenth-century paintings in the nave chapels about the life of St Gregory and the Camaldolese

Order. The chapel also contains Annibale Carracci's well-known painting of *St Gregory at Prayer* (1601–2).

On the right and left of the portal are two handsome sixteenth-century funerary memorials. The one on the left was originally made for the beautiful sixteenth-century courtesan 'Imperia', although all traces of her memory have since been erased from the monument.

THREE ORATORIES

S. Gregorio Magno has three oratories, located among cypress trees behind a grilled gate to the left of the church. They symbolize another moment of revitalization for the Roman Church – the Catholic Counter-Reformation, which responded to Protestantism by evoking the spirituality of the early Church. Pope Gregory I was an exemplary model for that spirit, and these three small chapels emphasized St Gregory's links with early Christianity and classical Rome. Cardinal Cesare Baronius had his architect Flaminio Ponzio (1560–1613) unify the chapels by a severely 'classical' portico, using antique columns and an architrave.

Inside the chapel of St Barbara (far left) is an apse statue of Gregory by N. Cordier (1567–1612), with all his Papal attributes, and in the middle of the room the stone table to which Gregory allegedly brought twelve poor men to feed every day. (The table was removed from the Lateran Palace, where Gregory lived and worked as Pope.) The fresco cycle on the walls by Antonio Viviano (1603–4) glorifies the saint in all his different aspects: as Doctor of the Church (with the ever-present dove of the Holy Spirit whispering in his ear); as a great missionary (sending forth evangelizers to England); as server of the poor (an angel is shown attending his charitable daily feast).

On the right is the chapel of St Sylvia, with an ecstatic statue by Cordier of Gregory's mother as an old woman, welcomed into heaven by frescoed angel-musicians (by Guido Reni).

Left: The site of St Gregory's cell in the sixth-century monastery he built on the Coelian Hill is now a small chapel containing the Pope's original marble episcopal throne.

Right: A seventeenth-century painting of Pope St Gregory giving his benediction, in the St Gregory Chapel in the church of S. Gregorio Magno on the Coelian Hill.

The middle chapel of St Andrew marks the probable spot of the original Oratory of St Andrew in Gregory's monastery. It was finished after Cardinal Baronius' death by Cardinal Scipione Borghese in 1607–8, and contains frescoes by Domenichino (Domenico Zampieri, 1581–1641) and Guido Reni (1575–1642). The chapel became the magnet for a heated artistic debate, beginning in the early seventeenth century and continuing until our own times. Some contemporary art critics praised Reni's *St Andrew Contemplates Martyrdom* for its 'higher', more idealized forms and style, while others preferred Domenichino's *Flagellation of St Andrew*, with its theatre-like setting and clear story-telling. Scholars today still debate the relative qualities of both artists – as transitional representatives from Counter-Reformation 'edification' (characteristic of the late sixteenth century) to the later (seventeenth-century) more emotional style of the Baroque.

S. MARIA IN COSMEDIN
Rome's Byzantine Centre
This church generated two important tasks for the Roman Church after the fall of the Western Empire: services of charity and patronage of the arts.

EARLY CHURCH WELFARE
We must retreat to the early days of the Roman Republic to find the first traces of S. Maria in Cosmedin. In those times this area, located on the edge of the River Tiber, was known as the *Forum Boarium*, the city livestock and grain market. Archaeologists have identified the foundations of ancient temples dedicated to Hercules and Ceres (third century BC) next to the present site of S. Maria in Cosmedin. During the fourth century, the imperial authorities deconsecrated Ceres' sanctuary and turned the loggia into the *Statio Annonae,* or headquarters of Rome's food supply organization. During the Empire, the *annona* had supervised imports of grain and other products and organized provision to the populace, either free of charge or at subsidized prices.

In the sixth century, the *Statio* was converted into a *diaconia*, or Church relief centre, with an oratory within. Quite a few of the columns from the ancient loggia are still to be seen in the church: four stand in their original position in the left-hand colonnade; others were incorporated into the left wall and both sides of the entrance. We have already described how Pope Gregory I revived imperial food distribution outlets and incorporated them into the *diaconiae*. There were eighteen of these deaconates in Rome, and S. Maria was the most famous and the most important. Here the poor were fed, the sick cared for, and services provided to the ever-increasing numbers of pilgrims from throughout the Christian world.

GREEKS IN ROME
History books tell us that from earliest antiquity the zone below the Aventine, between the Circus Maximus and the Tiber, was inhabited by a large and active Greek community. In the nearby 'sacred area' of the *Forum Boarium*, crowded with temples and altars – the Republican temples of Hercules and Portunus (sometimes identified as the shrines of Vesta and Fortuna Virilis) can still be seen; numerous rituals were celebrated there according to Greek cults.

S. Maria in Cosmedin's first name – S. Maria in Schola Graeca – reveals its origin. *Schola*, in fact, originally referred to an association or organization which could be a guild for artisans or a community centre for a foreign colony. As early as the late sixth century, tradition tells us, the neighbourhood's enterprising Greeks had persuaded the authorities to grant them, for their own Christian cult, the oratory in the former *annona*. The site, as mentioned above, also hosted an important Church relief centre.

Soon the Greek community began to swell, as thousands of refugees, fleeing first from Arab invaders, and then from Byzantine iconoclasts, came to settle in Rome. Under Pope Hadrian I (772–95) S. Maria in Schola Graeca was completely rebuilt and enlarged to meet the needs of its expanding congregation, who dedicated it to the Virgin 'in Cosmedin' (variously interpreted as referring to a district in Constantinople, or as a Greek term for decoration or ornament). Many of the newcomers who fled Asia Minor and Constantinople and settled around S. Maria in Cosmedin were persecuted Greek artisans and artists.

S. Maria in Cosmedin was built in the sixth century to serve Rome's foreign Greek community.

A second exodus surged into the West throughout the eighth and ninth centuries, as Byzantine Emperors pursued a ruthless iconoclast (the word means a breaker or destroyer of images) policy – forbidding the representation of human iconography in religious works. Previously lionized artists of the Byzantine Empire found themselves subjected to persecution, torture, and death or exile. During the iconoclast wars from 726 to 843, these masters found comfort with their fellow expatriates in the community of S. Maria in Cosmedin. The rich artistic traditions which were banned and demolished in the East flourished and proliferated in the West.

As the Emperors' successors, Roman Popes became major patrons of art from the fourth century on. And Christian art, inspired by spiritual fervour and religious iconography, expanded and diversified. First taking on the mantle of classical forms, the Church next turned to the Oriental resplendence of the Eastern Empire. Under Pope Paschal I (817–824), a remarkable artistic revival – known as the 'Carolingian Renaissance' because of the generous support received from Charlemagne and his successors – attempted to reflect both the early Roman Church and the magnificence of Byzantium. The dazzling mosaics Paschal commissioned for the churches of S. Cecilia and S. Prassede, and especially the chapel of Zeno, could have been the work of refugee-artists who had found asylum in S. Maria in Cosmedin.

BYZANTINE INFLUENCE

The jewel-like animals and flowers in S. Prassede's chapel of Zeno, S. Clemente's sumptuously-coloured 'tree of life', the Virgin Mary as an Oriental princess in the apse in S. Maria in Trastevere – there is reason to believe that much of this 'Byzantine' splendour had its cradle in this dusky little church of S. Maria in Cosmedin.

The adjective Byzantine derives from Byzantium, the ancient Greek city on the Bosphorus which the Roman Emperor Constantine rebuilt and renamed as Constantinople in AD300. Byzantine art was very different from the classical art of the West. While the Roman classical style strove for naturalism, worldliness and harmonious simplicity, Oriental art was formalized, transcendental and ornately decorative. Byzantine frescoes and mosaics were characterized by a strict iconography, highly formal structure, shallow pictorial space, immobile figures, and an opulence of gold and rich colour.

The seventh-century Muslim Arabs who invaded Syria, Palestine, Egypt and North Africa were desert warriors with an aversion to luxury and religious imagery. Gifted artisans of the conquered territories – predominantly Greek – made up the first wave of refugees to flow into Rome and pray in the shadows of S. Maria in Cosmedin.

S. MARIA IN COSMEDIN TODAY

There is little to remind us in S. Maria in Cosmedin today of the medieval Byzantine splendours generated by its early parishioners. Its frescoes are faded and its art works cannot compete with the treasures of many other Roman sanctuaries. But this church has an incomparable atmosphere of peace and antiquity, a comfortable self-confidence, a settled 'cosiness'. In the tranquil simplicity of its sagging floors and candlelit aisles, a pilgrim senses how ancient Greek artists must have felt 'at home', and found the strength to create masterpieces for later ages.

Happily, S. Maria in Cosmedin can now be appreciated in its simple medieval dignity (after Hadrian I, the church was remodelled by Popes Gelasius II and Calixtus II in the twelfth century). Restorations in the nineteenth century, carried out by the architect Giovanni Battista Giovenale from 1892 to 99, removed later Baroque façade and Neo-classical architectural elements and decor.

The two worn, fluted columns on the side of the entrance door were taken from the loggia of the *Statio Annonae*, and

96

craftsmen seemed to have the name 'Cosma', they bequeathed the appellation 'cosmatesque' to their type of marble-inlay work, which continued as an art form throughout the twelfth and thirteenth centuries in Rome and its surrounding areas. The intricate geometric patterns in dark reds and greens are distinctly Oriental in character – clearly influenced by the non-representational traditions of Islamic art. The graceful Gothic canopy over the altar is a work by Deodatus Cosma of the above-mentioned group, and is dated 1294.

The paintings in the nave and aisle apses are either very faded, or modern paintings in medieval style, yet they blend harmoniously with the ancient decor. In a chapel off the right aisle is a much-venerated thirteenth-century *Theotokos* image of the Virgin (the title means Mother of God's incarnate son), and, in the sacristy, an eighth-century mosaic of the Epiphany, originally commissioned by John VII in 706 for the first St Peter's (and donated to S. Maria in Cosmedin by Urban VIII when the new basilica was constructed). Beneath the church is the crypt built by Hadrian I into the foundations of the Roman Temple of Ceres.

THE MOUTH OF TRUTH

In S. Maria in Cosmedin's medieval portico is to be found one of Rome's most popular tourist attractions – the *bocca della verità*, or 'mouth of truth', a large round stone disc in the image of a monster with a gaping mouth. According to Roman legend, any liar who dares put a hand into this cavity will get a crunching finger-removing bite.

Apparently, this disc was used as a drain cover in imperial Rome, sculpted to represent (so latest research has it, according to a brochure in the sacristy) the Roman god Faunus, who was in turn derived from the Greek god Pan. Faunus' rites were particularly prominent in feasts for the goddess Ceres, whose temple was practically on the spot where S. Maria in Cosmedin now stands. In the Middle Ages the *bocca della verità* was used for trials by ordeal, since several dreaded prisons and execution spots were located nearby.

next to these, in niches, are two black marble stones which have been identified as Roman weights used in that ancient inspection station. The twelfth-century (opinions differ as to dates) marble choir, *pergola* (columns separating the choir from the presbytery), and bishop's throne behind the altar are lovely, as are the thirteenth-century Gothic altar canopy, and the mosaic candlestick, guarded by a surprisingly angry marble lion.

According to art historians, S. Maria in Cosmedin has the earliest 'cosmatesque' pavement to be found in Rome. This type of floor mosaic first made its appearance in the work of a group of medieval (twelfth-century) artisans from the neighbourhood. Since a disproportionate number of these

Left: A Romanesque lion and thirteenth-century Paschal candlestick in the choir of S. Maria in Cosmedin.

**Above: This disc, assumed to be a Roman drain cover, is now called the *bocca della verità*, or mouth of truth.
In a modern version of the trial by ordeal, tourists place their hands in the opening to prove they are telling the truth.**

S. GIORGIO IN VELABRO
Ministering to Rome's Poor

This mysterious church, seriously damaged in a 1993 bomb attack, has been almost miraculously restored to its early medieval state. Its origins and functions were very similar to those of S. Maria in Cosmedin.

BEYOND THE MISTS OF LEGEND

The origins of the church of S. Giorgio in Velabro are veiled in the mists of antiquity and legend. One myth holds that it was on this very spot that Rome was born. In ancient times, it is said, the twins Romulus and Remus were washed ashore in a basket to this marshy lowlands between the River Tiber and the Palatine Hill, were discovered and nursed by a she-wolf, and went on to found the city of Rome. Historians explain the term 'Velabro' as a combination of the Etruscan word *velum*, meaning marsh, and the Latin *aurum*, meaning golden. Classical writers such as Horace described the area as swampy, with yellow-coloured sand. The hollow was constantly flooded and was indeed a site of fog and mists.

In Republican and imperial Rome, the Velabrum, just a few steps from the Forum Boarium, was drained and became one of the city's liveliest commercial districts. The area hosted many temples catering to merchants and traders, as well as the residences of the industrious Greek community.

Early Christianity's popular soldier-martyr St Sebastian was allegedly martyred here in the late third century. A captain of the Praetorian Guard of Diocletian (284–305), Sebastian was shot with arrows and clubbed to death by his fellow officers. His body was supposedly thrown into the *Cloaca Maxima* (Rome's main drain) in the Velabrum market, and was recovered by pious Christians of the neighbourhood.

Today, a visitor approaching S. Giorgio in Velabro can still find reminders of the church's shadowy past. The building is surrounded by a broad paved hollow – the earlier Velabrum swamp, sloping from the Palatine down to the Tiber. Nearby, the massive Arch of Janus Quadrifons was used as a covered meeting place by fourth-century Roman merchants and shoppers. Adjoining the church, the Arch of the Money-Changers was built in 204 by Velabrum bankers and cattle traders in honour of the Emperor Septimius Severus (193–211).

MORE CHURCH WELFARE

S. Giorgio in Velabro, like its sister church S. Maria in Cosmedin just down the hill, was one of Rome's eighteen

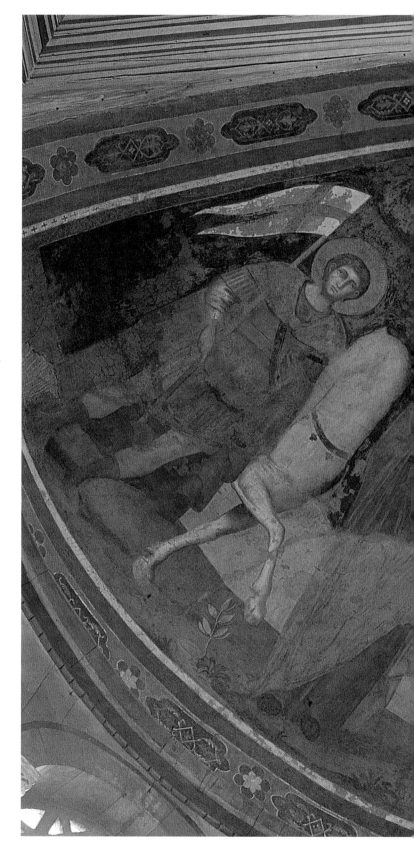

The apse fresco in S. Giorgio in Velabro, showing the church's co-patrons, St Sebastian (on right) and St Giorgio (on left), with Christ, Mary and St Peter.

diaconiae, or Church charity centres, established during and after the sixth century. Most of these have vanished from sight and memory. Some, such as the churches of SS. Nereo e Achilleo and SS. Cosma e Damiano, have merely changed their form and function.

Regarding the origin of the *diaconiae*, the Apostles (Acts 6:1–7) had chosen seven deacons (from the Greek word for 'to serve') to help them distribute alms to the poor. Later, the first official deaconates, which were originally monasteries with the

The thirteenth-century portico and bell-tower of S. Giorgio in Velabro, partially destroyed by a Mafia bomb in July 1993 and restored in record time.

specific apostolate of charity and relief, were founded in Egypt in the fourth century, expanding rapidly throughout the East. Byzantine monks who came to Rome probably helped the Church organize its first similar institutions.

According to tradition, S. Giorgio in Velabro had been serving Rome's poor from Paleo-Christian times. Excavations carried out in the twentieth century revealed, beneath the present pavement, a fifth- or sixth-century monastery (itself built on the foundations of an imperial-era home) with a typical *diaconia* layout: oratory, storage and distribution rooms, and a dormitory. Upon that structure, in the year 683, Pope Leo II (682–3) built the church that can essentially be seen today. This *diaconia*, officially recognized in the time of Pope Zacharias (741–52), functioned until around the year 900. In fact, Roman Church records indicate that by the tenth century the monastic *diaconiae* had already become diocesan parishes.

LATER HISTORY

Pope Leo II's church was dedicated to St Sebastian, in deference to the site of his martyrdom nearby. (The *Cloaca Maxima*, still visible through a grille, is across from the church portico.) In the year 749, Church chronicles relate, Pope Zacharias led a solemn procession from the Lateran Patriarchate (St John Lateran) to the Velabrum church, followed by almost the entire Roman population, all chanting and singing hymns. The occasion was the transfer of a precious relic, part of the skull of St George. On that occasion the Pope changed the dedication of the church and gave it the name it holds to this day.

A Christian soldier, St George is believed to have been martyred at Lydda (now Lod, site of Jerusalem airport) during Diocletian's persecutions, around 303. His cult was immensely popular in the East, where he was called *megalomartyros*, 'the greatest of martyrs'. By the eighth century the Velabrum's prosperous colony of Greek merchants had been flooded by even more Easterners fleeing the Arabs and Byzantine iconoclasts. It was fitting that Pope Zacharias, who came from a Greek family, should give the quarter its own Oriental saint. Furthermore, St George was the patron of Byzantine troops stationed nearby. (The legend of St George and the Dragon arose in the later Middle Ages, when – especially during the Crusades – the saint personified the ideals of Christian chivalry.)

The church was restored both inside and out by Pope Gregory IV (827–44). During the thirteenth century the bell-tower and portico were constructed, and in 1295 titular Cardinal Jacopo Stefaneschi commissioned the apse mosaic and other decorations. Subsequent centuries witnessed additional changes and renovations, but the most thorough restoration was undertaken by architect Antonio Munoz from 1923 to 6. Munoz removed Baroque and later embellishments, lowered the floor (raised in the 1800s) to its original level, and opened up the clerestory windows (closed since the late Middle Ages), using as a model one early selenite frame, discovered under the pavement and now displayed on the wall beside the sacristy.

A VISIT

S. Giorgio in Velabro's has a dignified Romanesque (thirteenth-century) portico and bell-tower. Its sturdy Corinthian columns, carved lions' heads, and Gothic-lettered inscription along the architrave (announcing renovations by the thirteenth-century Prior Stefano da Stella), all speak of a different age.

Inside, we find a small and tranquil Romanesque basilica: the unadorned nave is separated from two outer aisles by sixteen classical columns, all different and all taken from earlier classical buildings. In fact, S. Giorgio was used for filming the conclave scene of the film *Shoes of the Fisherman*, since its interior so closely resembles in form and spirit Rome's earliest Christian churches. The church has a charming irregularity, narrowing towards the apse, particularly in the right nave (as can be seen by observing the wooden ceiling). This unusual shape was probably due to the building's being squeezed into a crowded area of shops, warehouses and private homes.

S. Giorgio in Velabro is a peaceful place to rest and contemplate. Although at first the church seems to offer little in terms of art, upon closer inspection it contains some surprising treasures. The apse fresco is said to be the work of the celebrated medieval artist Pietro Cavallini (1273–1321). In bright colours against a turquoise sky, a triumphant Christ salutes the Virgin Mary, St Peter, and the church's co-patrons: handsome St George with his white horse and banner, and the older, bearded St Sebastian, also in military dress.

No one should miss the little marble relief on the left wall at the back of the church. This Annunciation scene has the usual angel – but the recipient of the divine message has a beard. The figure is said to be the Virgin's father, Joachim; in the background the head of a modest young Mary peeps from a balcony, straining to hear the news. In fact, that particular Annunciation iconography was used in the Orient, especially in St George's homeland in Palestine. On the back and nave walls, other delicately carved fragments probably formed part of the ninth-century marble choir; Munoz had found these turned upside down under the pavement. One particularly ornamental segment has been used as a lectern stand at the front of the church.

The twelfth-century marble altar and canopy have 'cosmatesque' decorations, that is, in the mosaic style developed by medieval artisans from the Schola Graeca district. Underneath the altar, the confessional contains St George's cranial bones, placed here by Pope Zacharias in the eighth century.

TRAGEDY STRIKES AND PEACE RESTORED

On the night of 27 July 1993, a powerful explosion almost completely destroyed S. Giorgio in Velabro's portico, opened a hole to the right of the façade, and seriously damaged the sixteenth-century monastery next door. The bomb, detonated from a car parked on the left of the porch, was later traced to the Italian Mafia, which had carried out a similar attack the same night at Rome's St John Lateran Cathedral. The Mafia 'warning' was assumed to be a response to Italian police round-ups, and to stern anti-Mafia statements made by Pope John Paul II during his pastoral trip to Sicily in May 1993.

The church has been meticulously and faithfully restored. Pieces of columns, capitals, inscriptions and carvings were carefully collected and catalogued, and the portico was reconstructed with all its original materials. In fact, the church once more appears, just as before, in all its sober Romanesque splendour.

CHAPTER

THE MURKY – AND MAGNIFICENT – MIDDLE AGES: PAPAL POLITICS AND MONASTIC MEMORIES

Violence and spirituality – even today the Roman skyline testifies to those aspects of medieval life and society. Fortress towers raised by warring medieval families stand among the gentle bell-towers of churches and monasteries. Arcaded cloisters still provide refuges of peace and prayer.

The Middle Ages stretched across 1,000 years, from the late fifth to the early fifteenth centuries. For much of that period Rome was a fractious battlefield, where Popes contested anti-popes, Roman barons fought among themselves and with the Papacy, and stormy dividing lines were drawn up between supporters of the Popes and those of the German Emperors. Popes were kidnapped, exiled, elected and deposed at the will of powerful Roman families. Papal prestige suffered from a string of corrupt and mercenary Pontiffs; at one point in the early tenth century, there had been eight Popes in eight years, and most of these had come to murderous ends.

Yet the Middle Ages was also a period of profound spirituality. Monasteries and convents kept culture and learning alive throughout centuries of warfare. In the thirteenth century, several new monastic orders brought about

a true spiritual regeneration for the faithful of the Church. The mendicant Franciscan Order, founded by St Francis of Assisi (1181–1226), gave the world a shining example of poverty and Christian charity. The preaching Order of the Dominicans, established by St Dominic (1170–1221), defended Catholic orthodoxy (sometimes excessively) throughout Europe. Other religious orders, such as the Augustinians and Carmelites, appeared on the scene as well. Rome hosted several important monastic centres in the High Middle Ages (thirteenth to fifteenth centuries).

Medieval Europe, and specifically the medieval Roman Church, was characterized by the struggle between Popes and emperors. According to the Papal theory of Christian society, eternal salvation was more important than worldly possessions, spiritual authority took precedence over temporal power, and secular rulers were thus subservient to the Pope,

S. Maria Sopra Minerva, designed by two Dominican monks in the late thirteenth century, is one of Rome's few Gothic churches.

God's representative on earth. But the Emperors never had an easy time accepting Papal primacy in politics.

When Charlemagne (742–814) revived the Roman Empire of the West on Christmas Day 800 in St Peter's Basilica, Pope Leo III (795–816) asserted spiritual over temporal authority by placing the imperial crown on his head. Later, Pope Gregory VII (1073–85), in one of the most dramatic events of the Middle Ages, compelled the Emperor Henry IV (1050–1106) to do public penitence. The image of Henry kneeling barefoot in the snow before the Pope at Canossa, Tuscany, in January 1077, was recalled for centuries as a symbol of imperial submission to spiritual sovereignty.

During the period of the Crusades, from the late eleventh through the thirteenth centuries, the Popes were able – intermittently – to lead Western Christendom in a vast effort to reconquer the Holy Land. For a while the Roman Church was a vigorous unifying influence in a cohesive Christian society, and this was a powerful stimulus for art and culture of every type.

Papal supremacy is said to have reached its high-water mark in the thirteenth century under Pope Innocent III (1198–1216). Innocent made the Papacy a force to be reckoned with in international affairs, deciding the succession of kings and Emperors and intervening with European monarchs in matters of marriage and morals. Yet the diversion of the Fourth Crusade to the capture of Constantinople, and Innocent's annihilation of the Protestant Cathars in southern France, were black marks against Innocent's pontificate. After the thirteenth century the Papacy began to decline.

In the early fourteenth century a series of French Popes moved the Papal court to Avignon, France. There the Pontiffs took up residence for almost seven decades (1305–78), while the Holy City sank into a period of anarchy and decay.

During the Middle Ages in Rome, craftsmen and artists created sparkling mosaics on church apses, walls and pavements. Marble canopies with pointed arches and delicate spires were raised over altars and tombs. Not many of these medieval marvels survive in twentieth-century Rome; but what is left is a joy for the eye and spirit.

SS. QUATTRO CORONATI (FOUR CROWNED SAINTS)
Popes vs. Emperors and a Quiet Cloister
The basilica of SS. Quattro Coronati contains a secret treasure – a work of art which was also a cogent political statement for

its time. Its medieval cloister is one of the most serene and meditative spots in all of Rome.

SETTING
Approached from the 'Street of the Oak Grove' (Via dei Querceti) – a reminder that in medieval times this was a secluded country area of woods and vineyards – the church of SS. Quattro Coronati appears as a medieval fortress emerging from the leafy heights of the Coelian Hill.

Along the steep Via dei Quattro Santi, the church presents high thick walls and embattled towers supported by buttresses. Above this mass looms a truncated belfry (ninth to twelfth centuries – historians differ), which seems more suited for defensive purposes than for ringing bells.

This is Rome's only surviving fortified abbey. In the late Middle Ages, the monastery was sometimes used as a refuge for Popes fleeing conspiracies and conflicts in the nearby Lateran Palace, and as a protected hospice for important visitors to the Papal court. In its architecture and atmosphere, SS. Quattro Coronati speaks of a troubled and dangerous phase in Roman Church history.

Residents recount a strange legend from the Roman Church's darkest days. A certain ninth-century English-woman, Joan, beautiful, brilliantly educated – and promiscuous – managed to have herself elected as Pope John VIII, succeeding Leo IV in 855. According to the folk tale, Joan–John gave birth at S. Clemente, on her way to be crowned Pope in the Lateran and was killed by the angry populace half-way up the Via dei Quattro Santi. For that reason, it is said, the Papal cavalcade always made a detour at one point on the street. ('Don't ask about the "Papessa Giovanna", the nuns of SS. Quattro Coronati will warn visitors. 'It's all nonsense!')

ART AND POLITICS
After passing beneath the menacing tower and several walled courtyards, the visitor will be sufficiently immersed in medieval ambiance for the church's first surprise.

Located in a small vestibule to the right of the church entrance is the amazing little chapel of St Sylvester. Before entering, ritual necessitates that the curious ring a bell, petition to a silent and faceless presence behind the dark grate, and accept a key from a wooden turntable mysteriously opening from the wall. A heavy door grinds open, lights go on, and a series of Byzantine-style frescoes become visible around the

top of the claustrophobic chapel. These illustrate the legend of how the Emperor Constantine (*c*.306–37) was cured of leprosy by Pope St Sylvester (314–35), and other miraculous events during the early Pontiff's reign. They have tremendous charm and narrative appeal, but their true significance lies in their thematic content and the date of their execution.

The paintings were completed and consecrated in the year 1246. They provide an astonishingly clear statement on the Church and its political situation in the mid-thirteenth century. We have already mentioned Pope Innocent III (1198–1216) and his successful assertion of political as well as, or rather as part of, spiritual authority. Innocent had Frederick II elected and crowned as Emperor; the Pope's successors then deposed and excommunicated Frederick when his actions threatened the Church.

By 1246, when the St Sylvester Chapel was consecrated, the power struggle between the Papacy and the Emperor was once more in full swing. In 1244 Pope Innocent IV, pressed by the imperial forces, had fled to Lyon, where in 1245 he also attempted to depose and excommunicate Frederick. But times had changed and Papal prestige had suffered in the intervening years. At that point the Church needed a mythical account to justify Papal supremacy over imperial ambitions. And that is just what we find in this small, off-the-beaten-track sanctuary.

The relationship between the first Christian Emperor and his Papal counterpart in the fourth century, as depicted by the chapel's thirteenth-century artist, exalts spiritual over temporal authority in no uncertain terms. The cycle relates Constantine's recovery from leprosy through Pope Sylvester's intervention, the Emperor's Baptism, and various miracles by which the Pope astounds the population. In one panel the Emperor has relinquished his throne to Pope Sylvester and is in the process of offering the Pope a new type of crown. In the next, the Emperor, on foot, humbly leads the Pope, on horseback, in triumph through the city. The political message in this chapel is clear: the Papacy has ultimate authority over Church and Empire.

Above the door of the St Sylvester Chapel is an inscription announcing that the room was purchased by the Rome Stone-cutters' and Sculptors' Guild in 1570.

SS. Quattro Coronati served as a refuge for medieval Popes fleeing the Lateran Palace nearby – thus its fortress-like exterior.

HISTORICAL SINGULARITIES

The very name of the basilica has been a source of confusion and controversy. The church is dedicated to 'Four Crowned Saints', that is, four Roman soldiers (according to tradition, Severus, Severinus, Victorinus and Carpophorus), who received the crown of martyrdom under Diocletian (284–305) for refusing to sacrifice to the pagan god Aesculapius. Five centuries later, the martyrs' relics were brought from a cemetery outside Rome and interred in the basilica along with the relics of five other martyrs from the same period, five sculptors (Claudius, Nicostratus, Castor, Sempronianus and Simplicius) from Pannonia (modern Hungary), who were martyred for refusing to sculpt a statue of the same god, Aesculapius. (Later researchers claimed that the interred saints represented a completely different group of unnamed martyrs from nearby Albano.)

Regardless of this hagiographic mix-up, the basilica of the Four Crowned Saints blithely and triumphantly continues to honour all nine of its supposed patrons. Behind the apse, seven panels tell the story of the sculptor-saints; four frescoes narrate the *Glory of All the Saints in Heaven* across the apsidal dome (all works are from the early seventeenth century). The martyrs' relics are contained in four urns in a ninth-century crypt below the altar.

Different versions of the martyrs' legends are found throughout the basilica complex – on the church walls, in side chapels, and in entrance lunettes and architraves. Even in the St Sylvester Chapel, the Mannerist painter Raffaelino da Reggio (1550–78), commissioned by the Stonemasons' Guild, frescoed the vault, pilasters and walls around the medieval Constantine–Sylvester cycle. Raffaelino's paintings differentiate and celebrate the church's two groups of crowned martyrs.

For centuries most Roman stonecarvers preferred to have their shops near the basilica. Important sculptors such as Maderno, Bernini and Algardi belonged to the SS. Quattro Coronati guild. Even today the *marmorari* meet every year on 8 November to celebrate the feast of their patron saints in the St Sylvester Chapel.

This thirteenth-century fresco was a cogent political statement for its time, asserting papal over imperial authority. Recounting a legend from the fourth century, the painting shows the Emperor Constantine on foot, leading the way for a triumphant Pope Sylvester.

MORE HISTORY

There was a church on this site by the end of the fifth century, dedicated to the four martyred soldiers, and it may have been built in the time of Pope Melchiades (311–14). For several centuries the basilica was also referred to as the *Titulus Aemilianae*, referring to the early Christian family who owned the original property and allowed its use for worship and assembly. In the ninth century, Pope Leo IV (847–55) collected the relics of all nine saints here and had the church extensively restored and embellished.

In the eleventh century the basilica became the victim of another episode in the imperial–Papal struggle. In 1084, Pope Gregory VII (1073–85), threatened by besieging armies sent by Emperor Henry IV (whom the Pope had forced into humiliating public submission at Canossa some years earlier), called to his aid Robert Guiscard and his Norman soldiers. After routing the imperial forces the Southern marauders laid sack to the city, burning Pope Leo's basilica almost to the ground.

The basilica was rebuilt (as was S. Clemente) by Pope Paschal II (1099–1118) in the early twelfth century – but on a much smaller scale. In fact, the present (Paschal's) basilica is just about half the size of Leo IV's. Leo's nave became the entire church: the left aisle was made into a cloister, while the right aisle was used for construction of the convent refectory. Since Paschal's reconstruction left the original presbytery intact, SS. Quattro Coronati's apse seems enormous and completely out of proportion to the rest of the church.

Five huge columns embedded in the outside right wall of the present courtyard (which was the back half of Leo's church) are lonely testimony to the church's shrinking structure – and to dwindling Papal funds. (Threatened by two anti-popes, investiture battles and imperial invasions, it is a wonder Paschal managed any construction at all. Paschal also constructed the *matronea*, or enclosed women's galleries, above the nave columns.

The church was restored again under Martin V (1417–31) and given a carved wooden roof in 1580 by King Henry of Portugal, who had earlier been the basilica's titular Cardinal. The last restorations were carried out by Professor Antonio Munoz who, first as a leading architect, and then as Rome's Superintendent of Monuments in the 1930s, tried to return so many Roman churches (including the basilica of S. Sabina) to their original pure state.

MEDIEVAL SPIRITUALITY

Access to the medieval cloister is gained by ringing a small bell in the basilica's left aisle. Through a wooden door is an unexpected world of silence and tranquillity: the smell of herbs and the sound of soft splashing water; the shade of an arcaded portico winding around the green garden; and in the middle a stone fountain carved with friendly lions' faces.

The cloister was built by renowned medieval (twelfth- or thirteenth-century) marble carvers and stonemasons, perhaps descendants of those 'cosmatesque' marble craftsmen who worked in S. Maria in Cosmedin, in honour of their martyred patrons. (The fountain, from one century earlier, originally stood in the church courtyard.) All the walls are covered with Paleo-Christian graffiti and sarcophagus fragments. The small chapel in the left gallery, dedicated to St Barbara, belonged to Leo IV's church and has faded frescoes from the ninth to twelfth centuries.

SS. Quattro Coronati's cloister, the 'cosmatesque' pavement in the church nave, and the Sylvester Chapel's Byzantine-style frescoes all testify to a flowering of art in Rome throughout the

Left: The thirteenth-century cloister of SS. Quattro Coronati is one of the most peaceful spots in Rome.

Right: The interior of SS. Quattro Coronati. The church was constructed by Pope Paschal in the early twelfth century to honour four early Christian martyrs; later five sculptor-martyrs were added to the dedication.

twelfth and thirteenth centuries. In those days, the city's painters, sculptors, goldsmiths, and marble workers were kept busy fulfilling the ambitions of Popes and nobles alike.

The spiritual harmony of SS. Quattro Coronati is deeply grounded in the contemplative life of the cloistered Augustinian nuns, who reside in the convent and have administered the basilica since Pius IV (1559–65) gave it into their keeping in the mid-sixteenth century. The Order is famous for its beautiful singing, and on Sundays Masses with music are sometimes open to the public.

S. MARIA IN ARACOELI
Rome's Monastic 'Altar of the Heavens'
An important monastic centre in the late Middle Ages, this church continues to be the pilgrimage site for a popular Roman ritual.

AN ANCIENT PROPHECY
S. Maria in Aracoeli, built on the site of the ancient Roman Capitol, rises above the ruins of a temple to Juno Moneta (home of the early Roman Mint, hence our word money). The transformation of this church dedicated to the Madonna from a temple to a pagan goddess was an early (and not infrequent) Christian coup, and was legitimized by an ancient legend.

According to this legend, the Emperor Augustus, disturbed by rumours that the Senate was about to honour him as a god, consulted the Tiburtine sibyl, who prophesied the descent from the skies of 'the King of the Ages'. As she spoke, the Emperor beheld a marvellous vision, the Virgin standing on an altar in a dazzling light and holding the Baby Jesus in her arms (according to later interpretation); he heard a voice which said: 'This is the altar of the Son of God.' The Emperor immediately raised an altar on the spot, the Ara Coeli, or altar of the heavens.

We have this legend from Rome's first guidebook, the *Mirabilia Urbis Romae*, written in the twelfth century. The

Mirabilia is known to be full of preposterous inventions. However, even now the official church brochure offers a photograph of John Malalas' eighth-century chronicle, which recites the same story, citing an even earlier (fifth- to sixth-century) Byzantine historian. Furthermore, one of the classical columns in the central nave bears the inscription *'a cubiculo Augustorum'* ('from Augustus' bedchamber'), and seems to have come from the Emperor's private palace.

A thirteenth-century altar, long believed to be Augustus' original construction, recounts the myth on its stone slabs, and displays in a porphyry urn above what are said to be the remains of St Helena, mother of Constantine. In sixteenth-century frescoes in the main apse, the pagan Emperor and his prophesying sibyl take their place among the angels and saints.

MEDIEVAL MONASTERY

Before long, a church grew up around the legendary Ara Coeli. We know for a fact that by 574 the site housed a monastery of Eastern-rite monks (in the late sixth century Rome was governed by Byzantine exarchs). From the ninth to the thirteenth centuries the church and monastery belonged to the Benedictines. Throughout the early Middle Ages, as Rome's patrician families fought each other and the Popes' followers in the city streets, and Emperors intermittently besieged the city walls, the Aracoeli monastery was a haven of scholarship and prayer.

In the thirteenth century, Innocent IV (1243–54) ceded the complex to the Franciscan Order, which had been recognized by his predecessor Innocent III (1198–1216). The Franciscans were already bringing about a spiritual renewal among Christians in cities and countryside. In Rome, they rebuilt and enlarged the Aracoeli complex and made it a centre of medieval culture and politics.

The monastery was also strategically located next door to the medieval headquarters of the 'restored' Roman Republic, or Commune, which the city's citizens had proclaimed in 1143. As in ancient times senators had met in the Temple of Jupiter (immediately adjoining the Temple of Juno Moneta), so

Above: S. Maria in Aracoeli (left) has always existed side-by-side and interacted with the Campidoglio, seat of Rome's municipal government (right).

Right: Pinturicchio's fresco series on the life of St Bernardino of Siena, painted in 1438, is one of the Aracoeli's greatest artistic treasures.

throughout the Middle Ages medieval 'Senators and Prefects' met to discuss politics and decide municipal affairs in the now-vanished Franciscan cloister.

It was Cola di Rienzo, the self-proclaimed Tribune of the Roman people, aspiring to restore Rome to its imperial glory, who first ascended the Aracoeli staircase, after it had been built in 1348 by the vote of the Roman people (in thanks for deliverance from the Black Death). Cola di Rienzo was later lynched as a demagogue in the place where his statue now stands towards the bottom of the Aracoeli ramp. Petrarch, the fourteenth-century poet who helped revive interest in the ancient world, received the laurel wreath on the Capitoline Square.

S. Maria in Aracoeli is still designated as the church of the Senate and the Roman people. Directly across from it, to one side, is the Capitol, or Campidoglio, the seat of the Roman city government. A pair of contrasting staircases leads to the church on one side and the Capitol piazza on the other – as if to contrast the spiritual and temporal powers which have sought an equilibrium here throughout the centuries.

TREASURES FROM ALL AGES

The austere, almost undecorated thirteenth-century façade of the Aracoeli soars like a mountain of rough brickwork at the top of its steep staircase. (The Campidoglio has a gradually inclining ramp leading to a harmonious Renaissance square designed by Michelangelo.)

Once inside S. Maria in Aracoeli, we find a typical early Christian basilica divided into three naves by columns, all of them taken from classical Roman ruins and each one different from the next. The floor is covered by tombstones of famous personages who have made their mark on Roman history throughout the centuries, and the side aisles are lined with the chapels of historic Roman families. A gilded ceiling, built between 1572 and 1586, commemorates the victory of Lepanto, when the Papal fleet helped defeat the Turks, checking Turkish expansion in the Mediterranean.

Like all Roman churches, S. Maria in Aracoeli is a repository of art and architectural treasures from every century. Those from the Middle Ages include a sad-faced Byzantine Madonna gazing out from the main Baroque altar. Although most art historians date the Madonna to the twelfth century, an Aracoeli legend claims that the image, painted on a piece of birch wood, was carried by Pope St Gregory the Great in the year 594 through the streets of Rome, and brought about the city's deliverance from a terrible plague.

The thirteenth-century master Arnolfo di Cambio (1245–1303) executed a Madonna and a sepulchral monument in the right transverse nave. In the left transept another Gothic-style tomb, by Giovanni di Cosma, honours a scholarly Franciscan Superior (Cardinal Matteo d'Acquasparta, d. 1302), mentioned in Dante's *Paradiso* (canto 12, verse 124). The Aracoeli's 'cosmatesque' pavement is not particularly beautiful, but it is all authentic thirteenth-century, and has some interesting medieval tombstones set between its mosaic strips.

The Aracoeli is full of tributes to the Franciscans and their founder. St Francis has his own chapel at the beginning of the left aisle; above the columns are medallions of Franciscan saints, twelve female saints on the left, and twelve male saints on the right. The tombstone of the thirteenth-century Franciscan 'Builder Aldo, who supervised the construction of this church', is near one of the columns. Towards the sacristy, a tall and slender – and very modern – bronze statue of St Helena, created by a Franciscan artist in 1972, stands over the shrine containing the saint's relics.

Above: The Emperor Augustus, legendary founder of the Aracoeli, as represented in a thirteenth-century altar table to the left of the main altar.

Right: The famous Santo Bambino, protagonist in Rome's favourite Christmas ritual, was stolen from the Aracoeli in 1994 and replaced with the copy shown here.

In the church can be seen a handsome Renaissance tomb by Andrea Bregno (1418–1503), a tombstone signed by Donatello (*c.*1386–1466), and other works attributed to Pietro Cavallini (*c.*1250–*c.*1330), Benozzo Gozzoli (1420–97) and Giulio Romano (1499–1546). An especially tender fifteenth-century Sienese Madonna, *Refugium Peccatorum* ('Refuge of Sinners'), is located on a column in the nave.

Probably the church's greatest treasure is the series of frescoes on the life of St Bernardino of Siena, painted by Pinturicchio (1454–1513) in the first chapel on the right. The glowing colours and serene perspective of these early Renaissance paintings make them some of the most beautiful in Rome.

THE SANTO BAMBINO

On 1 February 1994, a great tragedy befell the church of S. Maria in Aracoeli and the citizens of Rome. An icon dear to the hearts of the Roman people was stolen from its chapel of honour next to the sacristy. Down through the ages, that image, the Santo Bambino ('Holy Child'), had drawn the city residents to crowd the Aracoeli church, and these days the heartbroken Franciscans who guard the church will plead with visitors to pray for the return of their treasure. The lifelike replacement, dressed and crowned in gold, stands in his little chapel; his story is told on a plaque by the door.

It is hard to imagine that the original plump and rosy-cheeked child could have had such an adventurous past. Carved by a Franciscan monk in fifteenth-century Jerusalem (at that time parts of the Holy Land were under Franciscan tutelage), the sacred image was transported to Rome upon the orders of the Franciscan Curia, whose headquarters were then located in this church.

According to legend, the statue, carved from the wood of a Gethsemane olive tree, was miraculously painted by an angel as its Franciscan creator slept. Caught in a storm during the voyage to Europe, the wooden statue was thrown overboard. It bounced through the stormy seas, avoiding pirates and avaricious merchant ships, and finally landed at the feet of the Franciscan monk, who had been waiting anxiously on the shores of Livorno.

In Rome, until its theft, the Santo Bambino worked miracles down thorough the ages. Upon request, the statue was transported to hospitals or to the beds of Rome's sick and dying, and has been known to bring about inexplicable cures. Until this century, the Holy Child made his charitable visits in a gilded carriage donated by the people of Rome. From time to time the Bambino's jewels were sold, to fund relief efforts after floods, earthquakes or other natural disasters in Italy.

Because of the Bambino's services to the Roman people, Pope Leo XIII (1878–1903) ordered his coronation, which took place on 2 May 1897. Every year the Bambino is at the centre of Rome's favourite Christmas ritual. During Midnight Mass on Christmas Eve, he is unveiled and paraded to the Nativity crib in the left side nave, where he receives tributes from the children of Rome – poems, letters, and requests of all sorts.

S. MARIA SOPRA MINERVA
Rome's Uniquely Gothic Church

Rome's only Gothic church is filled to bursting with art treasures and with the ghosts of protagonists from medieval Rome – and almost every other period of Church history.

GODDESSES AND FRIARS

Who would guess that behind S. Maria Sopra Minerva's massive seventeenth-century façade lies Rome's one truly Gothic church? In fact, once past the basilica's severe Renaissance (1453) doors, the pilgrim encounters a sight completely unique in Rome: soaring pointed vaults, delicate ogival arches, predominant blues and golds, flickering lights from stained-glass rose windows. The Corinthian columns, marble floors and flattened vaults, however, suggest that even here the Gothic is not quite 'at home'.

The site of the present basilica originally hosted a temple to Minerva, built by Pompey the Great around 50BC, in thanksgiving for his military victories in Asia. Nearby, in ancient times, were other temples dedicated to pagan goddesses, including a shrine to the popular Oriental nature deity, Isis. It was among the ruins of Minerva's temple that Pope Zacharias (741–52) built the first church here, which he dedicated to the Virgin Mary and called St Mary over Minerva. This is not the first time – nor the last – we will encounter churches to Mary occupying the sites of former pagan sanctuaries.

Left: Filippino Lippi's frescoes of the Annunciation in S. Maria Sopra Minerva, executed between 1488 and 1492, are considered to be among Rome's most beautiful paintings.

Above: This appealing statue of an elephant supporting an obelisk was designed by Gianlorenzo Bernini (1598–1680) and stands outside the entrance to S. Maria Sopra Minerva.

Zacharias' structure has disappeared. The present building owes its existence to the Dominican friars, who received the property from Pope Alexander IV (1254–61) and made the church and adjoining monastery their powerful headquarters throughout the Middle Ages, (and then during the Renaissance, and the Counter-Reformation). The Dominicans administer S. Maria Sopra Minerva even today, and their influence is strongly felt throughout the church. (Medallions in the nave's upper portion portray Dominican saints; there is a richly decorated chapel to St Dominic; many chapels have paintings representing Dominican missionaries and other luminaries.)

A GOTHIC ENIGMA

Apparently, two talented Dominican monks, Sisto and Ristoro, who had worked on the Gothic church of S. Maria Novella in Florence, began the present structure in 1280, during the pontificate of Nicholas III (1277–80). This first Gothic church in Rome was completed in 1370, transformed in the Renaissance and Baroque periods, and then restored (badly, some say) in the nineteenth century (1848–55) by the Dominican Fra Girolamo Bianchedi to a semblance of its former medieval state. Unfortunately, the restorers covered the pillars and columns with fake marble and the walls and vaults with Neo-Gothic painting – so it is impossible to know how the church looked in Sisto's and Ristoro's days.

Anyone who stands amid the medieval heights and lights of S. Maria Sopra Minerva invariably asks the question: why? Why is this the only example of a Gothic church in Rome? Part of the answer is to be found in the history of the Roman Catholic Church. During the peak period of Gothic architecture, the Papacy, the city's principal artistic patron, was experiencing an all-time low. In the early fourteenth century, violent factionalism and empty coffers had forced a series of French-nationality Popes to flee to Avignon in France, where the Pontiffs remained for seven decades. In Rome, anti-popes, false popes, and rival Roman families fought fiercely among themselves. Roman architects, whose main benefactors had deserted them, ceased construction. The city became a slum.

There was another reason for the absence of Gothic buildings in Rome. Rome, a cradle of classical art and architecture, looked at Northern Gothicism with a wary and unappreciative eye. Even after centuries of barbarian invasions and internecine baronial struggles, much of the imperial city remained standing in medieval Rome. The imposing classical structures had a determinative influence on the culture and aesthetic tastes of the time. Throughout the Middle Ages, basilican churches were built on the model of their imperial antecedents; the 'barbarous' Gothic style never found much favour among Roman architects.

Thanks to powerful Dominican patronage, Rome did get one Gothic church. But even S. Maria Sopra Minerva – built upon the the ruins of Pompey's temple, in the shadow of Rome's most perfect classical structure, the Pantheon – is not a pure example of Gothic style. Its colonnade of marble Corinthian columns proudly parades its classical heritage beneath the slender ribs of the Gothic vaults.

A MEDIEVAL SAINT FOR A MEDIEVAL CHURCH

St Catherine of Siena (1347–80), an important medieval saint who was also one of the most influential women of her age, is buried beneath the high altar in S. Maria Sopra Minerva (her head is kept in Siena). This remarkable woman, who became patroness of Italy (in 1939, along with St Francis of Assisi as patron) and was named a Doctor of the Church (in 1970), was the youngest of twenty children of a Sienese dyer. At a young age, Catherine became a Dominican Tertiary and refused marriage to devote herself to prayer.

Catherine's personal holiness, mystical inspiration and copious writings made her a prominent spiritual leader of the late Middle Ages. She also played an important role in the political life of her times, through her letters and interventions with European rulers. She was considered largely responsible for convincing the Popes to return to Rome from their exile in Avignon. Broken-hearted by the Great Schism (1378–1417), which again pitted Popes and anti-popes against one another, Catherine died on 29 April 1380, in a house near S. Maria Sopra Minerva. She was canonized by the Sienese Pope Pius II in 1461. From the time of the saint's canonization in 1461 until 1887, Popes honoured her memory by making a commemorative procession to her tomb each year on the feast of the Annunciation.

St Catherine's sepulchre is beneath the main altar. A lovely reposing statue of the saint, sculpted in 1430 by Isaia of Pisa, is visible inside a golden casket below the altar table. The small circular plates with angels' heads above the altar, as well as paintings of the cardinal virtues on the sides, are the works of Francesco Podesti (1800–1895).

In 1630, Cardinal Antonio Barberini had the room where St Catherine died transported piece by piece (the walls, that is; the ceiling remains in the nearby Via S. Chiara) to S. Maria Sopra Minerva and installed as a memorial chapel at the back of the church. Frescoes on the walls are by Antoniazzo Romano (1461–1508) and his school; the saint's representation above the altar is a copy of a painting in Florence by Bronzino (1503–72). In the small corridor is the first funerary monument made for Catherine, a late fourteeth-century work attributed to a Roman sculptor identified simply as 'Paolo'.

GHOSTS FROM THE PAST

The superabundance of art treasures in S. Maria Sopra Minerva is so overwhelming that it is almost impossible to concentrate on individual works of art. Chapels and tombs of great Roman families, memorials and funerary monuments to Popes and Cardinals, present a dizzying procession of sarcophagi, statues, frescoes, paintings, portrait busts and mosaics. The ghosts of those who inspired the artistic spect-acle seem to circulate around the columns and corners.

In the Frangipane Chapel to the left of St Catherine's altar-shrine is the tomb of Fra Giovanni of Fiesole (1387–1455), known in art history as Beato Angelico. This gifted Dominican friar was also one of the most renowned painters of the early Renaissance. Nicholas V (1447–55), one of the first Popes actually to reside in the Vatican and a great patron of the arts, invited Fra Angelico from Florence to Rome to decorate his private Vatican chapels. While in Rome, the artist resided in S. Maria Sopra Minerva's adjoining monastery, where he died a peaceful death. Another reposing figure by Isaia of Pisa gazes from the the top of his tomb, and his paint-ing of the *Virgin and Child* hangs over the chapel altar.

To the other side of the main altar, in the Carafa Chapel in the right transept, S. Maria Sopra Minerva's most famous work of art honours a great Dominican and one of the most important theologians of the Middle Ages. On the right wall the magnificent Filippino Lippi (1457–1504) frescoes,

executed between 1488 and 1492, depict the 'triumph' of St Thomas Aquinas over paganism and heresy. On the altar is Lippi's *Annunciation*, while his *Assumption* and *Saints in Glory* fill the wall above. It is impossible to describe the beauty of these paintings. They must be seen.

To the left of the Carafa Chapel, in the right transept, is the Gothic tomb of the erudite Bishop Guillaume Durand Mende (d. 1296) with a mosaic of the *Virgin and Child between Sts Dominic and Privatus.*

Many other ghosts inhabit this church, most of them from eras later than the age of Catherine, Fra Angelico, St Thomas and Bishop Durand. From the left wall of the Carafa Chapel scowls the funerary statue of Paul IV (1555–9), the Carafa Pope and Great Inquisitor of Rome's Counter-Reformation. This severe and dreaded Pontiff was responsible for instituting the Index of Forbidden Books, and for confining Jews to ghettos in Rome and in other Italian cities.

Two of the Renaissance's most characteristic Popes, Leo X (Giovanni de' Medici, 1513–21) and Clement VII (Giulio de' Medici, 1523–34), are buried in the choir area behind the altar. These great humanists, munificent patrons of artists, political strategists – and vigorous hedonists – have imposing sepuchral monuments, worthy of their many achievements and huge egos.

The Chapel of the Annunciation, further towards the entrance in the right aisle, was commissioned by Cardinal Juan de Torquemada (1388–1468), a relative of the notorious Spanish Inquisitor. Torquemada's confraternity was responsible for one of the Dominicans' most appreciated charitable works in Rome, the provision of dowries for poverty-stricken young women. Nineteenth-century travellers such as Augustus Hare chronicled the yearly procession, when the girls, crowned with flowers, came to S. Maria Sopra Minerva to receive their gifts. The event is depicted in the chapel's painting by Antoniazzo Romano. In a delicate *Annunciation* scene, the Virgin presents purses to three tiny girls in white, while the gentle-faced Cardinal Torquemada looks on.

THE RENAISSANCE IN ROME: POWER AND PATRONAGE

By 1420 both the sojourn in Avignon and the Great Schism were over. The Papacy had returned to a rejuvenated Rome and greeted the new era with open arms – and pocketbooks. A series of Roman Pontiffs set about securing and extending the Papal territories and replenishing the Papal coffers. By dint of several decisive political (and even military) victories, and copious revenues from pilgrims streaming back into Rome, the Popes became more powerful and wealthier than ever before.

The new era was called the Renaissance, which literally means rebirth. After medieval warfare, plagues, famines and ecclesiastical schisms, the Western world was coming back to life. The Renaissance first emerged in the prosperous Italian city states, next made Medici Florence its artistic capital, and finally, attracted by the patronage of powerful Popes, moved to Rome.

The steady growth of urban society and a revived interest in the classics of ancient Greece and Rome were two important stimuli for this vibrant cultural renewal. Cities were more secure and open to new ideas than the lonely castles of feudal countrysides. Humanism, a movement resulting from the study of classical 'humanities', stressed the dignity of man – his ability to master his fate and live happily in the world.

From the mid-fifteenth century Peter's successors enthusiastically supported humanist scholarship and the fine arts in order to enhance the prestige of the Papacy and the city of Rome. They lured the finest painters, sculptors and architects of the day from Florence and other Italian cities and soon made Rome the unrivalled artistic capital of Europe. Often the Renaissance Curia exhibited the lavish extravagance typical of the most sophisticated princely courts.

The Renaissance Popes devoted themselves wholeheartedly to reconstruction of the city of Rome and to the propagation of Church doctrine. Their pontificates were full of activity on every level. Nicholas V (1447–55) made the Vatican the Papal residence, embellishing chapels with the works of Fra Angelico and establishing the first Vatican Library; Pius II (1454–64), a humanist scholar in his own right, attempted to organize a Crusade to retake Constantinople from the Turks; the Venetian Paul II (1464–71) delighted the Roman populace with generous entertainments; Sixtus IV (1471–84) rebuilt

Considered one of Italy's finest Renaissance buildings, the so-called Tempietto ('little temple') was constructed for the church of S. Pietro in Montorio by Donato Bramante in 1502.

bridges, widened roads, and filled the city with hospitals and public monuments; Alexander VI (1492–1503) extended and consolidated the Papal States; the military work was continued by Julius II (1503–13) who also commissioned Michelangelo's Sistine ceiling; Medici Pope Leo X (1513–21) obtained the services of Raphael and other brilliant artists and scholars.

In a speech from his deathbed in 1455 Pope Nicholas V advised his Cardinals: '…If the authority of the Holy See be visibly displayed in majestic buldings, imperishable memorials and witnesses seemingly planted by the hand of God himself, belief will grow and strengthen like a tradition from one generation to another, and all the world will accept and revere it.'

Although the Renaissance Popes could have provided their flock with a more saintly example, we are grateful to them for bequeathing to us some of the greatest works of art the world will ever know. Our inheritance would have been even greater but for a catastrophic historical event: the Sack of Rome.

In 1527 marauding troops of the Emperor Charles V swept down into Rome, putting the entire city to the torch, pillaging, raping and carrying off innumerable treasures. Many interpreted the devastation as a sign of divine retribution for Papal decadence and greed. The Protestant Reform had already been launched in the North. It was time for the Church to embark on an examination of conscience and genuine spiritual renewal.

S. MARIA DELLA PACE
A Renaissance Church for a Renaissance Pope

On this first stop of a Renaissance itinerary the visitor sees paintings by Raphael, visits a Bramante cloister – and encounters a Pope who exemplifies his period in many different ways.

Above: The façade of S. Maria della Pace was designed by Pietro da Cortona in 1656 and has a convex portico which mirrors the rhythm of the Renaissance interior.

Right: S. Maria della Pace's internal courtyard, designed by Bramante between 1500 and 1504, is a perfectly proportioned Renaissance cloister.

QUINTESSENTIAL RENAISSANCE

Approached by a tiny square which opens up from narrow medieval alleyways behind the Piazza Navona, the façade of S. Maria della Pace has a breathtaking effect. A graceful convex façade, with columns and a semi-circular portico, is flanked by two concave wings – the whole providing a wonderful play of light and curving lines. The church façade is actually a Baroque addition by Pietro da Cortona, commissioned by Pope Alexander VII in 1656. In fact, the impression made by this lovely structure is extremely 'classical', because of its use of Doric capitals and the way it mirrors the almost circular rhythm of the church interior. S. Maria della Pace's classical spirit is not surprising, since it was built by a Pope steeped in the scholarship of ancient Greece and Rome.

Sixtus IV (1471–84) was neither the first nor the last of Rome's Renaissance Popes. He was, however, a consummate example and advocate for the Papacy's new age. Sixtus attempted to reconcile the Church with the humanism of the early Renaissance. He strove to make Rome once again worthy of its classical past and of its position as capital of Christendom. The great revival of classical culture and learning which marked the Church's transition from the medieval to the modern world owed much to this Pope's activities. He helped raise the Papacy to a degree of artistic magnificence which rivalled the capitals of the world.

The church of S. Maria della Pace (St Mary of Peace) was built by Sixtus IV between 1480 and 1483 on the site of an earlier shrine, in fulfilment of a vow of thanks for the restoration of peace in Italy. The church celebrates several positive events in Sixtus' pontificate and eminently reflects his intellect and spirituality. Let us take a look at the man himself.

Francesco della Rovere was born in 1414 in a Ligurian fishing village near Savona, into a family of the impoverished lesser nobility. His mother had visions of a great future for her child; she named him after St Francis and dressed him in the Franciscan habit when he was only a toddler. Francesco joined the Franciscan Order at an early age and was known for his devotion and piety. At the universities of Bologna and Padua, and in his subsequent work as preacher, Franciscan Superior, and Roman Cardinal, he was admired as an outstanding scholar and acute theologian. The early fifteenth century was animated by a fervent renewal of classical studies, and Francesco was intimate with the greatest humanists of his age. He was particularly devoted to the philosophy of St Augustine.

Elected Pope in 1471, Sixtus IV became a 'typical' Renaissance Pontiff, in both the positive and the negative senses. His nepotism and attempts to aggrandize the Papal States were bitterly criticized even in his own times. His pursuit of della Rovere family interests – perhaps because of his humble beginnings – embroiled the Church in the turbulent intrigues of European politics.

On the other hand, Sixtus was a generous benefactor of scholarship and learning. A voracious collector of books and

A portrait of Pope Sixtus IV (1471–84), who sponsored many of Rome's Renaissance churches, on the right wing of the façade of S. Maria della Pace.

manuscripts, he contributed profusely to the Vatican library and constructed a new building to house the acquisitions. He founded the Sistine choir, established the Vatican archives, and returned many classical works of art to the Capitoline museum. His patronage of art and architecture benefited fifteenth-century Rome and the Roman people, and the fruits of that patronage are still enjoyed today.

Sixtus paved and widened the city streets and carried out extensive public works. He laid the foundations for a new bridge (Ponte Sisto) across the River Tiber and reactivated an important hospital (S. Spirito in Sassia). We are indebted to Sixtus IV for the world-famed Sistine Chapel (named, in fact, after him), for which he called to Rome the leading artists of the early Renaissance – Botticelli, Ghirlandaio, Perugino and Pinturicchio.

Known even in his own times as *Renovator Urbis* ('Renewer of the City'), Sixtus filled Rome with beautiful (both new and restored) churches: S. Agostino, S. Maria del Popolo, S. Pietro in Montorio and S. Pietro in Vincoli. S. Maria della Pace was probably his finest and most representative construction.

TEMPLE TO PEACE

In 1480 Pope Sixtus IV decided to build a splendid new church in gratitude for the conclusion of a war with Florence. In fact, the conflict was a rather disreputable affair for the Sistine Papacy. Hostilities began after the Pazzi Conspiracy (1478), in which the great Lorenzo de' Medici and his brother Giuliano were brutally attacked (Giuliano was killed) during Mass in Florence Cathedral. The action, undertaken to advance della Rovere family politics, was evidently known in advance, if not approved, by the Pope himself. Besides his eventual negotiation of a truce with the Florentines (1480), the Pontiff had a few other victories to celebrate: the (modest) successes of his campaign against the Turks in the Aegean Sea, and the end of warfare with Venice and the Kingdom of Naples. To declare the pacification of Italy, Sixtus IV commissioned a 'temple to peace' on the site of a former miraculous Marian shrine.

Sixtus IV's church has an odd and unusual history. In former times a popular Marian sanctuary stood here. First the shrine had belonged to the early church of St Andrew of the Water-Vendors, which was renamed St Mary of the Water-Vendors in the twelfth century. The *acquaioli*, or water-sellers, were a large group in medieval Rome, where the aqueducts were in complete disrepair and potable water quite scarce.

In the fifteenth century, a venerated painting of the

Madonna and Child, in the porch of the medieval church, miraculously shed blood when accidentally hit by a stone (or perhaps by a ball during a neighbourhood game, or by a drunken soldier's sword – legends disagree). Sixtus had officially visited the venue of the miracle, and promised to build a new church in honour of Mary, whose help he beseeched in ending the wars. The miraculous painting now hangs above the main altar (constructed by Carlo Maderno in 1614).

INNOVATION AND TRADITION

Besides marking several important events in the Sistine pontificate, S. Maria della Pace also reflects the Pontiff's passionate interest in new forms of architecture. Built (art historians assume so, although there are no records) by the Pope's favourite architect, Baccio Pontelli (1450–92), the church has an unusual shape: an almost square nave terminating in an octagonal transept-apse, with two very shallow chapels on each side, and topped by a striking cupola.

The interior space of this church, almost circular in its rhythm, is graceful and harmonious. The architect has achieved a Renaissance ideal of dignified simplicity and serene proportion, made 'to the measure of man', very distant from the massive early Christian basilica, as well as from the exuberance of later Baroque decorations. The church of S. Maria della Pace excited much interest among artists and architects of the day. It was generally considered to be the most significant and 'modern' religious building in fifteenth-century Rome.

A closer study of S. Maria della Pace reveals a more profound aspect of Sixtus IV's artistic patronage. A devout Augustinian philosopher and scrupulous scholar of the Scriptures, Sixtus IV incorporated theological concepts and biblical symbols into the architectural works he commissioned. Sixtus' religious structures are often based on a spiritual 'numerology', which has been studied by art historians but is somewhat difficult for the layman to comprehend.

According to several Sistine scholars, the structure and proportions of S. Maria della Pace were to have a symbolic function. For instance, the proportional number seven was used by St Augustine to represent the Old Testament, while the number eight stood for the New Testament's further revelation. The S. Maria della Pace nave equals seven-eighths of the apsidal space: i.e. representing the Old Testament leading to its final fulfilment in the Eucharist. The presbytery's four chapels symbolized the Gospel's diffusion to the cardinal points of the globe.

TEMPLE TO ART

As a testimonial to Sixtus' humanist interests, S. Maria della Pace was originally rich in classical decor. The purity and clarity of the structure, with its centralized – almost circular – floor plan, owes much to classical Roman buildings such as the nearby Pantheon. A piece of the original flooring suggests a Roman-style mosaic pattern.

Several of the most eminent High Renaissance artists worked in this church, among them Bramante and Raphael. To the left of the church we find Bramante's first Roman construction, a perfectly proportioned cloister, commissioned by the Neapolitan Cardinal Oliviero Carafa (1430–1511) and built between 1500 and 1504. Although completed several decades after Sixtus' death, the courtyard's classical grace would certainly have met with his approval.

Donato Bramante (real name Donato d'Angelo, 1444–1514) came to Rome around 1500, his heart full of longing to study the city's classical vestiges, and his head brimming with new architectural ideas. The ambitious Pope Julius II (1503–13) put him to work designing a new St Peter's Cathedral, which was to rival the greatest of pagan monuments in scale and splendour.

Bramante earned himself the title of 'ruinante' (the ruiner) as he set about tearing down the fourth-century basilica, disposing of its ancient and medieval accoutrements. Julius left the scene, other Popes and other artists intervened, and almost nothing survived of Bramante's original plan for St Peter's (completed by Sangallo, Michelangelo, della Porta, Maderno and Bernini).

Luckily, the great architect's cloister in S. Maria della Pace is still intact. This very classical courtyard has arcades of rectangular piers and attached Ionian pilasters on the first floor. Above, an open gallery has slim columns, alternating with piers and pilasters which mirror the design below.

Renaissance additions superbly correspond to the Sistine spirit and design of S. Maria della Pace. The famous frescoes of sibyls and prophets, commissioned by the wealthy banker Agostino Chigi were painted by Raphael and his school around 1511–14 above the first chapel on the right. They continue Sixtus' theme of Old Testament preparation for the New Word. In fact, the sibyls and prophets, are shown each receiving a revelation from an angel, foretold the coming of Christ among men. (The chapel directly across has Baldassare Peruzzi's New and Old Testament scenes in the half-dome (1516–17). Apparently, Raphael painted his sibyls and prophets in S. Maria della Pace after seeing Michelangelo's Sistine Chapel ceiling. And, indeed, the figures do have a very recognizable 'Michelangelesque' type of musculature and force.

Other Renaissance treasures include Jacopo Ungarino's octagonal cupola (1524); an ornate funeral chapel for the Cesi family by Antonio da Sangallo the Younger (1484–1546); and the four large presbytery canvases with scenes from the life of the Virgin (by G. M. Morandi, R. Vanni, B. Peruzzi and Carlo Maratta), which carry out the Marian programme Sixtus IV envisaged for his church.

S. MARIA DEL POPOLO
A Renaissance Treasure Chest

S. Maria del Popolo was built and beautified by powerful Renaissance families. It is a veritable museum of artistic and architectural masterpieces of the period.

GATE TO ROME

Beside the Porta Flaminia, which in former times was the city gate for pilgrims arriving from the north, is the church known to Romans as S. Maria del Popolo, or St Mary of the People. Both the church and its panoramic square are true layer-cakes of history. The shrine has seen early Christian martyrs, medieval monks, Renaissance princes, imperial invaders, the premier Baroque artists, Napoleonic city planners, and the invasions of twentieth-century tourism.

Nevertheless, it is to several Renaissance Popes and their wealthy families that this church owes its greatest glories. Pope Sixtus IV (1471–84) completely rebuilt the sanctuary between 1472 and 1478. Sixtus' nephew, Pope Julius II (1503–13), expended enormous sums on the church, commissioning for its decoration the most renowned artists of his day.

Rising over the piazza, the sober exterior clearly announces its early Renaissance origin. The façade's three doors all have

The cloister attached to S. Maria della Pace was constructed by Donato Bramante around 1504 and is considered an almost perfect example of Renaissance proportions.

classical tympanums. The two side entrances bear Sixtus' name and the date of the façade's completion (1477), while the middle door has his (and Julius') della Rovere family coat-of-arms. This emblem, the ubiquitous oak tree, can be seen throughout the church (della Rovere means 'of the oak' in Italian). Later, the Baroque era Pope Alexander VII (1655–67) placed his own family insignia, the Chigi mounds, atop the entire structure.

IMPERIAL DEMONS AND MEDIEVAL MONKS

According to legend, the church stands over what was originally the tomb of the Roman Emperor Nero (37–68). This notoriously evil ruler, who sent thousands of early Christians to their gruesome deaths, was believed to have committed suicide and been buried on this site at the foot of the Pincian Hill. Medieval Romans were convinced that Nero's vicious spirit haunted the area, and that crows inhabiting a huge walnut tree nearby were his demon servants. At night these escaped to terrorize the neighbourhood, swirling about as malevolent witches and phantoms.

In 1099 Pope Paschal II (1099–1118) decided to put a stop to such goings-on. After receiving a vision and guidance from the Virgin, he chopped down the walnut tree, exhumed the supposed grave of the wicked Emperor – throwing his remains into the Tiber – and built an oratory over the formerly accursed spot. These events are depicted in five gilded stucco panels inside an arch over the main altar.

It was Pope Gregory IX (1227–41) who dedicated the shrine to the Virgin Mary, rebuilding and enlarging the oratory around 1230. From that time, the church has been known as S. Maria del Popolo, from *populus*, referring to the people of the local parish. (Some historians claim that the name should be traced to an ancient 'poplar' grove.) Gregory built an important monastery for the church and brought from St John Lateran a much-venerated thirteenth-century icon of the Virgin and Child, now over the main altar.

From its position at the foot of the Pincio, S. Maria del Popolo holds sway over an even earlier period of history. Across the piazza stands an imposing obelisk, dating from the thirteenth century BC, and brought from Heliopolis to Rome by the Emperor Augustus (27BC–AD14). In 1589 Pope Sixtus V had the Egyptian monument set up in the piazza across from the church, once more reasserting Christianity's pre-eminence over the ancient world.

RENAISSANCE INTRIGUE AND INSPIRATION

It was during the Renaissance that S. Maria del Popolo took on the internal and external form we know today. Pope Sixtus IV transformed Rome's tribute to Mary of the People into one of Rome's most celebrated basilicas. Pope Julius II remodelled the apse, choir and side chapels, and filled the church with the works of his favourite artists.

It would require an entire book to do justice to the art treasures contained in S. Maria del Popolo. The first chapel off the right-hand aisle, the Della Rovere Chapel, has lovely paintings by Pinturicchio (1454–1513): a Nativity over the altar and scenes from the life of St Jerome in the lunettes. The atmosphere conveyed by this early Renaissance master is very special: distant fairy-tale landscapes, humbly devout figures and endearing animals. Two della Rovere Cardinals are buried here, both nephews of Sixtus IV; their tombs are attributed to the famous early Renaissance sculptors Andrea Bregno (1418–1503) and Mino da Fiesole (1430–84). The Basso Della Rovere Chapel has paintings by Pinturicchio's school (the lunettes with scenes from the *Life of the Virgin* are especially appealing), and more della Rovere tombs, also attributed to Bregno.

The memory of another powerful Renaissance family lingers in this church. To the right of the altar, in the chapel now dedicated to St Rita of Cascia, are buried Duke Juan of Gandia and his mother Vanozza Cattanei. Here nothing marks the spot; their funerary inscription was mysteriously discovered this century under the portico of St Mark's church at Piazza Venezia. Vanozza was the mistress of the Borgia Pope

Alexander VI (1492–1503) and the mother of his children: notorious Lucrezia, ruthless Cesare, and tragic Juan, assassinated, most say, by his own brother. In later years Vanozza spent her time and money in good works and pious endowments, generously remembering S. Maria del Popolo. Bregno's marble altar in the sacristy was commissioned by the Cardinal Rodrigo Borgia – before he became Pope Alexander VI.

Sixtus' reconstruction of S. Maria del Popolo was probably carried out by either Baccio Pontelli or Andrea Bregno (art historians differ). When Julius II decided to extend the apse and choir, he called in Donato Bramante, who was also working on the new St Peter's. In the choir, Julius commissioned almost identical tombs by Andrea Sansovino (1460–1529), one for a relative, Cardinal Girolamo Basso Della Rovere (d.1507), the other for a former enemy, Cardinal Ascanio Sforza (d. 1505).

Left: The church of S. Maria del Popolo, seen here from the adjoining piazza, has been the scene of historic events since the first century AD.

Above: S. Maria del Popolo was embellished and enriched by some of the Renaissance's most powerful Popes.

The ceilings were covered by more beautiful frescoes by Pinturicchio and his school. These artists and architects emblazoned the family oak symbol in every space and corner.

The sumptuous Chigi Chapel on the left aisle of the church was sponsored by Raphael's favourite patron, the wealthy banker Agostino Chigi (1465–1520). The chapel and dome mosaics were designed (1513–16) by Raphael (1483–1520) and then executed by others. Sebastiano del Piombo (1485–1547) did his last painting, *Nativity of the Virgin*, for the altarpiece, and is supposedly buried in the church.

S. Maria del Popolo participated in another event which actually hastened the end of Renaissance Rome. When Martin Luther (1483–1546) visited Rome in 1510 he stayed at the Augustinian monastery attached to the church. Shocked by what he saw, Luther was convinced that the Church needed a thorough reform. His disgust with the worldly life of the Renaissance Popes and clergy was one incentive for his Wittenberg Theses (1517) and the Protestant Revolt which followed. Later, when the imperial army sacked Rome in 1527, S. Maria del Popolo's monastery was burned to its foundations. (The square bell-tower is all we have left of the fifteenth-century monastic structure.)

BERNINI, THE BAROQUE, AND – CARAVAGGIO

Although S. Maria del Popolo has a Renaissance form and structure, the Baroque hand of Gianlorenzo Bernini (1598–1680) is everywhere to be found. First the Master added some curved half-volutes over the austere early Renaissance façade. Next, he scattered his typical angels throughout the church; they recline, or flutter their wings and draperies above the nave arches and beneath the organ lofts.

The pyramidal tombs in Raphael's Chigi Chapel are said to have been Bernini's idea; he definitely sculpted the funerary busts of the Chigi brothers Agostino (d.1520) and Sigismondo (d.1526) which decorate the monuments. Two other Bernini works adorn the Chigi Chapel: statues of the prophets Daniel and Habakkuk. A youthful angel tweaks Habakkuk by the hairs on his head and points in one direction, while the prophet seems intent on setting out in another (see title page). In fact, according to Daniel 14:33–9, Habakkuk, on his way with a basket of food for workers in the field, was commanded by a heavenly apparition to rush instead to the aid of Daniel, expiring in the lions' den in Babylon. On the opposite wall, a beseeching Daniel and drooling lion are looking very hungry. Other statues in the chapel are by Lorenzo Lotti (1490–1521).

Of course, S. Maria del Popolo is most famous for the works of another exceptional seventeenth-century figure, Michelangelo Merisi da Caravaggio (1573–1610). His *Conversion of St Paul* and *Crucifixion of St Peter*, commissioned by Tiberio Cerasi (1544–1601) and painted in 1601, have been photographed and described perhaps more often than any other canvas in Rome. No photograph, however, and certainly no description can do justice to the psychological drama of these paintings. The journey must be made to S. Maria del Popolo. In the same chapel, to the left of the altar in the transept, is the brightly coloured, slightly worldly *Assumption* (1601) of Annibale Carracci (1560–1609), very different in spirit from Caravaggio's dark spirituality.

…AND AFTERWARDS

In 1809 Guiseppe Valadier (1762–1839) and Napoleon's Prefect Count de Tounon began the transformation of the Piazza del Popolo into a Neo-classical plaza worthy of the Napoleonic Empire. (Valadier imposed a Neo-classical shell on S. Maria, thus harmonizing the exposed side with the rest of the piazza.) Even later, the church stood by as the piazza's sedate nineteenth-century carriages metamorphosed into tourist buses disgorging citizens from every country on earth.

A SECOND LOOK

No sightseer can be disappointed in this treasure house of history. Nevertheless, the pilgrim would be well advised to throw the guidebook aside and take a more leisurely stroll up and down the aisles. The spirits of less illustrious personages, evoked by less famous memorials, will tug at the coat-sleeve and plead for attention.

Gianlorenzo Bernini's statue of *Daniel and the Lion* in the Chigi Chapel of S. Maria del Popolo.

Near the main altar, the head of a wide-eyed boy appears over an inscription lamenting his early death and his parents' 'profuse tears'. Towards the back, a somewhat frightening monument with snarling lions and the profile of a young woman, tells us that the Princess Odescalchi died at the age of twenty giving birth to her third child. The bust of another ringleted girl practically leans out of her niche with a distressed expression ('Why me?'); her inscription has been completely effaced. We come across bewigged eighteenth-century courtiers, Pre-Raphaelite matrons, and churchmen of both severe and kindly mien. So many stories, so many destinies.

S. PIETRO IN MONTORIO
Peter's Pavilion
This church was rebuilt by Ferdinand and Isabella of Spain and boasts Rome's most famous example of High Renaissance architecture.

WAS THE APOSTLE HERE?
From a ridge on the Janiculan Hill, which the ancient Romans called *Mons Aureus* (golden hill) because of its yellow sandy soil, there is a sweeping view of Rome's towers and cupolas, fading gradually into a hazy background of blue Alban hills. Turning round, the visitor faces the simple but striking façade of a medium-sized Renaissance church.

It is due to a fallacious interpretation of the Apostle Peter's death that the church offers one of Rome's (and the world's) finest Renaissance treasures: Bramante's *Tempietto*. The church of S. Pietro in Montorio (St Peter's on the Golden Hill) was built and dedicated to St Peter because of an erroneous but centuries-long legend that the Apostle had been martyred on this very spot.

The source of the story is a bit complicated, but goes something like this. According to tradition, St Peter had been

Left: S. Maria del Popolo is most famous for two works by Michelangelo Merisi da Caravaggio (1573–1610). Here is his *Crucifixion of St Peter*, painted for the church in 1601.

Right: The Renaissance façade of S. Pietro in Montorio, funded by the Spanish monarchs Ferdinand and Isabella in the fifteenth century.

crucified (upside down) *inter duas metas*, or between the two posts (*metas*) which marked the ends of the classical arenas where many Christians met their martyrdom. In St Peter's case, the term referred to the two ends of Nero's Vatican Circus, where he was, in fact, almost certainly martyred.

Nevertheless, since the *metas* were shaped somewhat between an obelisk and a pyramid, it was calculated during the Middle Ages that the Apostle had died between the Pyramid of Cestius on the Ostian Way and an obelisk (or another pyramid) close to the Vatican. The *Mons Aureus* was equidistant from these two markers, so a church was erected on the alleged spot of the Fisherman's crucifixion.

BRAMANTE'S TRIBUTE

The church may have had a dubious birth, but its legend inspired a Renaissance masterpiece: the *Tempietto*, or 'little temple', of Bramante. The small dimensions of this monument and its inconspicuous location – crammed into a small court-yard beside the church – belie its importance in the history of art and architecture. This little temple, built in 1502 at S. Pietro in Montorio, is one of the architect's few buildings to come down to us intact.

Behind the grated gateway to the right of the church (on a lucky day it may be open), is a small circular pavilion on steps, ringed by a peristyle of sixteen Doric columns and surmounted by a graceful balustrade and hemispheric dome on a drum, with recessed windows echoing the columns below.

A true Renaissance classicist, Bramante had carefully studied and measured Rome's ancient monuments; the beauty of this monument derives from its classical harmony and perfect proportions. The ratio of height to width on the first level, for instance, reappears in the second storey. The structure admirably expresses the Renaissance ideals of pure form and ordered space, and is considered by many art historians to be the finest example of Italian High Renaissance architecture.

In the underground chapel (now closed), a hole marks the spot where the cross was supposedly placed at the time of St Peter's crucifixion. The upper and lower chapels have many statues and reliefs relating to the Apostle's life.

OTHER STORIES

Around 1480 Pope Sixtus IV (1471–84) bequeathed the church and monastery of S. Pietro in Montorio to Spanish Franciscans. Even today the coat-of-arms of the Kings of

Spain is prominently displayed on S. Pietro's façade. For it was the Spanish Catholic monarchs Ferdinand (1452–1516) and Isabella (1451–1504) who commissioned the new S. Pietro in Montorio, since the earlier ninth-century structure was falling apart, and engaged Bramante to build a shrine on the supposed site of St Peter's crucifixion.

The sixteenth-century Papacy was deriving many financial benefits from the discovery of America in 1492, and we know that Julius II used American riches granted him by the Spanish monarchs to help finance his grandiose projects for St Peter's. Philip III (1598–1621) had the piazza and the church's double staircase constructed (1605); a stone tablet on the stairs bears his name. Today the sixteenth-century monastery (to the right, adjoining the church) houses the Spanish Academy of History, Architecture and Fine Arts. Here young Spanish artists live and study, immersing themselves in the beauties of classical Rome, as Bramante did centuries before them.

The church guardian will point out bullet-holes in various walls, and a rather frightening crack running down the church façade. These were the results of Garibaldi's defensive battles against the French (1849) at the nearby San Pancrazio Gate. Garibaldi's short-lived Italian Republic served later as the model for a united Italy in 1870.

A tragic spirit haunts the area: Beatrice Cenci (1577–99), whose remains are buried beneath S. Pietro in Montorio's main altar steps. This young girl was accused of collaborating in the murder of her tyrannical father and, after a controversial trial, was beheaded publicly in a Roman square. A procession led by hooded members of Rome's Confraternity of S. Giovanni Decollato (St John the Beheaded) carried her body to the church, where she was entombed without gravestone or inscription, as was the custom for those condemned to death.

Also buried in the church are three Irish patriots who fled to Rome after the failure of their uprising against Queen Elizabeth I of England: Hugh O'Neil, Earl of Tyrone (d. 1616), his son, Hugh O'Neil II, Baron of Dungannon (d.1609) and Roderick O'Donnel, Earl of Tyrconnel (d. 1608).

A BOUNTY OF ART

As is the case of most Roman churches, S. Pietro in Montorio has an over-abundance of Renaissance – and other – art treasures. In the altar to the right of the entrance is Sebastiano del Piombo's *Scourging of Christ* (1519). This work has a powerful three-dimensional effect; the frescoed columns appear to be an integral part of the chapel architecture. The second right-hand chapel has, behind glass, Pomerancio's (1564) *Madonna of the Letter*, brought here from an outdoor street shrine in Trastevere.

Baldassare Peruzzi painted the *Coronation of the Virgin* (*c.*1509) in the chapel's half-dome; it glows with golden haloes and is populated with angels playing various musical instruments. The lovely cardinal virtues (*Fortitude, Prudence, Temperance,* and *Justice*) frescoed on the chapel's outside arch are also Peruzzi's. It is entertaining to imagine Peruzzi popping back and forth between decorating this church and the famous *Farnesina* just down the hill. This luxurious pleasure villa, designed by Peruzzi (1508–11) for Julius II's wealthy banker Agostino Chigi, was the sixteenth-century centre of fashion and festivity.

S. Pietro in Montorio also contains, to the right of the transept, a monumental chapel designed by Giorgio Vasari (1511–74) upon orders by the late Renaissance Pope Julius III (1550–65), containing statues and a balustrade by Bartolomeo Ammannati (1511–92). *Saint Ann with Virgin and Child*, in the third chapel on the left, is a lovely early Renaissance work by Antoniazzo Romano (1461–1508).

The stucco-work in this church, mostly by Giulio Mazzoni (1525–89), is especially elegant, and even those who don't particularly like that type of decoration should take a close look. Originally, Raphael's *Transfiguration* graced the church's main altar; Napoleon carried it off to France in 1809, and when it was returned it went to the Vatican Museum.

The Raimondi Chapel, second on the left, was designed by Gianlorenzo Bernini (1598–1680) and is dramatically lit by a hidden window above. The tomb of Girolamo Raimondi (d. 1628) has two *putti* looking into his open casket; while the monument to Francesco Raimondi (d. 1638) by Andrea Bolgi (1601–56) contrasts reliefs of carnival festivities with an Ash Wednesday ritual, a death and a burial.

Sebastiano del Piombo's *Scourging of Christ,* painted around 1519, in S. Pietro in Montorio.

CHAPTER

THE CATHOLIC COUNTER-REFORMATION: ROME'S SPIRITUAL RENEWAL

The Protestant Revolt in Northern Europe and the Sack of Rome had a traumatic effect on the Roman Church. When in 1517 Martin Luther posted his ninety-five theses of protest on the doors of Wittenberg Cathedral, the Holy See was occupied by the Medici Pope Leo X. This pleasure-loving humanist, inveterate nepotist and munificent patron of the arts had recklessly sold indulgences along with his palace furniture in order to pay his huge debts. Unhappily, he was typical of the Popes of his day.

Ten years later, in 1527, the Sack of Rome reduced the Eternal City to rubble and ashes. By then Protestantism had snatched half of Europe away from the Mother Church. For most of the sixteenth century a string of Renaissance Pontiffs had emphasized luxury and the arts at the expense of piety and moral leadership. Much of the clergy was corrupt and the populace lacked spiritual guidance. It was time for a thorough reform of the Church.

The reform and revival we now call the Counter-Reformation – generated by a series of energetic Popes and by the decisive Council of Trent – was carried out in the last three-quarters of the sixteenth century. In 1535 Pope Paul III (1534–49) commissioned a report, the *Consilium…De Emendanda Ecclesia (Advice for Reforming the Church)*, which severely indicted the Papacy and led to his convening the Council described below. His work was continued by Julius III

(1550–55), and by the austere and ascetic Paul IV (1555–9), who vigorously (and often excessively) implemented the Roman Inquisition against heresy. Pius IV (1559–65) brought the Council of Trent to its conclusion.

Post-Council Pontiffs continued the work of Catholic reform. Pius V (1566–72) imposed strict moral discipline on the Curia, the clergy and even Roman citizens. Gregory XIII (1572–85) was responsible for the new Gregorian Calendar and encouraged missionary activities. Sixtus V (1585–90) changed the face of Rome with his ambitious building and urban planning projects.

The Council of Trent, meeting intermittently under five Popes for almost twenty years (1545–63), was the most far-reaching achievement of the Counter-Reformation. The Council defined the Church position on all major points, drawing a sharp line between Catholic and Protestant doctrines. Disciplinary decrees were set forth for the clergy,

St Ignatius of Loyola (1491–1556) founded the Counter-Reformation Jesuit Order in the sixteenth century. His chapel-tomb in the Jesuit mother church Il Gesú was designed a century later. Its Baroque magnificence was a departure from the founder's ascetic and reformist ideals.

requiring priests to undergo solid doctrinal and spiritual training, and insisting that bishops reside in their sees. Mystics of the period, such as Teresa of Avila and John of the Cross, inspired believers with their writings and example.

The emergence of several new religious Orders proved to be a dynamic influence in the Catholic revival. Different in their outlooks, but united in their defence of the Church, Jesuits, Oratorians, Theatines and other reformist congregations intensified and disseminated the Counter-Reformation. These groups exercised a profound influence on art in general, and particularly on the building of Roman churches.

The Council of Trent provided guidelines for art and architecture as well as religion. Paintings and sculptures were to be clear and intelligible in style, moral and didactic in subject matter, and in purpose should provide an emotional impetus to piety.

Church decorations stressed Catholicism's reasserted tenets: the indispensable mediation of the Church between God and the faithful, the veneration of Mary and the saints, and the necessity of the sacraments for salvation. Early Popes and saintly bishops, martyrs and missionaries, thus paraded their stories around the naves and presbyteries.

The new churches were designed to accentuate the altar where the priest celebrated the Eucharist – and for the preaching of Tridentine Catholic reforms. New forms of liturgical music were composed and added to church services to heighten the emotional impact on the participating faithful.

It is true that the more rigid – and sometimes intolerant – Counter-Reformation produced no geniuses such as the Renaissance's Pinturicchio, Bramante, Michelangelo or Raphael. Nevertheless, the much-needed reforms imbued the Church with renewed confidence – resulting one century later in a plenitude of Baroque artistic glories in Roman churches.

IL GESÚ AND S. IGNAZIO
The Jesuits
The mother churches of the Jesuit Order were dedicated to the Name of Jesus and to St Ignatius of Loyola. The sanctuaries contain shrines of the Order's founder (St Ignatius), its chief missionary (St Francis Xavier), and several young Jesuit martyrs.

A NEW MILITANCY
Reformers have a way of showing up at critical points in Catholic Church history. Like Francis and Dominic in the Middle Ages, Ignatius of Loyola could not have chosen a

better time to appear on the historical scene. By the mid-sixteenth century, the Papacy had recognized the urgent need for internal reform and an external counter-attack against Protestants in Europe. The Church found a brilliant standard-bearer in St Ignatius. His new religious Order, the Jesuits, helped accomplish a consolidation and regeneration of the Church from within.

The youngest son of a Basque nobleman, Ignatius of Loyola (1491–1556) was brought up to be a knight. He set off to become a valiant soldier, but was wounded in the French siege of Pamplona. During a long convalescence period in his Loyola family castle, young Ignatius recuperated by reading *Lives of the Saints* and *The Imitation of Christ*. It was at that time that he experienced his profound religious conversion. Afterwards he spent almost a year of intense asceticism in a cave near Manresa, praying on his knees for seven or more hours a day.

After more years of penitence and prayer, a pilgrimage to Jerusalem, run-ins with the Spanish Inquisition, and university studies in Spain and Paris, Ignatius arrived in Rome with several followers in 1537 and offered his services to the Pope. His new religious Order, the Society of Jesus (Jesuits) was approved by Pope Paul III in 1540. Ignatius was chosen as the first Jesuit 'General' and spent the rest of his life in Rome directing the Society he had founded. By the time of Ignatius' death in 1556, the Jesuits numbered 1,000 in nine European provinces, and, following the pioneer work of Francis Xavier in the Far East, were sending missionaries far and wide.

Ignatius transposed his warrior ideals to the religious sphere, creating a tightly structured, rigorously trained, and deeply committed organization. The Society became the Pope's 'army' in the Counter-Reformation, using as its weapons advanced academic studies, the education of youth and zealous missionary activities. The Jesuits almost immediately began to argue against Protestant theologians in Church councils, set up excellent schools throughout Europe, and were soon preaching the Gospels in Africa, Asia and the Americas.

IL GESÚ
Il Gesú (the church of the Holy Name of Jesus) is the Jesuit Mother Church. It occupies the site St Ignatius chose for his headquarters shortly after he founded the Society of Jesus in 1540. That year Pope Paul III Farnese (1534–49) gave the Society a small neighbourhood chapel, S. Maria della Strada (Our Lady of the Wayside), which although conveniently located soon proved much too small for the expanding order.

beginning, St Ignatius placed a great deal of emphasis on the location of the Society's churches. He located his headquarters in urban centres, where the Society could easily carry out its preaching, teaching and social ministries. In Ignatius' time, Il Gesú was situated at a perfect crossroads between the Pope and his court, the Campidoglio (centre of city government), and the teeming life of the city.

Il Gesú stands carefully oriented to the surrounding streets and piazza. Ignatius wished the church exterior to appear as a great gateway, from where the Jesuits would set forth for apostolic activities in the city and in the world, and from where the city would be drawn into the sacramental life of the church. Il Gesú's façade was the first of its kind. Giacomo della Porta's sober tripartite front has classical elements, although its enormous side volutes already anticipate the Baroque. The façade clearly exhibits the IHS monogram of the Holy Name of Jesus – and the name in large letters of its donor, Cardinal Alessandro Farnese (1571–5).

Any visitor is struck by the difference between Il Gesú's interior and that of earlier Roman churches. Here we have the nave as one huge hall, a shallow apse with the altar moved up front, and interconnecting side chapels clearly separated from the main body of the church. All attention is drawn up front, across the transept illuminated by light pouring in from the cupola above, to the high altar where the priest celebrates Mass. In fact, Il Gesú's interior accentuates the two main functions of Catholic worship as defined by the Council of Trent. The wide nave with laterally placed pulpit serves as a great auditorium for preaching; the prominent altar provides a theatrical stage for the Eucharistic ceremony.

Il Gesú is a Counter-Reformation church, but its decor is almost all Baroque, dating from the late seventeenth century. In fact, Ignatius' church was largely undecorated, since the Jesuits prefered austerity in church decor – and also lacked funds and patronage – in their earliest years. Giovanni Battista Gaulli (1639–1709), known as 'Il Baciccia', was the artist responsible for Il Gesú's innovative ceiling frescoes – cupola, pendentives and vault, which he painted between 1672 and 1685. The vault fresco, representing *The Glory of the Holy Name of Jesus*, seems to open up a hole in the ceiling, through which heavenly light pours on to downwards-cascading colossal figures and into the nave and altar. Thus, according to the Baroque interpretation, the Jesuit church becomes not only a gateway to and from the world, but a window into paradise as well.

St Ignatius' chapel-tomb, off the left aisle, is an explosion of

Ignatius' dreams for an appropriately large and magnificent church were not realized in his lifetime. It took over forty years, three foundation-stone ceremonies, and six architects (Nanni di Baccio Bigio, Michelangelo, Vignola, Giovanni Tristano, Giovanni de Rosis, Giacomo della Porta) before Il Gesú was consecrated in 1584.

Spiritually, Il Gesú incorporates Jesuit values and articulates Catholic doctrine as reaffirmed by the Counter-Reformation. Architecturally, it marks the clear transition between Renaissance and Baroque. The plan of the Gesú became the model for Jesuit churches throughout the world.

Il Gesú stands in the heart of downtown Rome, on one of the city's busiest and noisiest intersections. It is a meeting place for all classes and generations of the city's population. From the

The façade of Il Gesú, designed by Giacomo della Porta (1571–5) for the Jesuit headquarters in Rome, which served as the model for Roman churches for centuries afterwards, and for Jesuit churches worldwide.

Baroque magnificence, with lapis lazuli, alabaster, semi-precious stones, all kinds of coloured marbles, gilded bronze and silver plate. The original solid silver statue was carted off and melted down by Napoleon's French officers in 1798, and supposedly was even more splendid than what we now behold. It took more than 100 artists, under the direction of Andrea Pozzo, to accomplish this luxurious frenzy. Would St Ignatius have approved?

More to the saint's taste, perhaps, would be the intimate little chapel of the *Madonna della Strada* in the left transept, which hosts an image from the façade of Ignatius' first church. In a round jewel-like setting, scenes from the *Life of the Virgin* by the Jesuit artist Giuseppe Valeriano (1542–1606) circle the tiny altar.

Directly across from St Ignatius' Chapel is that of the first Jesuit missionary saint, Francis Xavier (1506–52), designed by Pietro da Cortona (1597–1669) and Carlo Maratta (1625–1713). A plaque tells us that the saint's arm, 'which blessed so many converts in far away lands', now resides in the silver and lapis reliquary above the altar. Paintings depict St Francis' death off the China coast, St Francis finding his lost crucifix, baptizing an Indian princess, and St Francis in glory.

We should mention that the lateral chapels, which are separated from the nave and all connected by a candlelit corridor, are serene little corners, each attracting a coterie of faithful devotees. One chapel (the third on the right) is completely dedicated to angels.

S. IGNAZIO

The church of S. Ignazio was built in the next, that is the seventeenth, century. It is entirely Baroque in style, and can be said to represent the Jesuits' triumphant phase, and that of the Counter-Reformation.

This was originally part of the Roman College, one of the Society's earliest and finest educational institutions. Founded in 1551 as a 'school of grammar, humanities, and Christian doctrine, free of charge', the Roman College realized St Ignatius' conviction that 'all the good of Christianity and the world depends on the good education of the young' (as his spokesman wrote to Philip II of Spain in 1556).

In S. Ignazio's Baroque vault fresco (1693–4), Andrea Pozzo portrays Jesuit missionary activities in the four continents known in the seventeenth century.

By the early seventeenth century, the Roman College's original chapel had become too small for its bustling 2,000 students. Gregory XV Ludovisi (1621–3), who was a Roman College alumnus and had canonized Ignatius in 1622, nudged his nephew Cardinal Ludovico Ludovisi into funding a new church. (The Ludovisi amply recompensed themselves by emblazoning their names and family crest throughout the church. The inscription on their tomb states: 'One raised St Ignatius to the altar, while the other raised altars to Ignatius.') Work was entrusted to the College's own mathematics professor, Orazio Grassi, and the church was opened in 1650.

As mentioned above, the church of S. Ignazio originally formed part of the large complex of the Roman College. It now faces on to one of Rome's loveliest and most unique – Rococo – piazzas. Its tripartite façade is very similar to that of Il Gesú, which, as we have said, provided the model for most Jesuit churches worldwide.

S. Ignazio's floor plan repeats that of Il Gesú, but on a greater and grander scale. Originally the church served as both a college chapel and an auditorium, and its wide hall-like nave is functional for both purposes. Here famous theologians expounded on doctrinal matters and students defended their doctoral theses. In the seventeenth century the church was also an important cultural centre, hosting concerts and public ceremonies for the Roman population.

One important characteristic of S. Ignazio is that it has always been the Jesuit sanctuary for youth. Here two of the Jesuits' most beloved young saints are buried: St Aloysius Gonzaga (d.1591), who refused the honour of becoming a Spanish prince to study at the Roman College, and died at the age of twenty-three after ministering in Rome's plague hospitals; and St John Berchmans (d.1621), a young Jesuit student at the Roman College, who passed away here at twenty-two years of age. The elaborate Baroque tombs of these appealing saints face each other from both sides of the transept.

Much of the transept and pendentive painting was done by young art students at the Roman College, under the guidance of their professor, Andrea Pozzo. With the sacristan's help, we can identify portraits the students did of each other and of their teachers. The large figure of Judith, for instance, has the face of one collegian's mother, her maid is his grandmother, and Holofernes' severed head is the likeness of a too-strict school-caretaker

S. Ignazio is particularly famous as an example of Baroque illusionism. When money ran out before a dome could be built,

the clever Jesuit artist Andrea Pozzo painted a fake dome over the altar (1681–1701) . The *trompe l'oeil* perspective is the biggest joke in Rome (the uninitiated standing underneath never guess that the ceiling is really flat). Pozzo's luminous nave fresco is one of Rome's great experiences. As the visitor progresses under the nave, the painted sky seems to open out, figures of saints and angels fly outwards into space, and several colossals (infidels and heretics) tumble downwards,

Above: The family tomb of Pope Gregory XV Ludovisi, who canonized St Ignatius in 1622. The tomb is located in S. Ignazio to the right of the main altar.

Right: The main altar of S. Ignazio has frescoes by Andrea Pozzo depicting scenes from the life of St Ignatius.

desperately grasping at the billowing clouds. The fresco shows the Society of Jesus's missionary activity throughout the world, and has four monumental women, appropriately dressed to represent the four continents which were being converted by the missionary work at that time.

S. MARIA IN VALLICELLA (CHIESA NUOVA)
A 'New Church' for New Times

Rome's popular saint, Philip Neri, made S. Maria in Vallicella the reference point for Church revitalization and assistance to the poor of Rome. In gratitude, Romans have always called it their 'new church'.

THE BEACON

When S. Maria in Vallicella was rebuilt in the late sixteenth century, Rome was just emerging from a dark period of Papal corruption, spiritual indifference and social decay. Reformist Popes, a newly disciplined clergy and several dynamic new religious Orders were bringing about a Catholic revival from within.

The Institute of the Oratory was one of these new religious congregations, and its founder, St Philip Neri, was perhaps the Counter-Reformation's most appealing personality. S. Maria in Vallicella, the Oratorians' headquarters and centre of Philip Neri's reforming activities, became a beacon of spiritual and social renewal. It was immediately dubbed Chiesa Nuova (new church) by enthusiastic Romans. That is still its preferred name today.

Philip Neri (1515–95), son of a Florentine lawyer, was born in a period of profound crisis for the Church and for Catholicism. He grew up in Renaissance Florence, and a love of art and beauty inspired his entire life. As a boy he spent much time with the Dominican friars of St Mark's.

At the age of seventeen, Philip was sent by his family to be apprenticed to his wealthy uncle Romolo near what is now Monte Cassino. The vista of a prosperous commercial career repelled him, and the next year (1533) he left for Rome as a penniless young pilgrim. There he tutored his landlord's sons to make a living. Although beloved as a kind and innovative teacher, Philip spent much of his time praying and meditating in the Catacomb of St Sebastian, where he was inspired by memories of the fervour and sacrifice of the early Christian community.

In 1551, while the Council of Trent was still in session, Philip was ordained a priest. Eventually he founded a brother-hood of laymen, who devoted themselves to the care of pilgrims, and of the city's poor and needy. Many flocked to attach themselves to Philip's apostolate – Romans of all ages and social strata. Philip was, however, a shrewd judge of character. To exclude the possibility of false, show-off piety, he reportedly required several aristocratic hopefuls to go about in ragged cloaks, or with foxtails attached to their breeches.

Father Philip moved into the church of S. Girolamo, where he soon became one of the city's most sought-after confessors. He strolled the streets, playing games with the local orphans and loafers, instructing and inspiring them with his customary humour and informality. To further encourage his penitents, Father Philip initiated a series of afternoon services – liturgy, readings, prayers and discussions, enriched by beautiful music. All of Rome seemed to gravitate to these sessions – pious old ladies and neighbourhood toughs, theology students and artists, society women in silks and furs, prostitutes, top Curia Cardinals and religious reformers. A new room, called the Oratory, was constructed above the church to accommodate the clamouring overflow.

Philip and his fellow priests became known as the Oratorians. Their Order was approved in 1575 by Pope Gregory XIII (1572–85), who also gave them the dilapidated church of S. Maria in Vallicella as their new headquarters. The Oratorians immediately set about restoring and reconstructing their new home, handing bricks and mortar to experienced workmen and spoiled noble postulants alike, to raise the Chiesa Nuova in record time.

On the day of the big move, the Oratorians marched in a bizarre procession from their interim headquarters at another church, ceremoniously brandishing an assortment of battered household implements – frying pans, wooden bowls, brooms and dustbins, chairs and spits – to the delight of the Roman populace. Philip interrupted his parade to kick a few soccer balls – one of his favourite pastimes – with the neighbourhood youth.

When Philip Neri died in 1595, all Rome mourned. He had truly contributed to the reform of the Church – purifying it with the simplicity of his thought, the charity of his actions, and the exuberance of his spirit. One of his greatest contributions to the Church was his stress on beauty as an aid to devotion, and especially on good music. The 'oratorio' (a dramatized form of sacred music) originated in the Oratorians' services.

In the Chiesa Nuova, one tomb inscription for a simple parishioner commented aptly: 'In gratitude to Saint Philip

Neri, who was able to render cheerful the paths of the Lord, even in the most difficult of life's adversities.'

BACKWARDS IN TIME

In Philip Neri's days, S. Maria in Vallicella was known as 'the joyous house', but that had not always been the case. St Philip's Chiesa Nuova rose on the site of an earlier church called 'in Vallicella' because it had stood in the valley of a small stream flowing into the nearby marshes. In remote times the hollow depression was characterized by stagnant waters, sulphurous odours, and damp mists – perhaps even a cavernous hole.

The area was so disagreeable that pre-Republican Romans believed it covered the Gates of Hell; they built a temple in honour of two important underworld deities, Dis and Proserpina, on that very spot. In fact, during the Oratorians' zealous excavations for their new centre, they discovered – and reused or sold – some of the pagan marbles and statuary.

The earlier S. Maria in Vallicella was supposedly founded by St Gregory the Great in the sixth century (his statue and inscription decorate the church façade, along with those of St Jerome). Twelfth-century Church annals mention the building in relation to the sale of indulgences. (We suspect St Philip would not have approved.) Throughout the Middle Ages the district was called Pozzo Bianco (white well), after its pride and joy – a marble drain top from imperial Rome standing in front of the church.

By Philip Neri's time, the neighbourhood had become a melting (probably boiling) pot of different classes and professions: bankers and thieves, painters and printers, courtesans and innkeepers, Cardinals and functionaries in the pontifical Curia. The bustling and heterogeneous population offered ideal conditions for the Oratorians' apostolate.

The church boasted its customary miraculous icon. The Vallecellian Madonna and Child, frescoed on a hovel across the street (the site of the present apse), had been venerated throughout the Middle Ages. In 1535, after losing out in a hotly-contested street competition, a resentful ball-player hurled (or kicked) a stone at the revered image, which began to bleed from the cheek and neck. The picture was removed and placed inside the sacristy, where it continued to work miracles. According to tradition, during construction of the Chiesa Nuova, the Vallecellian Madonna appeared to Philip Neri in a dream, warning him to replace a rotting wooden beam. Pietro da Cortona's nave-vault fresco shows the Virgin holding up the perilous rafter, thus saving workers and worshippers from a terrible catastrophe.

Philip had the original S. Maria in Vallicella pulled down and replaced, according to plans by Matteo da Città di Castello and Martino Longhi the Elder, by a bigger and more beautiful construction. Work continued, with the generous patronage of Cardinal Pier Donato Cesi (his dedication is at the back of the church), and later of his brother, Bishop Angelo Cesi of Todi (an even larger inscription emblazoned over the main portal), from 1575 until Faustolo Rughesi completed the façade in 1605. The palazzo on the left of the church (now called the Oratory) was built between 1637 and 1650 after a design by Francesco Borromini, as a residence and library for the Oratorians.

INSIDE THE CHIESA NUOVA

S. Maria in Vallicella is very similar – inside and out – to other Counter-Reformation churches in Rome. Like the Jesuits' Il Gesú and S. Ignazio, and the Theatines' S. Andrea della Valle, it has a double-storeyed tripartite façade with scrolls. The

S. Maria in Vallicella, another important Counter-Reformation church in the centre of Rome.

worked there for twenty years, on and off, from 1647 to 1669. His frescoed vaults over the nave (the above-mentioned *St Philip's Vision of our Lady and the Falling Beam*), cupola (*Trinity in Glory*), and apse (*Assumption of the Virgin*) are bright, dramatic and immediately appealing. He also painted the pendentives and the ceiling of St Philip Neri's former chambers.

Apart from these frescoes, the Chiesa Nuova's greatest treasures are three early (1607–8) paintings by Peter Paul Rubens (1577–1640): over the main altar, *Virgin, Child, and Angels*, and, on either side, *St Gregory the Great with SS. Maurus and Papius*, and *St Domitilla with SS. Nereus and Achilleus*. St Gregory is represented as the supposed founder of the church; Sts Maurus and Papius are Roman martyrs whose relics were brought to the church and placed beneath the main altar in 1599. Under Rubens' oval Madonna (removable) is hidden the Vallicellian Madonna, protagonist of the two miracles mentioned earlier.

Philip's church is filled with many other lovely – if little-known – paintings. Worthy of note are the splendid *Presentation of the Virgin* (in the left transept) and *Visitation* (in the fourth chapel from the entrance on the left) by Il Baroccio (Federico Fiori di Urbino, d.1612). The latter was Philip's favourite painting. According to his biographer, the saint sometimes went into ecstasy in the Visitation Chapel. The *Assumption* by Aurelio Lomi di Pisa, (d. 1622), (in the fifth chapel on the right from the entrance), caused a great stir in 1796, when the Virgin miraculously moved her eyes. The phenomenon was noted by almost all the Oratorians in residence. With pomp and processions they declared a month-long festival, during which the miracle repeated itself, to the delight of Roman devotees.

Also worth a visit are the *Portrait of St Philip* by Guido Reni (d.1642) now in the saint's restored chambers (open to the public annually on 26 May), and two works by Alessandro Algardi (d.1654) – the famous statue of St Philip Neri and Angel and the bronze bust of Pope Gregory XV (who canonized St Philip in 1622), both in the sacristy.

interior appears to be one large hall-like nave (with side aisles), transepts, a shallow apse and five lateral chapels.

Philip Neri had wished the walls and vaults of his church to be left white and undecorated. The Baroque century which followed had other preferences, however. As is the case with the above-mentioned churches, the Chiesa Nuova's interior presents us with a wealth of stucco and gold, whirls of painted angels and spiralling clouds, and swirls of blue and crimson draperies.

Pietro da Cortona (Pietro Berrettini, 1597–1669), seventeenth-century Rome's most sought-after ceiling painter, was commissioned to decorate the Oratorians' church; he

Left: Pietro da Cortona's famous fresco for the nave ceiling in S. Maria in Vallicella shows
The Vallicellian Madonna Saving the Chiesa Nuova from Collapse.

Above: St Philip Neri's chapel in the left transept of the Chiesa Nuova, with a copy of
Guido Reni's portrait of the saint.

S. ANDREA DELLA VALLE
The Operatic Church

Not far from Il Gesú and the Chiesa Nuova, S. Andrea della Valle was the centre for yet another new Counter-Reformation religious congregation.

AN OPERATIC BASILICA

It is not at all hard to imagine why Giacomo Puccini set the first act of his opera *Tosca* in S. Andrea della Valle (in the Barberini Chapel, first on the left after the entrance). In fact, it would be hard to imagine a more theatrical church. The airy majesty of the great white marble hall (one wide nave with barrel vault and Latin cross), glittering with gold and awash with bold paintings, seems to call for some kind of orchestral accompaniment. By the time S. Andrea della Valle was reconstructed (beginning in 1591), the Counter-Reformation already had quite a bit to celebrate – and this lovely church certainly makes the point.

The drama unfolds as soon as one enters the basilica. Mattia Preti's enormous paintings (1650–51), spreading the story of St Andrew's martyrdom across the curving apse, have an almost unbearable impact. The three frescoes, *St Andrew Raised on the Cross*, *St Andrew's Crucifixion*, and *St Andrew's Burial*, are both uplifting (lofty classical architecture and spacious landscapes) and tragic (the saint's fearful expression and mocking crowds). Above the apse, Domenichino's frescoes (1624–1627), less dramatic but even more beautiful, also depict episodes from the life of the saint, including the famous *St Andrew Brings Peter to Jesus* and *Jesus's Call to the Fishermen Andrew and Peter*.

EARLY ORIGINS

The site of S. Andrea della Valle was originally occupied by the tiny but famous Church of St Sebastian. The sanctuary existed here from the fourth century, and was an immensely popular pilgrimage site. As a reminder of the church's origins, Sebastian's statue can be seen on the church façade; he also appears in a rather dingy altar painting by Giovanni de Vecchi (1614) in the third chapel on the left.

In 1582 the devout and widowed Donna Costanza Piccolomini, Duchess of Amalfi and last heir of the Roman family branch, bequeathed to her favourite Order of Theatine Fathers her palazzo, her property, and the adjacent crumbling Church of St Sebastian. Costanza stipulated only that a much larger basilica be constructed on the site, and dedicated to the patron of Amalfi, St Andrew.

The Theatine Fathers for whom S. Andrea was founded, and who administer the basilica to this day, were one of the new

S. Andrea della Valle (above), where enormous paintings by Mattia Preti (1650–51) show the martyrdom of St Andrew (right).

religious Orders of the Italian Counter-Reformation. Established in 1523 as the Congregation of Regular Clerks (they were known as the Theatines because the first Superior General was the Bishop of Theate – and later Pope Paul IV), they attempted to instil virtue in the laity and to reform the clergy. From the beginning, the Theatines emphasized study of the Scriptures, the dignity of worship, and care for the sick and poor.

In 1591 the palazzo and church were demolished and construction began on the new church, which the Theatines made their centre of oratory and catechesis. A chapel in S. Andrea's left transept is dedicated to the Theatine founder, St Cajetan of Tiene (1480–1547), while the chapel directly opposite in the right transept venerates another member of the Order, Andrew of Avellino – and has a painting by Giovanni Lanfranco (1581–1647) of the saint suffering an attack of apoplexy. The two saints are also represented by statues on the church façade (along with Sts Andrew and Sebastian).

The Theatines kept their promise to honour St Andrew. Anyone who enters the church will be moved by the drama and heroism of this saint's martyrdom, as depicted in the splendid apsidal frescoes described above. The fisherman Andrew from Capernaum (d.60), was a disciple of John the Baptist before becoming one of Christ's first Apostles. He was the brother of Simon Peter and, in fact, introduced Peter to Jesus. Andrew preached the Gospel in Greece (Scythia and Epirus) and, according to tradition, also founded the Churches in Scotland and Constantinople. He supposedly died in Patras, crucified on an X-shaped cross.

After the fall of Constantinople (1204) the Crusaders took Andrew's body to Amalfi, and the Pope obtained his head in 1461. The latter was considered one of the Vatican's greatest treasures, until it was returned to the Patriarch of Constantinople by Pope Paul VI (1963–78). Andrew is the great patron of the Eastern Churches, almost on a par with St Peter in the West. The basilica's cupola (Carlo Maderno, 1622, with the assistance of his nephew Francesco Borromini) is Rome's second largest after St Peter's, and second in evidence on the Rome skyline.

INSIDE THE BASILICA

Many impressive works and monuments ornament S. Andrea della Valle. Perhaps the most important are the tombs of the early Renaissance humanist Pope Pius II Piccolomini (1458–64) and his nephew Pius III, who reigned for only twenty-seven days (1503). Located high in the walls of the nave, to the right and left before the transept, the tombs have bas-reliefs on four different levels (school of Andrea Bregno, late 1400s), which tell the life stories of the two Pontiffs.

S. Andrea della Valle was the scene for one of Rome's great pre-Baroque rivalries – between the Bolognese Domenichino (1581–1641) and Giovanni Lanfranco (1581–1647) from Parma. Domenichino's *Four Evangelists* in the dome pendatives were greatly praised and admired in their day. But it was Lanfranco who received the commission for painting the cupola. His *Glory of Paradise,* with its whirl of golden clouds and swirling angels, set the pattern for many other dome frescoes in Rome.

The Ginetti Chapel (first on the right) was designed by Carlo Fontana (1670) and has a white marble – and very graceful – relief of *The Angel Tells the Holy Family to Flee to Egypt* by Antonio Raggi (1624–86). Across the nave, in the Barberini Chapel (the *Tosca* chapel, first on the left), stands a statue of St John the Baptist, sculpted by Pietro Bernini (1562–1629), with the help of his son, the much more famous Gianlorenzo, for Cardinal Maffeo Barberini, who later became Pope Urban VIII (1623–44). The Strozzi Chapel (second on the right) is full of sombre bronze plagiarisms of Michelangelo's *Pietà, Leah* and *Rachel.*

White ribbing and gold stucco work (1650–52) between the apse paintings is by Alessandro Algardi (1595–1654). Carlo Rainaldi (1611–91) completed S. Andrea's façade, slightly altering Carlo Maderno's original design.

There are two explanations for the church's name. According to one, 'of the Valley' referred to the area where the church was built. The other refers to Cardinal Andrea della Valle, who had palaces and property across from those of the Piccolomini, and could have given his name to the piazza and church.

**Domenichino (Domenico Zampieri) painted beautiful scenes from the life of St Andrew
in the apse vault of S. Andrea della Valle.**

THE BEST OF BAROQUE: THE CHURCH TRIUMPHANT

By the beginning of the seventeenth century, the Council of Trent (1545–63) had achieved clarification of Church doctrine, reform of the clergy, and spiritual revival. The spread of Protestantism had been checked in Europe, and portions of Germany, Switzerland and the Low Countries returned to the Mother Church. Jesuit efforts curbed the Northern Reformation's progress in Eastern Europe; in France religious wars ended with a Catholic victory; a Catholic (Spanish–Italian) fleet inflicted a historic defeat on the Turks at Lepanto in 1571.

The Roman Church seemed to have every reason to exult, and a new spirit pervaded art and architecture in Rome. The triumphal new art form which responded to Catholicism's newfound confidence was known as the Baroque. Churches were to be celebrative and festive, full of splendour and pageantry. To accentuate the contrast between Catholicism and Calvinist puritanism, and to give an idea of the type of heaven awaiting the Catholic faithful, the Church enlisted Baroque artists to adorn and enrich chapels and cathedrals – within and without.

Baroque churches provided the framework for dramatic presentations – with displays of gold and precious stones, clouds of angels and saints in glory – of the even greater wonders of heaven to come. These great showpieces were meant to sweep the onlooker off his feet. These were not the times for Renaissance harmony and proportion – or for Counter-Reformation austerity and preaching. Emotional intensity was called for to bring about spiritual conviction and conversion.

A succession of exuberant Papacies ushered in the new age. Paul V (1605–21) commissioned a façade and parts of the interior for the new St Peter's and beautified Rome with many monumental fountains. The prodigality of Paul's favourite nephew, Cardinal Scipione Borghese (1576–1633), resulted in an art and antiquities collection, assembled in his pleasure villa within the vast Borghese park, which surpassed even those of his Renaissance precursors. Perhaps to assuage his conscience, the Cardinal also restored many Roman churches in the Baroque style: for example S. Sebastiano and S. Gregorio Magno.

The pontificate of Urban VIII (1623–44) attracted painters, sculptors and architects from far and wide and made Rome once more the artistic centre of the world. The Pope built magnificent family palaces and entertained the Roman populace with outdoor festivals which were famed throughout the Western world. Innocent X (1644–55) rivalled Urban VIII in his patronage of great artists, and converted his family

Pietro da Cortona's SS. Luca e Martina was Rome's first completely Baroque church, pre-dating even the creations of Bernini and Borromini.

properties in Piazza Navona into a Baroque showplace for Rome and for all of Europe.

Under Alexander VII (1655–67), Bernini made of St Peter's – both within and without – the most imposing shrine in all Christendom. Clement IX (1667–9) befriended Sweden's extravagant Catholic convert, Queen Christina of Sweden (1626–89). Finally, with the election of the stern economical reformer Innocent XI (1676–89), called 'Papa Non' by Romans because of his frugality, the most euphoric phase of the Baroque seemed to be at an end.

By the end of the seventeenth century the physical aspect of Rome's churches had changed beyond recognition. Catholicism's capital had become a theatre of the Baroque – and it is thus that the pilgrim will find the city even today.

Rome's Baroque transformation was due primarily to a trio of remarkable artists: Gianlorenzo Bernini, Francesco Borromini and Pietro da Cortona. Some of the most appealing works of these architects were small, centralized structures, next on this pilgrimage to the churches of Rome.

S. ANDREA AL QUIRINALE
Church as Theatre
Bernini's church for St Andrew, with its oval shape, theatrical altar and splendid dome, epitomizes the Baroque at its height. Not far away, another church contains Baroque sculpture's most famous representation of mystical experience.

CONSUMMATE BAROQUE
Many history and art history books include a chapter entitled 'Bernini and the Baroque'. Rome gave birth to the Baroque style – and in Rome (and for a while in the entire Western world) Bernini was the Baroque.

Gianlorenzo Bernini (1598–1680), architect, sculptor, painter, playwright, stage designer, actor, impresario, was born in Naples. Brought to Rome by his father, the respected sculptor Pietro Bernini, Lorenzo spent his childhood feverishly studying and drawing Roman monuments and art works. At the age of eight he sculpted a marble head which astounded Italy's foremost painter of the day, Annibale Carracci, who praised him publicly. Still in his teens, Bernini executed a portrait bust for Pope Paul V, who declared that the artist would become the 'Michelangelo of the seventeenth century'.

Gianlorenzo Bernini executed commissions for a long succession of Baroque Popes (Paul V, Gregory XV, Urban VIII,

Innocent X, Alexander VII, Clement IX, Clement X, Innocent XI). His churches, palaces, squares and fountains changed the countenance of medieval–Renaissance Rome to that of the city we see today. St Peter's Basilica also owes its most spectacular elements – both inside and out – to Bernini's interventions. From his brief posting as court artist to Louis XIV of France, the Italian genius helped spread the new Baroque style from France throughout Europe – and beyond.

Bernini was a brilliant conversationalist and a prized guest in seventeenth-century Rome's aristocratic circles. Besides his buildings, sculptures and paintings, he also produced theatrical performances which were the wonder of the civilized world. At the same time, he was also a man of intense personal piety. In his later years he asserted that his secular masterpieces – palaces, piazzas and fountains – had been a complete waste of

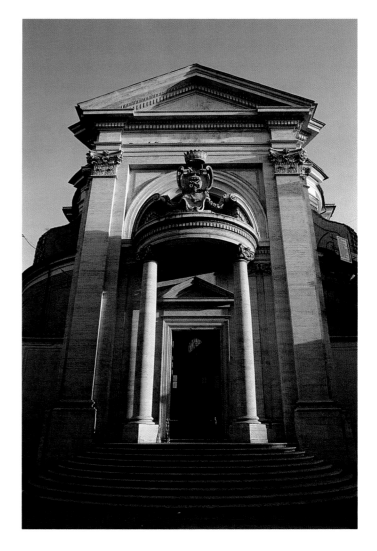

time. It was only his religious sculptures and churches which gave him satisfaction in his old age.

Bernini loved one church in particular, where (according to his son Domenico's biography) he often went to relax and 'console myself with my work' in the last period of his life. That church was S. Andrea al Quirinale, a shrine dedicated to the Apostle St Andrew and built (from 1658 to 1670) as part of a Jesuit novitiate on the Quirinal Hill.

FERVOUR AND DRAMA

S. Andrea's façade, looking on to the busy street which now serves Rome's main government quarter, invites the visitor up a graceful, semi-circular flight of stairs and through a classical portal. Entering the church, one feels that Bernini's theatrical experience has provided him – even for religious architecture – with an amazingly rich source of inspiration. S. Andrea opens on to the short side of an elegant elliptical space, propelling onlookers directly in front of the main altar. And there, framed by a 'curtain' of glistening fluted, pink-speckled columns, the drama of St Andrew's martyrdom is taking place.

A highly emotional painting by Guillaume Courtois (1668) shows the Apostle, the church patron, being nailed to an X-shaped cross, while mothers and children grieve and gesticulate in the foreground. But a happy ending is already in sight. To

Left: The graceful façade of Gianlorenzo Bernini's S. Andrea al Quirinale (1658–70) and its elliptical interior, designed as a stage-like setting.

Above: The Titular Cardinal of S. Andrea al Quirinale, Cardinal Kozlowiecki of Poland, 'takes possession' of his church in February 1998.

THE JESUITS AGAIN

In 1658 the Society of Jesus commissioned S. Andrea to replace a former novitiate (church and quarters occupied by religious novices during their period of probation) on the Quirinal Hill. By this time the Society, because of its superior schools and association with the ruling classes, had become influential throughout Europe, and the Order's missionary activities had spread Catholicism to South America, India, Japan and the Philippines.

The Jesuits were thus able to obtain for their new building the services of Pope Alexander VII's own architect, Bernini. Expenses were born by Prince Camillo Pamphili, nephew of the former Pope Innocent X, who had his family symbols carved over the inside and outside doors. The church was opened for services in November 1670.

The Jesuit presence is evident throughout the church. Side altars are dedicated to the Order's sixteenth-century pioneer saints. The second chapel, clockwise on right, honours the great Jesuit missionary St Francis Xavier, with paintings by 'Il Baciccia', who did the vault in Il Gesú. In the second chapel, counter-clockwise on the left, we view a painting of the Jesuit founder, St Ignatius of Loyola, depicted along with St Francis Borgia (1510–72), who established the first novitiate here, and the young St Aloysius Gonzaga already encountered in S. Ignazio.

The next chapel on the left is dedicated to the church's favoured saint, St Stanislaus Kostka (1550–68), a young Polish nobleman who walked over 600 miles – against his family's wishes and in very fragile health – to join the Jesuit novitiate on the Quirinal Hill. Stanislaus studied and died in rooms behind the church. These are open to visitors upon request. S. Andrea al Quirinale is still served by the Jesuits, and the pastor is often of Polish descent.

ULTIMATE BERNINI

Bernini preferred S. Andrea to all his other churches. But he considered his religious sculpture *St Teresa in Ecstasy* the finest

one side of the frightened saint, a cloud-perched cupid is calmly watching as the tragedy turns to triumph. Above the gruesome painted scene, a spectacular 'glory', in the form of a great bronze relief executed by Giovanni Rinaldi between 1668 and 1670, depicts three charming angels and froths of countless cherubs about to whisk the martyr to paradise in a gilded blaze.

In fact, there he is again, St Andrew, alighted even higher on the broken pediment as a statue by Antonio Raggi (1624–86), about to take off to heaven through the golden dome. From a hidden source, an opening above the altar and behind the pediment, a diffuse light heightens the dramatic effect.

There is something amazingly intimate about S. Andrea's small size and oval shape. The impression of a theatre is carried through in the almost musical procession of arched side chapels and niches. Up in the golden dome, composed of hexagonal coffers with different types of flowers, cherubs peep over the edge to see what is going on below. Around the drum, more playful *putti* drape garlands and festoons, and semi-recumbent fishermen (St Andrew was a fishermen) relax, dangling their nets over the drum windows.

As an architect Bernini used sumptuous means, opulent colours and textures, yet achieved almost classical proportions and unity. Marbles in the richest tones, bronze, gold, lapis and mosaics – all are controlled by a harmonious repetition of form, and by light pouring in from the cupola.

Above: A recumbent polychrome statue (1796–1802) of the young Polish Jesuit, St Stanislaus Kostka, who died in the S. Andrea novitiate.

Right: The interior of S. Carlo alle Quattro Fontane, built (1638–67) by Francesco Borromini, is full of technical innovations and architectural surprises.

piece of art he had ever accomplished. The setting for this statue in the Cornaro Chapel (1645–52) of the church of S. Maria della Vittoria heightened even further the theatrical effects Bernini achieved in S. Andrea al Quirinale.

Here architecture interacts with sculpture, painting and decor for a dramatic presentation of an ecstatic experience. Again, shining columns act as a curtain frame; the curved pediment is like the proscenium arch of a stage. 'Box seats', carved to both sides of the altar, have sculpted portraits of the Cornaro family as spectators of – or participators in – the spiritual event. The whole scene is lit by a dramatic, concealed source of lighting.

The 'event' is a mystic vision recounted by the sixteenth-century Spanish nun St Teresa of Avila (1515–82). In a famous description, the saint tells how a divine angel pierced her heart with a flaming arrow, filling her with pain and rapture. In Bernini's rendition, the use of startling white marble for the saint and angel, the rapturous face and writhing draperies of the swooning nun, the vivid but invisible light, all produce an intense emotional effect that represents the Baroque at its height.

A visit to S. Andrea should be followed by another to S. Maria della Vittoria, which is not very far away. Carlo

Maderno's church was built between 1608 and 20 and dedicated to St Paul in honour of Pope Paul V. It was then 'renamed' St Mary of Victory in 1622 for its miraculous painting, *The Madonna of Victory*. The image had been carried by victorious Catholic armies when they routed the Protestant forces in Prague's decisive Battle of White Mountain – and then brought to Rome in pomp and splendour and given its very own, rededicated, church.

S. CARLO ALLE QUATTRO FONTANE
Architectural Surprise Package
Francesco Borromini's small church dedicated to St Charles Borromeo is full of surprising, even bizarre, effects. Upon closer examination, we discover a profound spiritual symbolism.

RIVALRY AND RENOWN
At the highest point of Rome's Quirinal Hill stand two monuments to the great seventeenth-century rivalry of Baroque architecture: Gianlorenzo Bernini's S. Andrea al Quirinale, described earlier, and Francesco Borromini's

S. Carlo alle Quattro Fontane. These remarkable churches emblematically mirror their creators' personalities and histories. S. Andrea, harmonious and richly spectacular, could only have been the work of the sociable and sophisticated Bernini; while the convoluted and brilliantly unorthodox S. Carlo reflects Borromini's eccentric and tormented genius. (Another Roman site which demonstrates this famous rivalry is Piazza Navona, with Borromini's church of S. Agnese, and, opposite, Bernini's Fountain of the Four Rivers.)

Francesco Borromini (1599–1667), of Lombard origin, was born in Bissone on Lake Lugano. For more than twenty years he worked as a stonecutter, draughtsman and architectural assistant, first on Milan Cathedral and later on St Peter's. His St Peter's apprenticeship under Carlo Maderno (1556–1629), his uncle, was apparently fairly happy and fruitful (their tombs lie beside one another in Rome's church of S. Giovanni dei Fiorentini). But upon Maderno's death, his experience as underling to Bernini, who took over the direction of St Peter's, gave rise to the bitter rivalry which tortured him for the rest of his life. It is said that Borromini resented Bernini's easy success, and claimed that Bernini exploited his (Borromini's)

technical skills to become the preferred architect of Rome's high society. Painfully conscious of his humble origins, Borromini dressed in workman's clothes and derided Bernini for his smart clothes and fashionable life.

S. Carlo was Borromini's first architectural commission. Some say it was Bernini who recommended him for the job, and that Borromini accepted his competitor's challenge to construct the church within the space, which was (and still is) equivalent to one of the four pillars which support St Peter's dome. In any case, in 1634 the Spanish Discalced (meaning 'without shoes', i.e. barefoot, or poor) Trinitarians turned to the thirty-year-old Borromini to design their monastery and church, dedicated to the Holy Trinity and St Charles Borromeo (the saintly Counter-Reformation Bishop of Milan).

S. Carlo was the only building Borromini ever achieved from beginning to end. The artist realized the monastery, church and convent from 1634 to 1641. He worked on the façade from 1664 until the time of his death in 1667; by then, most of his works had been completed or changed by other architects. Borromini's dealings with his clients often ended in quarrels, and he was a demanding and violent master (beating one assistant so brutally that he later died from his wounds). In the summer of 1667, the rancorous and frustrated Borromini committed suicide by plunging a sword through his chest. The bell-tower and last touches to S. Carlo's façade were finished, according to the artist's instructions, by his nephew Bernardo Borromini in 1675.

A GEOMETRICAL GEM

S. Carlo alle Quattro Fontane is, most agree, not a beautiful church. Compared to the almost musical harmony, unity and opulence of Bernini's S. Andrea down the street, S. Carlo's interior seems agitated, unconventional, convoluted. For one thing, Borromini satisfied the Trinitarians' conditions for using only 'poor' materials, in keeping with the Order's mission and simple lifestyle. For another, there appears to be no focal point; one architectural element grows out of another with almost dizzying caprice and diversity.

Left: The Baroque façade of S. Carlo alle Quattro Fontane exhibits Borromini's love for convex and concave movement in his designs.

Right: S. Carlo's cupola and odd, geometrically coffered dome.

But wait a minute. That is just the point. Borromini has departed from the Renaissance ideals of humanist balance and unity; he is more interested in producing innovative solutions and a dynamic, flowing use of space. Anyone who gives S. Carlo a chance will be pleasantly overwhelmed by a cornucopia of architectural surprises.

S. Carlo's biggest surprise is its unusual shape, a diamond with convex curves instead of diagonal lines. The resulting octagon was Borromini's solution to the problem of squeezing the church into a corner between two busy streets. (Because of its small size, S. Carlo is often called by its diminutive, 'S. Carlino'.) To round off the angles (he hated corners), Borromini used paired columns and niches, which gave the walls an undulating effect.

Upon the octagonal (sometimes described as elliptical) body of the church, Borromini placed an oval dome which seems to float over a series of horizontal windows, cleverly disguised by a curious circle of foliage. Within the dome are honeycombed coffers with striking geometric designs – octagons, crosses and hexagons.

There are more surprises. Niches for the statues of the Trinitarian founders (Sts John of Matha and Felix of Valois) are crowned with leaping flames, rather than the usual subdued scallops favoured by Roman Church tradition. The entablature over the altar is tweaked up into a playful pinnacle, and this pattern is repeated in the four wooden confessionals with their bizarre peaked 'caps'

Passing into the two-tiered cloister, we are again struck by Borromini's obsession with geometry. While the lower columns support arches and convex bulges, the upper order carries a flat cornice sectioned horizontally. A balustrade between the two levels is composed of small bottle-shaped pillars – and every second pillar is placed upside down. The sacristy next door has a ceiling that seems very Rococo, with curling white mouldings and cheerful cherubs.

BORROMINI'S METAPHYSICS

Borromini's architecture is not a mere expression of capricious imagination and technical skill. We have reason to believe that the artist's concern with geometrical form was moved by a profound sense of metaphysics.

The monastery and the church of S. Carlo were commissioned by the Discalced Trinitarians, that is the Order of the Holy Trinity, and dedicated to the Most Holy Trinity. Borromini's emphasis on tripartition is particularly noticeable in the façade, but even the interior clearly favours groups of three (columns, shells in niches, Trinitarian emblems).

The octagon, the matrix shape of the church and cloister, is only one of the three root forms used by Borromini in S. Carlo: the cross and the oval are continually integrated with this, providing a tripartite artistic range. Because of the presence of these three geometrical forms, S. Carlo has been recognized as the architectural expression of the dogma of the Holy Trinity.

The architect's ultimate statement for his church is the dome lantern image of the Holy Spirit (inside an equilateral

triangle). This image is accentuated by a flood of light from the dome windows, and by the perspective of diminishing geometrical coffers towards the top.

A BAROQUE FAÇADE

S. Carlo alle Quattro Fontane, or St Charles (Borromeo) at the Four Fountains, is located at the south-west corner of one of Rome's busiest crossroads: Via delle Quattro Fontane (named for the intersection's four monumental Baroque fountains) and Via Quirinale (which runs along a street of governmental palaces). Unfortunately, the revolutionary character of S. Carlo's façade is rarely savoured – because of the smog, congestion, and danger of murder by motorcycle on the almost non-existent pavements.

Borromini was working on S. Carlo's façade in the year of his death. The result is the culmination of the artist's mature talent – and the epitome of Baroque architecture. Borromini used traditional (classical) elements, such as columns, pilasters, cornices and pediments – but in completely unorthodox ways – curving and contorting these to achieve an unsettling and constantly moving effect.

The curving, wavelike impression of S. Carlo's interior is even more pronounced in the façade. The two-tiered front is partitioned into three sections by columns and niches, providing a lively undulation of convex and concave spaces. Statues of the Trinitarian founders occupy the two side niches, while in the centre, St Charles Borromeo is crowned by the soaringly distorted wings of two Art Nouveau-like angels.

Other fanciful (almost bizarre) elements abound: at the top, a huge oval (formerly containing a painting) leans forward precariously from the featherweight grip of floating cherubs; just below this, a curious 'kiosk' opens over a brief balustrade; the whole is surmounted by an oval drum bearing the curvy octagonal dome with its spiral cap. The bell-tower, completed by Borromini's nephew, is completely faithful to S. Carlo's style and spirit.

Left: The cloister in S. Carlo, which uses architectural elements of different shapes and patterns.

Far left: S. Carlo was built for the Trinitarian Order, and this statue of one of the founders, St Felix of Valois, stands in a niche to the right of the main altar.

SS. LUCA E MARTINA

The Artists' Church

Many art historians hold that Pietro da Cortona's shrine for Sts Luke and Martina was, chronologically, the first Baroque church to be built in Rome. It is dedicated to the patron of artists and to a virgin martyr, who later inherited the architect's fortune.

POMP AND PIETY

By the end of the seventeenth century, Rome's architectural horizon had been profoundly changed, with Baroque church domes and cupolas replacing the fortress-like towers of medieval warlords. The third of the trio of architects who were largely responsible for making Rome a Baroque city was Pietro da Cortona (1597–1669). Like his contemporary and rival Gianlorenzo Bernini, Cortona was extremely versatile. He was Italy's most sought-after ceiling painter, a renowned architect, and master of the city's largest decorative workshop.

Son of a humble stonemason, Pietro Berrettini (called da Cortona, after the town where he was born), came to Rome at the age of fifteen. Cortona's biographers tell us he arrived in the Papal city poor and shabbily clad, and that for more than a decade he braved hardship and indifference to study both classical art and new figurative trends.

Timid and taciturn, Cortona worked for St Philip Neri's Oratorians and himself engaged in many charitable works. The Oratorians later trusted the decoration of their entire mother church, S. Maria in Vallicella, to Pietro da Cortona, who worked there intermittently from 1633 to the end of his life. Cortona's paintings in the Chiesa Nuova spread over the church's apse and nave vaults, dome, tribune pendentives, and even the ceiling of St Philip's former chambers (*see* p.145).

After long years of dogged work and study, the artist was finally noticed, and Rome's aristocracy and high clergy were soon scrambling for his services. He became the chosen painter of four Popes: Urban VIII, Innocent X, Alexander VII and Clement IX. His work was requested by the Medicis in Florence and by the monarchy in France. It was Pietro da Cortona who launched what we now call the Baroque style of painting.

The richly-decorated chapel of St Martina is located in the lower church of SS. Luca e Martina.

Pietro da Cortona died at the age of seventy-two, an honoured and wealthy man. He bequeathed nearly his entire fortune to an obscure Roman saint, whose relics he had discovered and whose church he had designed.

SAINTLY INSPIRATION

As the most esteemed artist of the day, Pietro da Cortona was elected head of Rome's Fine Arts Academy in 1634. From the very day of his election, he determined to restore the Academy of St Luke's next-door parish church, SS. Luca e Martina, which had fallen into a sad state of neglect and disrepair.

Built in the sixth century on the ruins of ancient Rome's Secretarium Senatus (Senate Secretariat), the tiny sanctuary of S. Martina was dedicated to a Roman virgin allegedly martyred in the early third century. According to legend, St Martina's martyrdom was especially gruesome. After being flogged with iron hooks and showered with boiling water, she was thrown to wild beasts. Still remaining unhurt and true to her faith, the brave maiden was tied to a funeral pyre. When she emerged miraculously unharmed by the flames, she was finally killed by decapitation.

St Martina's sanctuary was given to the Academy of St Luke when its former church near S. Maria Maggiore was razed in 1588 (for construction of Sixtus V's family villa). At that time, the name of the Academy's patron, St Luke, was added to that of the early Christian virgin martyr. In several Church traditions, St Luke the Evangelist appears both as a physician and as an accomplished painter; he supposedly fashioned several miraculous icons of the Virgin (some of which adorn Roman churches to this day).

Even in its earliest days as a medieval university, the Academy had venerated St Luke as patron of artists, and throughout its history, the feast-days of St Luke (and later those of St Martina as well) were celebrated with processions and the distribution of candles. Cortona probably had a long-standing devotion to St Martina, since records show his frequent contributions to keep a candle always burning at her shrine.

At his own expense, Cortona began to excavate enthusiastically in SS. Luca e Martina's lower crypt, and one fine day his workers came upon a clay sarcophagus – containing the head of St Martina and the remains of three other contemporary martyrs: Concordius, Epiphanius and another unnamed saint. (The martyrs were confirmed by a Paleo-Christian inscription.) Historians hypothesize that Cortona was intent

on discovering the holy relics in order to attract financial assistance from important patrons. Indeed, the artist had been working on frescoes for the church of S. Bibiana, when her bones and those of the Sts Bibiana, Dafrosa and Demetria were exhumed, prompting Pope Urban VIII to undertake an ambitious restoration (*see* p.70).

In the façade of SS. Luca e Martina, Pietro da Cortona used architectural forms to create a rhythm of linear movement and light.

St Martina's discovery naturally caused great excitement. The Pope wrote hymns in the saint's honour, a procession was organized for the pious people of Rome, and a reburial was held with great fervour and ceremony. Both Urban VIII and the church's protector, Cardinal Francesco Barberini, came forth with significant contributions, and Pietro da Cortona was commissioned to reconstruct both the crypt and upper church of SS. Luca e Martina.

The artist himself was deeply moved by the discovery of St Martina's relics. He contributed heavily to the refurbishing of the saint's shrine in the crypt, making it one of the city's most richly ornamented chapels, and planned for his own tomb in an adjacent room.

Upon his death, Cortona bequeathed most of his not insubstantial fortune to St Martina. The bequest was to be used by the small Order of Sisters of Sant'Eufemia, whose convent was nearby, for maintaining the saint's tomb. Now the sisters live far away in a Roman suburb, and the yearly procession, willed by Cortona to bear St Martina's head from the sisters' convent to the church, no longer (since 1970) takes place. Yet the Cortona fund still exists and draws interest in a Roman bank, and St Martina often makes incongruous appearances in the bank's computer files.

A BAROQUE CHURCH

Pietro da Cortona sometimes referred to himself as an architectural amateur. Yet Rome proudly displays his façades (S. Maria della Pace and S. Maria in Via Lata) and domes (S. Carlo al Corso), and most agree that it was in the field of architecture – rather than painting – that he accomplished his most original work. The church of SS. Luca e Martina was Cortona's acknowledged masterpiece; it is also the only church finished according to his designs.

Moreover, SS. Luca e Martina can be regarded as Rome's first completely Baroque church, antedating even the creations of Bernini and Borromini. At first glance that would not seem to be the case. If by Baroque we think of swarms of angels and saints in glory, precious materials and lush colours – then Cortona's church is bound to be a disappointment.

The church is of a unified travertine material, painted white inside and out, and almost without decoration. The plan is a Greek cross with four shallow apses, reminiscent of the centralized classical forms (Pantheon, mausoleums) favoured by Renaissance architects. However, Cortona's 'Baroque' is to be found in the intense play of light and shade, and the rhythmic movement of convex and concave forms.

These aspects are already announced in the façade, where the front section swells gently outward, and there are strong contrasts between the soft curving lines of the dome, columns and decorative elements on the top, and the more austere lines of the pilasters and windows.

These rhythmic features are repeated in the deceptively unembellished interior. The harmoniously white walls seem to undulate around the church. A strong *chiaroscuro* effect is achieved by the protruding and receding columns and pilasters and ribbing in the ceiling vaults. Although Cortona's upper church lacks the richness and intimacy of the saint's shrine below, its spiritual impact cannot be denied. At times, the light in the large white empty space is so bright, the entire building seems to become suspended.

CORTONA'S SCHOOL

In his later years Cortona had more work than he could possibly handle. Following a long-established tradition, he established an extensive workshop of students and apprentices who faithfully carried out commissions in their master's style. Cortona's *atelier* was so much in demand, however, that he transformed it into a veritable factory – turning out paintings, sculptures, and designs for stuccoes and every type of decoration imaginable. (There was even a foundry in the garden.)

After Cortona's death the decoration of SS. Luca e Martina was completed by his workshop, under the guidance of his most faithful follower, Ciro Ferri (1634–89). Another student, Lazzaro Baldi (1624–1703), painted one of the church's three art works, the *Martyrdom of St Lazarus*, the eighth-century Christian artist who had his hands burned with hot irons in the Byzantine campaign, known as the iconoclast wars, against sacred images. The other paintings are an *Assumption* by Sebastiano Conca (1680–1764), and a copy of Raphael's *St Luke at His Easel* on the main altar (the original is in the Academy gallery).

In the 1930s most of the neighbourhood surrounding SS. Luca e Martina was destroyed to make room for Mussolini's vast parade avenue through the imperial forums. At that time, the Academy of St Luke moved to a new palazzo near the Trevi Fountain. The church of SS. Luca and Martina, showpiece of the Academy's Baroque master, Pietro da Cortona, still remains its parish church.

CHAPTER

THE EIGHTEENTH CENTURY: REASON VERSUS DEVOTION

At the dawn of the eighteenth century, the era of Rome's splendid monuments to the Italian Baroque seemed to be coming to an end. Virtuoso creations by Bernini, Borromini and Pietro da Cortona had been inspired by the fervour of the Catholic Counter-Reformation and the Church's triumph over Protestantism in much of Europe. The splendour and pageantry of seventeenth-century Baroque architecture had been fuelled by Catholic confidence and spiritual conviction. However, by the early eighteenth century, the Church's self-confidence was being sorely tried

The eighteenth century was not a propitious era for Rome and the Papacy. During the 1700s, the Popes witnessed their authority and influence dwindle on the world stage. Throughout the century, national monarchies throughout Europe began nibbling away at the Church's temporal power, forcing the Popes to retreat increasingly to the purely spiritual sphere. The humiliating reality of Papal weakness became clear when Pope Clement XIV (1769–74), constrained by the European monarchies, decreed the dissolution of the Jesuit Order in 1773.

The Popes faced a challenge to their spiritual power as well. Known as the Age of Enlightenment, the eighteenth century was dominated by French thinkers such as Voltaire, who insisted on a critical examination of previously accepted ideas and authorities. The *philosophes* declared the ascendancy of reason over faith and launched a fierce offensive against many traditional Christian beliefs and practices.

In contrast to the rest of Europe, the Roman response to the Enlightenment – and to the later French Revolution and Napoleonic occupation – was decidedly lukewarm. As citizens of the Pope's capital and the centre of Christendom, Romans were not about to give up their traditional faith and popular devotions. Eighteenth-century travellers often wrote of Papal processions by candlelight, saintly feast-days when the city was strewn with flowers, and Assumption Day fireworks. Roman neighbourhoods took particular care of their tiny Madonna wall-shrines. As a reflection of this particular brand of emotional piety, Roman churches produced their own versions of eighteenth-century architecture, as we will see below.

The Papacy's decline was reflected in art and architecture. The Eternal City became the haunt of scholars, collectors and travellers on the Grand Tour, but Rome no longer led Europe in artistic innovation. Not many new churches were built in Rome in the eighteenth century, although quite a few were rebuilt or restored. Several important basilicas, for instance, received their present-day façades: S. Giovanni in Laterano,

The church of S. Maria Aventina, with its altar covered in creamy white stucco and marble, and its very shallow nave, creates the effect of an elegant eighteenth-century salon.

completed by Alessandro Galilei in 1735; S. Maria Maggiore, designed by Ferdinando Fuga in 1741–2; S. Croce in Gerusalemme, transformed by Pietro Passalacqua between 1743 and 1744.

In the early 1700s, the drama and passion of the Baroque subsided into the more intimate and decorative style known as Rococo. Originating in France around 1715, the Rococo was the ultimate refinement of the Baroque, emptied of its artistic vigour and religious content. The word 'Rococo' is an Italianized version of the French *'rocaille'*, or shell-work. Shells were a typical Rococo decoration, but in general the term also connotes elegance, delicacy and grace. In the city of the Popes, the Rococo style was rare and short-lived.

In the second half of the century, revived interest in classical archaeology of the ancient world launched the artistic movement known as Neo-classicism. In place of the emotional fervour of Baroque art, Neo-classicism insisted on clarity and sobriety. Balanced proportions and noble simplicity replaced the complex extravagance of Baroque figures and forms. Very few Roman churches were built in the Age of Reason, and in these Roman devotion managed to invade the Neo-classical structures.

As mentioned earlier, eighteenth-century churches are rare in Rome. In fact, only two are really exceptional; these belong to the two very different, almost antithetical, architectural styles described above.

LA MADDALENA
Roman Rococo

Rome's Rococo churches are rare and the finest example is La Maddalena. In this charming structure, Roman piety manages to overcome Rococo tendencies towards superficiality and frivolity.

ROCOCO AND BAROQUE

In a small square a few blocks from the Pantheon in Rome stands the church of St Mary Magdalen. 'La Maddalena', as the building is affectionately known to Romans, is an example of a very rare style of religious architecture in Rome – the Rococo. For the visitor accustomed to Rome's usual robust classical and Baroque aspect, La Maddalena's eighteenth-century concave façade, light salmon colours and frilly stucco decorations breathe the spirit of a different age.

What is unique about La Maddalena's façade, completed (according to most art historians) in 1735 by Giuseppe Sardi?

Sardi reportedly used Borromini's S. Carlo as his model, and the impression of constant movement, due to the curving and contorted surfaces, certainly owes much to that Baroque master. But Sardi replaced many of Borromini's classical elements with more decorative, curvilinear forms and decoration. The narrow, deeply concave façade rises to a shell-like oval and wavy pediment; the cornices, corbels and statue niches are adorned with playful cupids and lacy stucco-work.

Before entering La Maddalena, the visitor might enjoy taking a look at another Roman Rococo jewel not far away. Just behind the Piazza Farnese, in a tiny square shaded by a leafy oak, is the equally tiny church of S. Maria della Quercia (St Mary of the Oak). The graceful convex façade (1728) is peach-coloured, with creamy stucco trimming. Here we have the Rococo at its most delightful – small in scale, delicate and dainty.

The architect was Filippo Raguzzini (1680–1771), protégé of Pope Benedict XIII (1724–30). Raguzzini also designed the

lovely Rococo Piazzetta S. Ignazio, in front of the seventeenth-century Jesuit church dedicated to St Ignatius, several blocks away towards the Corso (Rome's main shopping street).

ASSISTING THE SICK

Although the church we see today results from its eighteenth-century renovations, La Maddalena dates from a much earlier period. As far back as the year 1320 we have historical records of a small oratory here dedicated to St Mary Magdalen. The chapel and adjacent hospital belonged to a confraternity called 'the Disciplined', which in 1486 was absorbed into the larger confraternity of the Gonfalone (banner-bearers).

Similar to guilds in other cities, Rome's confraternities were lay religious organizations, usually related to a specific profession or craft (basket-weavers, bankers, tailors), frequently devoted to the cult of a saint or relic (St Catherine of Alexandria, the stigmata, the Holy Cross), and almost always engaged in social assistance to the city's poor and needy. This background is very important for an understanding of La Maddalena's true character.

Since the late sixteenth century La Maddalena has been the mother house of the Order of the Servants of the Sick, called the Camillians after their founder Camillus of Lellis (1550–1614). Camillus was a tall, hot-tempered,

Left: La Maddalena (church of St Mary Magdalen), a rare example of the Rococo style in Rome.

Above: The interior of La Maddalena was completely renovated in the Baroque style in preparation for Camillus of Lellis's canonization in 1746.

heavy-gambling young man. After serving in the Venetian campaign against the Turks, losing all his money in a gambling debt, and suffering from an apparently incurable disease of the leg, he experienced a conversion under the influence of Rome's beloved patron and spearhead of the Counter-Reformation, St Philip Neri.

In 1582 Camillus, now a priest, founded a congregation of male nurses who pledged to serve the city's sick and plague-stricken, even at the risk of their own lives. Attending a parish feast-day at St Mary Magdalen in 1586, Camillus was inspired to acquire the church for his religious congregation. There, at Christmas of the same year, he settled with a dozen companions to establish the Order of the Ministers of the Sick.

Wearing as their badge the sign of a red cross, the Camillians circulated throughout Rome, bringing comfort to hospitals, to houses of the dying, to the homeless in the shadows of classical ruins, and to victims of the plague quarantined in special shelters. La Maddalena became a distribution centre for food, clothes and medicines for the city's diseased and afflicted. Eventually the Camillians extended their activities to the battlefields of Hungary and Croatia and founded hospitals in various Italian cities.

We should mention here that the lovely Rococo church of S. Maria della Quercia also belongs to a confraternity. Since 1532 this dainty little edifice (in a different form, of course) has been the headquarters of the Roman Butchers' Confraternity, and a centre for their various devotional and charitable activities.

PIETY AND ART

The Rococo church of St Mary Magdalen was completely renovated and decorated in preparation for Camillus of Lellis' canonization (1746). The work was carried out by various artists and architects under the guidance of the Camillians themselves (Carlo Fontana from 1668, then Giovanni de Rossi from 1695, completed by Giulio Carlo Quadri in 1699). La Maddalena is thus anything but frivolous and superficial, in spite of its sumptuous decoration. It is imbued with the sincere piety of Camillus and his followers. The church has a graceful elliptical nave, transept, luminously frescoed dome and apse.

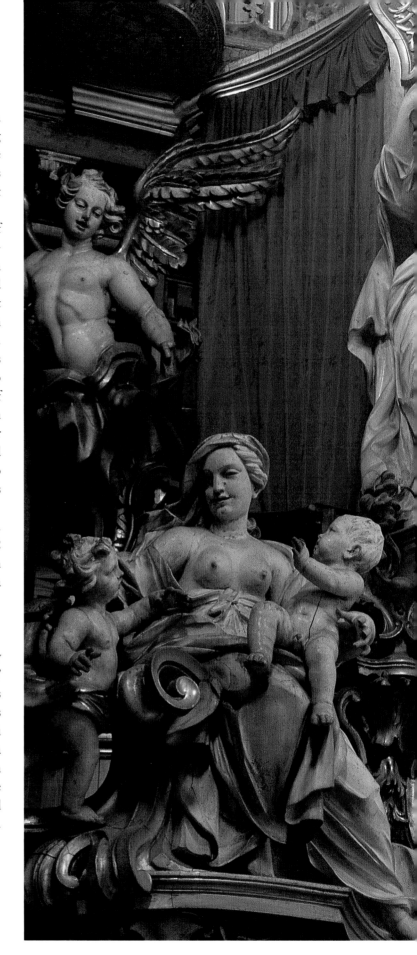

La Maddalena's organ loft of gilded carved wood is considered to be the most representative Rococo work in Rome.

Polychrome marbles, gilded wood and large paintings create an overall richness of effect, but the interior remains intimate and reverent in spirit. The nave statues above the confessionals illustrate qualities necessary for penance: *Sorrow*, *Fidelity* and *Shame* on the right, and *Humility*, *Secrecy* and *Simplicity* on the left. Frescoes by Michelangelo Cerruti (1732) depict episodes from St Mary Magdalen's life on the vault (the raising of Lazarus) and in smaller panels around the window.

Some of the church's special devotional attractions include a sixteenth-century icon of Our Lady Health of the Sick in the second right-hand chapel (donated in 1616 by a pious noble matron), the crucifix which spoke to St Camillus in 1582 ('Continue with your work, I will assist you. This work is mine not yours') in the right transept chapel, and an extremely beautiful fifteenth-century life-size wooden statue of Mary Magdalen across from the crucifix. The third chapel on the right contains an urn with St Camillus' remains.

Along with the above-mentioned façade, La Maddalena's organ and sacristy are cited by art historians as the quintessential representation of eighteenth-century Roman Rococo. The organ, designed by Hans Conrad Werle in 1773, and located over the entrance, is of carved and gilded wood and decorated with lively stucco angels and allegorical figures. The sacristy is also richly decorated with gilt and woodwork and has Girolamo Pesce's painting of *Sts Camillus and Philip Neri* (1739) in the vault. The church also contains late Baroque paintings by Sebastian Conca, 'Baciccia' (Giovanni Battista Gaulli) and Luca Giordano.

S. MARIA AVENTINA (KNIGHTS OF MALTA PRIORY)
Piranesi's Priory
Rome's only masterpiece of late eighteenth-century architecture also represents a separate sovereign state with its origins in the Crusades.

A NEO-CLASSICAL RARITY
S. Maria Aventina or S. Maria del Priorato (St Mary on the Aventine or St Mary of the Priory) is one of a kind in several ways. It is perhaps the only architectural masterpiece of the later eighteenth century in Rome. It is also the only architectural work of the world-famous engraver Giambattista Piranesi. Although usually described as a prime example of the

Above: Gardens behind the Knights of Malta Priory.

Right: S. Maria Aventina is also the Priory of the Sovereign Order of the Knights of Malta. Along the nave hang the banners of the Knights' original provinces.

eighteenth-century Neo-classical style, the church has its origins in Rome's remotest and most mysterious past. Finally, it is the Priory of the Order of the Knights of Malta, a unique institution with no territory but worldwide diplomatic relations and significant prestige and influence in the Catholic Church.

Few Roman churches were built in the later eighteenth century – S. Maria Aventina is an important exception. This tiny building, renovated and decorated by Piranesi in 1765, soon became, for those who knew it, a first-rate example of the Neo-classical style.

La Maddalena escaped Rococo frivolity by means of its truly reverent atmosphere. S. Maria Aventina was not entirely Neo-classical either. Thanks to Piranesi's imaginative genius, his church managed to convey a mysterious spirituality not at all consistent with eighteenth-century Enlightenment logic. Piranesi inherited some of this mystery from the church's location and origins.

ANCIENT ORIGINS

In ancient times the Aventine was a sacred place, covered by snake-infested woods, and the site of several important temples (including those to Diana and Juno Regina). Here, the first-century historian Titus Livius tells us, Roman legions deposited their weapons for ritual purification after the summer campaigns, in a religious ceremony known as the *Armilustrium.*

Barbarian invasions laid waste to the Aventine temples and shrines in the fifth and sixth centuries. Soon, however, the zone recovered its spiritual mission with the construction of some of Christianity's earliest churches: S. Prisca – a house church founded by the two saints mentioned in St Paul's Epistles; S. Saba – built upon ancient ruins; S. Sabina – one of Rome's first basilicas; and the ancient monastery of Sts Bonifacio and Alessio.

In the tenth century, the Aventine served as headquarters for the fractious warlord Albericus. Thundering down from Spoleto, Albericus terrorized and took charge of Rome, placed his eighteen-year-old son Octavian on the Papal throne, and then had a change of heart. In 932 he donated his Aventine

palace to a group of Benedictine (some historians say Basilian) monks for a monastery, which became one of Rome's twenty most important abbeys in the early Middle Ages. The original S. Maria Aventina dates from that period.

By the twelfth century, the Benedictine monastery had become the property of the Templars, a military–religious order founded by Crusaders in Palestine; upon their suppression in 1312 by Pope Clement V, it passed into the hands of the Hospitaller Order of St John of Jerusalem. Like the Templars, the Order of St John had been established during the Crusades, first for assistance to pilgrims and protection of the Holy Sepulchre, and later as a fighting force to recover the Holy Land from Muslims. At this point, the history of S. Maria Aventina becomes almost as complicated and difficult to follow as that of its owners.

Through pious donations, the Knights of St John of Jerusalem eventually obtained vast property and wealth throughout the Near East and Europe. After the Crusades, they settled down to hospital and charitable activities (with occasional military forays against the Turks from their head-quarters in Rhodes and later Malta). In Rome, the Knights' main centre for centuries was the monastery of St Basil in the Forum of Augustus. Yet it seems that by the mid-sixteenth century they had moved into the Aventine estate and made S. Maria Aventina their priory (the main church of a religious order).

In the 1600s, under Cardinal Prior Benedetto Pamphili, the Aventine estate was famous for its sumptuous feasts and important cultural events. The Pamphili emblem, the dove, can

Left: The façade of S. Maria Aventina was completed by G. B. Piranesi in 1765. Although austerely Neo-classical in style, it also uses strange exotic elements as decoration, as shown in the detail (right).

Rome, and during visits to Pompeii, Herculaneum and Paestum, he passionately studied and sketched the classical ruins and every vestige of the ancient world.

Piranesi's famous cycles of engravings (*Grotesques and Caprices*, *Roman Views*, *Prisons of Fantasy*, *Roman Antiquities*, among others) combine an incredibly precise rendition of classical details and architectural forms with a startling, almost surrealistic atmosphere.

Through his Venice connections Piranesi met a powerful Venetian, Cardinal Rezzonico, who recognized his talent and entrusted him with the renovation of the entire Knights of St John (now Malta) estate: the church of S. Maria Aventina, the priory villa, gardens and adjacent piazza.

The artist has been credited with transforming the church (at the time a small and unremarkable Renaissance structure, as we can see from early eighteenth-century engravings) into one of the masterpieces of Roman Neo-classicism. In fact, this work reflects all the artistic currents of Piranesi's era: the transition from Baroque to Rococo and then to Neo-classicism, and finally to nascent Romanticism towards the century's end. In the final analysis, however, Piranesi's creation remains totally personal and unique, as a visitor discovers when exploring the Aventine church.

still be seen in the elegant 'coffee house' Benedetto built in the spacious gardens. The church, now alternatively called S. Maria del Priorato, reached its peak of glory in 1765 when the Cardinal Prior, Pope Clement XIII's nephew Giovan Battista Rezzonico, commissioned G. B. Piranesi to radically renovate the entire monastery complex

PIRANESI'S MASTERPIECE
Giambattista Piranesi (1720–78) was celebrated worldwide as a master engraver. S. Maria Aventina was his first and only architectural venture, but anyone who visits the church will certainly wish the artist had not limited himself to this Aventine shrine.

Piranesi was born in Venice and studied art there before arriving in Rome in 1740. Here he remained (except for a certain amount of travel in Italy) for the rest of his life. In

A statue of S. Maria Aventina's architect, G. B. Piranesi (1720–78), dressed in a toga to indicate his interest in classical archaeology and culture.

A SPIRITUAL CAPRICE
Visitors to Rome's Piazza dei Cavalieri di Malta (Square of the Knights of Malta) usually hurry directly to the famous 'keyhole view'. A small aperture in the door leading to the Knights of Malta estate offers, indeed, a striking perspective of St Peter's bluish dome, framed by the arc of a long green arbour. However, merely by turning around, the observer could behold something just as amazing.

The piazza is enclosed on two sides by a dazzling white wall, fantastically ornamented by small obelisks, steles, urns, grimacing masks, overripe cornucopias – and many sculpted images of weapons and antique trophies. This is Piranesi's reference to the ancient *Armilustrium* ritual. Since Piranesi was working on the Order of Malta complex long after the Knights' glorious Crusading era had passed, he obviously wished to compare their productive peacetime with the Romans' laying down of arms after a period of warfare.

On the main entrance to the Knights of Malta property, Piranesi carved symbols of the Order's history: military and naval reliefs and esoteric images from ancient rituals and religions. In fact, in spite of the warlike references, the overall impression here – particularly by moonlight – is mysterious, almost mystical. The artist's devotion to classical details is obvious, yet according to his own fanciful, sometimes bizarre interpretation.

Once inside the gate, the visitor confronts the austerely classical façade of S. Maria del Priorato (Aventina) standing high on the Aventine Hill. Four fluted pilasters with Corinthian columns support a triangular tympanum. However, a closer look at this model of Roman austerity reveals winged sphinxes, serpents and magical symbols relating to ancient rites and rituals.

Beyond the predominantly Neo-classical exterior is a space that is almost Rococo in its impact. One broad nave flanked by shallow niches, all executed in creamy white marble and stucco, gives the impression of an intimate salon. The graceful oval of the small presbytery cupola (and altar front) is ringed by rose garlands in the early eighteenth-century style. Yet as the eye travels to the altar, the contorted statue of St Basil in Glory, surmounting a Madonna and Child surrounded by a cloud of angels, seems to gather all entering light into a hazy conflagration that is truly Baroque. (St Basil, the fourth-century Bishop of Caesarea, was founder of Eastern monasticism and patron of the Order's first church in the Roman Forum. His image represents a link to important aspects in the Order's history.)

Reliefs of the life of St John the Baptist (patron saint of the Knights of Malta, formerly the Knights of St John) decorate the ceiling. In the niches are a medieval altar from the time of the Templars, tombs of a humanist and Grand Masters, two Roman sarcophagi and Piranesi's tomb. A statue by Piranesi's student, Giuseppe Angelini, shows the artist dressed in a Roman toga. This is obviously how Piranesi wished to be remembered, and, along with the many Roman and Etruscan references in the church, attests to his dedication to classical art. On the other hand, S. Maria's wealth of esoteric signs and symbols (stuccoes by Tommaso Righi) presage nineteenth-century Romantic art, and even the Art Nouveau of the early twentieth century.

Of course, the church's primary artistic references are to the Sovereign Order of the Knights of Malta itself. To one side of the main altar we find the Grand Master's throne, and along the nave hang bright banners of the Knights' *langues* ('languages', referring to the Order's original provinces: France, Provence, Castile, England, Italy, etc.). The Order's heraldry – Maltese crosses and castles – is omnipresent.

Passing through the lovely gardens the visitor enters the priory villa, also renovated by Piranesi, with its conclave hall decorated with portraits of every Grand Master from the twelfth to twentieth centuries. Ultimately, Piranesi was called to commemorate the history and spirituality of this extraordinary – by now almost millennary – institution.

THE ORDER OF MALTA YESTERDAY AND TODAY

The Sovereign Order of the Knights of Malta had previously been known as the Military Hospitaller Order of St John of Jerusalem and as the Sovereign Order of the Knights of Rhodes. These appellations designate different phases in a history which goes back 900 years.

Traditionally, the Order is said to have begun even before the Crusades, as a hospice–infirmary in Jerusalem (*c.*1070), dedicated to St John the Baptist. Soon, because of the need of armed protection for pilgrims and the sick, the monastic community began to take on military functions. With the Crusades, the Knights of St John (along with the Templars and the Teutonic Knights) were recognized in 1113 as a religious–military order, renowned for their religious devotion and fighting skill. From European monarchs and religious institutions they received a steady flow of privileges and donations, including substantial property.

The Knights of St John fought in the Holy Land until the last Crusader fortress fell to the Muslim Mamelukes at Acre in 1291. They moved to Cyprus and in 1310 captured the island of Rhodes, from where they transformed themselves into a naval force for battling the Ottoman Turks in the Mediterranean. Finally, after a series of fierce wars, the Turks drove the Knights from Rhodes in 1522.

In 1530 the Holy Roman Emperor Charles V ceded them the island of Malta as their territorial base, thus conferring on the Order the status of an internationally recognized sovereign state. Although the Knights lost Malta to the French under Napoleon Bonaparte in 1798, they retain their title of Sovereign Order of the Knights of Malta to this day. (In December 1998, an accord with the Government of Malta granted the order the right to use their former fortress, St Angelo, as their Maltese headquarters.)

Since 1834 the Knights of Malta have had their official headquarters in Rome, in a *palazzo* in the city's downtown commercial area, and their priory church and representational villa high on the Aventine Hill. The Order is internationally recognized as a sovereign entity.

CHAPTER

THE NINETEENTH CENTURY: THE CHURCH CEDES TEMPORAL POWER

The 1800s were not very auspicious years for church building in Rome. Opening with a French occupation (1796–1813), called 'the Napoleonic interlude' by the city's disdainful citizens, the century advanced towards Italian unification, a particularly tumultuous and painful episode for the Pope's capital. During the nineteenth century, the Church witnessed the diminution of its political power and the disappearance of its territorial possessions. The Papal States were incorporated into the new Italian Kingdom and the Popes had to content themselves with a spiritual domain.

One figure dominated the Roman religious stage in the nineteenth century: Pius IX (1846–78), the longest-ruling Pontiff in Church history. The son of a count, Pius IX was elected into a period of revolution and Italian national aspirations. Considered a liberal and nationalist at the beginning of his pontificate, Pius soon made it clear that he was not about to set up a constitutional Papal State. He firmly and unwaveringly believed that the temporal power of the Holy See was indispensable to its spiritual independence.

After years of turmoil and upheaval (and even exile), Pius finally witnessed the fall of Rome in September 1870 to King Victor Emmanuel's invading troops, and its designation one month later as the capital of the new Italian Kingdom. With the Guarantees Law of 1871, the Pope was deprived of the Papal States territories but retained the honours and immunities of a sovereign in his Vatican property. Pius,

however, never accepted the *fait accompli* and died a self-styled prisoner in the Vatican.

Although historians may view Pius IX's long pontificate as a political disaster, it was a period of internal consolidation and spiritual regeneration for the Catholic Church. Under Pius IX, the Vatican I Ecumenical Council (1869–70) affirmed Papal infallibility in faith and morals. In 1875 the Pope dedicated the Catholic world to the Sacred Heart; two decades earlier, in December 1854, he had declared the dogma of the Immaculate Conception (the Virgin Mary's freedom from original sin).

The nineteenth century witnessed a spiritual revolution within Catholicism − a reaction against eighteenth-century rationalism and unbelief towards a more emotional manifestation of popular devotion. Marian apparitions drew crowds of believers to La Salette in 1846 and Lourdes in 1858. There was a new emphasis on the Virgin Mary, on the saints, on ceremony. In ritual, believers demonstrated a predilection for

The church of S. Cuore del Suffragio was built in the Neo-Gothic style popular in the nineteenth century.

the Middle Ages – Gregorian Chant, the Latin liturgy, and Gothic Revival architecture. In fact, fascination with the Middle Ages was a tendency in many artistic, as well as spiritual, movements of the nineteenth century.

Pius IX was tireless in his restorations and embellishments of Roman churches (S. Maria in Trastevere, S. Agnese Fuori le Mura, his own funeral chamber in S. Lorenzo). Yet throughout the entire nineteenth century, very few new religious edifices were raised in the city of Rome. The next church on this itinerary was an exception and has several interesting characteristics of its age.

S. CUORE DEL SUFFRAGIO
The 'Purgatory Church'

Pointed arches, stained-glass windows and souls returning from the beyond – this church has a unique type of architecture and tells a story of the after-world.

UNIQUE IN ROME

A visitor who drives or walks along the Lungotevere road leading out of Rome is certain to notice a strange spectre rising from the banks of the River Tiber: a shimmering and soaring French Gothic façade among the usual earthy-toned houses and Baroque domes of the Roman horizon. This is the church of the Sacred Heart of Suffrage (S. Cuore del Suffragio). Although the church, begun in 1894 and open to the public in 1917, is one of a kind for Rome, its style, spirit and devotional activity are generally characteristic of nineteenth-century Catholicism.

The architecture of the building is described as Gothic Revival. This style, popular in Europe throughout the nineteenth century, marked a romantic return to the Middle Ages in reaction to the cold rationality of eighteenth-century Neoclassicism. In its dedication, the church also signified a response to Pius IX's calls for devotion to the Sacred Heart of Jesus, which had produced an ardent following and a flurry of construction in the last years of the century. Furthermore, the Confraternity of Suffrage which sponsored the church was part of the mystical and visionary current in the Catholic Church of the day.

STILL IMPERFECTLY PURIFIED

The church originated – and continues to this day – as the seat of an association for 'suffrage', that is, prayers and petitions to the Sacred Heart of Jesus for the assistance of souls in

Purgatory. Founded by the French Father Victor Joet, the Confraternity acquired a piece of property on the River Tiber, hired the Bolognese architect Giuseppe Gualandi, and here raised a Neo-Gothic edifice.

According to the Catechism of the Catholic Church, Purgatory is a condition or place in which the souls of those dying penitent are purified from lesser sins. It is a state of expiation through which spirits are purged of residual attachments to the earth in preparation for entrance into heaven. Suffrage, or prayers for the souls in Purgatory, can

Six pairs of stained-glass windows and six pairs of popular saints in Neo-Gothic style can be seen in S. Cuore del Suffragio.

accelerate their passage to God's grace. 'From the beginning the Church has honoured the memory of the dead and offered prayers in suffrage for them, above all the Eucharist sacrifice, so that, thus purified, they may attain the beatific vision of God' (*Catechism of the Catholic Church*, nr. 1032).

The Confraternity brochure relates that in November 1897, while the church was still under construction, a fire broke out during a feast-day Mass. Many among the crowd in the temporary chapel claimed to see, among the flames, the outline of a suffering face upon the left-hand wall. To this day the faithful continue to believe that a soul appeared from Purgatory, and the outline is still preserved behind a painting by the sacristy door in the present church.

A GOTHIC REVIVAL
The church of the Sacred Heart of Suffrage has a beautiful Gothic façade, with pointed-arch portals and windows and a lacy rose window. Seventeen statues of various saints decorate the exterior and represent those saintly individuals who expressed particular concern for the souls in Purgatory.

The inside, with its towering central nave, pointed arches and reddish-grey gumdrop columns, provides a cool, silent refuge from the incessant growl of the Lungotevere traffic outside. The church is dimly illuminated by light spilling through colourful stained-glass windows under the cross-vault roof. A lapis lazuli rose window hangs above the door like an exotic earring, while the two windows on its side, red and blue and green, carved in floral patterns, provide soft light for the entering visitor's initial meditations. The floor is of Veronese marble, orange and white, laid out in a pattern of fish-fin zig-zags.

The church is divided into three aisles. Looking towards the apse, the right-hand nave is distinctive because of its series of six stained-glass windows depicting twelve saints (from door to apse: St Frances of Rome and St Catherine of Genoa, St Bridget and St Ambrose, St Bonaventure and St Thomas Aquinas, St Efrem and St Peter Damian, St Joan of Arc and St Sebastian, and finally St Robert Bellarmine and St Francis de Sales). The faces (particularly of Sts Bridget, Ambrose, Sebastian and Joan of Arc) are expressive and the colours glowing.

The apse is dominated by a large canvas painting by Giuseppe and Alessandro Catani representing the Catholic doctrine on Purgatory, reminding worshippers of the church's purpose – to pray for the souls in Purgatory. In the centre of the work, amid a cloud of celestial spirits, the Sacred Heart of Jesus radiates light from his chest. Below, simple faces animated by love and hope implore Jesus's grace; above, with arms wide open, the Saviour prepares to accept them into his kingdom. Mary and Joseph kneel in intercessionary poses. The Archangel Michael can be seen on the right, bringing the symbolic flame of purification to the souls in Purgatory.

The art works here are minor but pleasant. In the right-hand aisle there are altars dedicated to the Archangel Michael, St Margaret Mary Alocoque, and St Joseph, and paintings treating the subject of grieving angels. In the left aisle is a quite lovely painting of *Mary of the Rosary*, and the sombre funeral monument of Monsignor Pietro Benedetti MSC, first parish priest of the church. The sculpture represents the *Pietà* and was done in bronze by G. B. Conti.

THE MUSEUM OF THE SOULS OF PURGATORY
One eccentricity has endowed the church of the Sacred Heart of Suffrage with a certain prestige: it possesses a 'museum' of eso-terica documenting the return of souls from Purgatory to earth.

The appellation 'museum' is really a misnomer for what is on display here. The entire collection, comprised of a little over ten artifacts, is housed in a glass case measuring about three metres by 1.2 metres. Nevertheless, there is something terribly eerie about the exhibit. The pieces on display present documented evidence of the appearance of souls from Purga-tory to those left behind on earth. There are imprints made by spirits on various items, such as Bibles, nightcaps, linen and money. Particularly macabre is item number two, displaying the marks left by three fingers on a Bible. The story goes that on 5 March 1871, the deceased Palmira Rastelli appeared before Maria Zaganti, begging her to have the parish priest perform a Mass on her behalf. As proof of her visit, she grasped Maria Zaganti's Bible, charring it with her fingertips.

Another account tells of the pious Sister Maria of San Luigi Gonzaga, who appeared before Sister Margaret of the Sacred Heart between 5 and 6 June 1894, clouded in shadow. Sister Maria disclosed that she was in Purgatory to expiate her impatience in the face of God's will. She had been sick for two years and had frequently expressed a desire to die. Upon recovering she repented, but still had some purifying to do before entering God's beatific vision. As a proof of her appari-tion, Sister Maria branded a fingerprint on to a pillow.

It is often the Purgatory display which draws visitors bent on the macabre to the church of the Sacred Heart of Suffrage. But the church has its own merits and it is worthwhile to sit and enjoy both its serene atmosphere and its modest works of art.

OUR TIMES: THE CHURCH ADAPTS TO THE MODERN WORLD

This book is being written as both a century and a millennium are coming to an end.
It is always difficult to evaluate the times in which we live – and the twentieth century has
probably been the fastest-moving, most eventful and most contradictory in Christian history.

The Papacy began the century shorn of its territorial possessions, the Papal States, and – on the surface at least – much circumscribed in its political influence. Furthermore, in this most secular and materialist of ages, the Church found itself confronted with unprecedented challenges on every front.

New scientific theories, atheist philosophies and critical Bible exegeses threatened religious certainties. Totalitarian dictatorships trampled human rights and national sovereignties; the *Shoah*, an attempt to annihilate European Jews in gas-chambers and death camps, was the declared policy of the Nazi regime. Nations perfected nuclear bombs and tools of biological and chemical warfare which were capable of wiping out the entire human race. At the same time, science developed new methods of conception and promised the imminence of cloning human life itself.

The Church has been called upon to speak out on these urgent issues, as a moral conscience in a confusing and frightening world. Restricted to a state of less than 0.44 square kilometres, lacking weapons or army, and not at all wealthy (despite the popular mythology), the Vatican is still a force to be reckoned with in the moral, cultural and sometimes even political spheres. In fact, with almost a billion faithful, Catholicism claims the planet's largest and most widespread religious membership.

Four centuries after the Council of Trent (intermittent sessions from 1545 to 1563) had answered the challenge of Protestantism with a profound Church renewal, the Second Vatican Council (inaugurated by Pope John XXIII in 1962 and concluded by his successor Pope Paul VI in 1965) was convened to bring about a Church rapprochement with the modern world. Council directives insisted on greater openness to different religions and other Christian confessions, more collegiality within the hierarchy, and the implementation of a pervasive liturgical reform.

The Council had a tremendous impact on all aspects of Church life, including the design and decoration of churches. Pomp and complicated ritual were discouraged, and a simpler,

The Church for the Jubilee of the Year 2000 is a modern structure of glass and white concrete,
designed by American architect Richard Meier.
(The photographs in this chapter are published with the kind permission of Richard Meier and Partners.)

more participatory liturgy (generally using the vernacular rather than Latin) was introduced. Altars now faced the congregation; church decor was more down-to-earth, sometimes even remarkably bare.

On the other hand, the Pope who has guided the Church's decades-long entrance into the third millennium has also brought a high-profile charisma and worldwide exposure to the Papacy and Catholicism. John Paul II has travelled to the furthest corners of the earth, establishing a close rapport with audiences of every race and creed.

Sadly, in Rome, home of the Popes and head and heart of the Catholic faith, twentieth-century church building has not responded adequately either to the needs of modern times or to the important role of the universal Church. For many, Rome's new religious structures lack both the beauty and the spiritual inspiration of earlier centuries.

Even John Paul II, speaking through the Vicar of Rome in October 1997, complained of the ugliness and deficiencies of modern churches, 'where there is little harmony between form and content and where it is difficult for the faithful to have a sense of the sacred'. The Pope's remarks were transmitted during a presentation of the Rome Diocese's project for fifty new parish churches in the Roman suburbs.

As part of that project, one parish church in the outskirts of Rome has been designated the 'Jubilee Church', or 'Church of the Year 2000'. It is that church, representative of the twentieth century and yet looking forward to a new millennium, which will conclude this pilgrimage to the churches of Rome.

These photographs of the architectural model for the Jubilee Church show the planned façade of three white concrete arches, which have been compared to giant sails.

THE CHURCH OF GOD
THE MERCIFUL FATHER
Rome's Jubilee Temple for the Year 2000

Rome's church of the future has three white concrete arches for a façade and a luminous and austerely bare interior.

A SUBURBAN PARISH CHURCH

At the time of writing, Rome's 'Church for the Year 2000' exists only on paper and in the form of a model now on tour of the US and Italy. Controversy persists concerning designs for the so-called Jubilee Church among architects and Catholics of every rank, including the parishioners for whom the church is being constructed. For this is no ordinary church. It is to be the symbol of Christianity's bimillennial anniversary, the model for sacred architecture on the threshold of the third millennium.

The Jubilee Church, named for God the Merciful Father, will rise in the low- to middle-income community called Tor Tre Teste (so called after a classical ruin there with three sculpted heads) on the outskirts of Rome. It is to be the jewel in the crown of the above-mentioned Rome Diocese project, endorsed by the Pope and the Vatican, for Rome's neglected suburbs: 'Fifty Churches for the Year 2000'.

In early 1996 the Rome Vicariate committee invited six internationally recognized architects to submit projects for a 'Church for the Year 2000', to represent Rome's (and Christianity's) passage into the new millennium. A Jewish American, Richard Meier, won the contest two years later with his plan for a stark white edifice of soaring arched walls and glass ceilings.

The Jubilee Church has been designed as a two-part precinct, with the church occupying the south half of the site, and a community centre occupying the north half. Construction began on 1 March 1998. The church will seat 400 worshippers and has a budget of $5 million.

AN IMAGINARY VISIT

A visit to the rather squalid Tor Tre Teste neighbourhood will convince anyone that this parish is badly in need of some beauty and spiritual inspiration. The drab housing complex raised in the 1970s was obviously not planned for aesthetics or cheer. High lacklustre apartment blocks dominate the site earmarked for the Meier church; a small, shabby green field is a poor attempt at a park.

According to project designers a paved plaza, called the *sagrato* (parvis) will lead to the main entrance on the east side of the church, nearest the effective centre of the housing project. The architect and the Vicariate hope that the tiny

The architectural model for Richard Meier's Jubilee Church. The church will be built in a low-income community on the outskirts of Rome.

piazza will become a magnet for parishioners, similar to the churchyards (*sagrati*) which were centres of community life in medieval Italy. The square is to be 'embraced' by curving walls on both sides and delineated by benches and greenery.

Many feel that the church exterior will be the most eloquent aspect of the project. Three curving walls of white reinforced concrete arch upwards like huge sails, or like the wings of a bird about to take flight. The walls are joined by perpendicular glass walls and glass ceilings, with white vertical and horizontal grids.

According to architect Meier's project presentation: 'The most striking feature of the church design is its openness.' Seen from the entrance plaza, the east façade is a vertical wall of glass. The roof of the church is a glass skylight running the length of the building. As shown in photographs of the model, the church interior will be wonderfully luminous, with light streaming in from the translucent glass surfaces of walls and ceilings. Meier's project description states: 'The nave comes into being through the interplay between the straight north wall and the concave shells on the southern side of the volume. Where the former is faced in stone and acoustic wood panelling, the latter is executed out of architectural concrete.'

The curved walls articulate different spaces within the building: the baptistery, a weekday chapel, separate rooms for confessionals. The sanctuary contains a box-like pulpit and simple altar table. A stained-glass *oculus* above the sacristy provides backlighting for a slender cross.

ARCHITECTURAL INTENT AND SPIRITUAL SIGNIFICANCE

The Vicariate's choice of competing architects who were not experts in sacred buildings, and not known to be especially religious themselves, manifested an emphasis on talent and creativity rather than on religious belief. That accent has given rise to both praise and censure.

Although Meier was furnished with few spiritual guidelines by the Rome Diocese, Vicariate officials feel the finished church will communicate both the spirit of the Second Vatican Council and the teachings of Pope John Paul II. The choice of an American Jewish architect, they say, is a sign of twentieth-century Catholic universalism and of the Church's new dialogue with other religions, especially Judaism. Furthermore, the very ecumenical' dedication of the Jubilee Church to God the Merciful Father is an absolute first for Rome and corresponds to John Paul II's consecration of 1999, the final year of Rome's Jubilee preparations, to God the Father.

Meier has suggested that the three ascending concrete arches represent the Trinity, and that the conspicuous baptismal font, which is large enough for immersion, is a clear link with Christianity's past. The use of reinforced concrete and stone represents the solidity of the Church of Rome, while the transparent walls and ceilings make this an 'open space for an open society'.

Meier's ultimate spiritual statement comes from the pure whiteness of the materials, the soaring vertical arches, and above all the great luminosity of the interior. The views of the sky above, at different times of day and in all types of weather, should lead the faithful to reflect upon the difference between those things made by man and those created by God.

CRITICISMS

Not all are enthusiastic about Rome's 'Church for the Year 2000'. The most virulent criticism is that the sanctuary will not have a prominent cross on its exterior. Apparently a cross will be etched into the left-hand wall around the piazza entrance, beside the church dedication to God the Merciful Father. But Romans and pilgrims alike will miss Christ's most important symbol above its facade or bell-tower. The bell-tower, represented in the model by a rectangular block of white concrete, is in itself quite disappointing.

Traditionalists mourn the fact that the church exterior looks more like an abstract art museum than a temple of God. Tor Tre Teste parishioners lament the lack of customary statues, paintings, stations of the cross and other liturgical decor. And architects complain that the church's internal space is fragmented and that the focus on the altar is interrupted by distracting objects or architectural elements.

This is an important moment for the Church to regain its lead in society's cultural life. With its modernist Jubilee Church for the Year 2000, the See of Peter has made a courageous break with its artistic past. Many worshippers, however, feel that religious spaces should not attempt to reflect the spirit of modern times – that is secularism and materialism – but rather the timeless values and ancient traditions of the faith. Some architects now fault modernist structures for stressing function over beauty and exalting abstract, occasionally incomprehensible, forms.

Richard Meier has described his church as a sacred ship with white sails unfurled, ready to take the faithful into the third millennium. Will posterity judge the Jubilee Church as the reflection of a troubled age, or as the expression of a higher spirituality to which believers can aspire?

ROME'S PILGRIMAGE BASILICAS:CHRISTIANITY'S MAJOR SHRINES

Introduction: Jubilees and Pilgrimages

On Christmas Eve 1999 the reigning Pope opens the Holy Door into St Peter's Basilica in the Vatican and inaugurates the Great Jubilee of the Year 2000. Ever since the Middle Ages, Jubilees have commemorated special holy years in Rome, drawing pilgrims from every corner of the earth to pray at the martyrs' tombs and other sacred sites. The Jubilee of the Year 2000, however, will be a uniquely important event for the Roman Church – a Jubilee celebration for both the end of a century and an entire millennium.

The term 'Jubilee' derives from the Hebrew word *jovel* or *jobel*, which designated the year in which the *shofar*, or ram's horn (trumpet), was sounded to begin a period of peace and social equality. References to our words 'jubilant' and 'jubilation' indicate the spirit of rejoicing which characterized the Hebrew Jubilee – as well as Church Jubilees down through the ages.

In the Old Testament a Jubilee was to be commemorated every fiftieth year, which was to be consecrated to God (Jahweh). Regulations for the Jubilee observance were laid down in Leviticus 25:1–55 and were evidently an extension of regulations for Jewish sabbatical years (Leviticus 25: 1–7). In both cases there were three conditions: the freeing of slaves, the cancellation of debts, and a year-long cessation of agricultural activities. Since there are no historical records of Jubilee years being strictly observed in ancient Israel, we assume that the tradition remained an Old Testament ideal rather than a customary practice. The Jubilee year was conceived as a purification, a restoration of social justice, an attempt to establish equality among all the children of Israel.

In the New Testament (Luke 4:16–30), Christ announces that he will usher in a 'year of the Lord's favour', when he will free captives and prisoners and proclaim good tidings to the poor. In the Christian tradition the Jubilee is a year of penitence, conversion and the remission of sins, and is based on these Old and New Testament passages.

**The dome of S. Pietro in Vaticano, built above the tomb of the First Apostle,
has become the emblem of the Roman Catholic Church throughout the world.**

PILGRIMAGES

Throughout history, pilgrimages have been the most characteristic means of celebrating Church Jubilees. During Christianity's first centuries many believers undertook long journeys to the Holy Land, where Jesus Christ was born, crucified and resurrected, and to Rome, where Peter and Paul had preached and died. After the seventh century, when the Muslim conquest of Palestine made Christians' access to the holy places there almost impossible, pilgrims flocked in ever greater numbers to Rome. Here the pious faithful could pray at the Apostles' tombs, visit the sites of early conversion and martyrdom, and even touch with their own hands numerous sacred relics.

Both the Scriptures and Catholic teaching emphasized the pilgrimage as a reminder that believers have no fixed abode upon the earth, but are on a continual path towards reunion with God in heaven. The privations and difficulties involved in the long journey (fifty days was the normal duration from Paris to Rome, and many trips were much more lengthy) were to be accepted as gestures of repentance and expiation. Many travellers gave up their customary attire to don the rough, cowled pilgrim's habit as a sign of penitence and detachment from worldly concerns. Many pilgrims died along the way because of the difficult conditions or from attacks by bandits and robbers.

Certain roads leading across Europe evolved their own legends, shrines and hostels to inspire and assist pilgrims on their travels. From the seventh century onwards, detailed itineraries were compiled by medieval monks to guide visitors in their search for Rome's holy sites and relics. Veritable citadels grew up around Rome's pilgrimage basilicas: monasteries, stables, hospices and hostels, wine-cellars and souvenir shops. Innkeepers and merchants developed a lively business; regional and local guilds, as well as charitable confraternities, were organized to help the sick and unfortunate during their sojourn in Rome.

JUBILEES IN HISTORY

The Catholic Jubilee celebration is not a direct offshoot of the biblical tradition, but rather developed in the context of popular devotion in the late Middle Ages. The first Jubilee, announced in 1300 by Pope Boniface VIII (1294–1303), might have been a surprise to the Pope himself.

At the close of the century, a spirit of guilt and fear was pervading the Christian world; rumours of possible Papal indulgences brought pilgrims flocking in great numbers to

Rome. In fact, on New Year's Day 1300 the most massive crowd in the history of the Eternal City tried to push its way into St Peter's Basilica in hopes of a Papal announcement. For over a month Boniface studied, conferred and meditated in search of a historical precedent. Finally, on 22 February, without a specific tradition to back him, the Pope proclaimed the granting of plenary indulgences for pilgrims who visited the Apostles' tombs in a state of penitence – and the first Jubilee was born. Giotto painted a commemorative fresco, a fragment of which now graces a dusky pillar in the basilica of St John Lateran.

Boniface had envisioned the celebration of Jubilees, also called Holy Years, once every century. Already by the year 1350, however, from his exile in Avignon, Pope Clement VI (1342–52) had launched the observance of Jubilees every fifty years in accordance with Old Testament tradition. With the Jubilee of 1390, Boniface IX (1389–1404) changed the Jubilee periodicity to every thirty-three years, in deference to the length of Christ's life on earth. And finally, insisting that every generation should benefit from the grace of Jubilee celebrations – and indulgences – with the 1450 Jubilee, Nicholas V (1447–1455) fixed the observance of Holy Years for every twenty-five years. And so the custom has remained ever since.

This fresco, now located on a pillar in the right aisle of S. Giovanni in Laterano, is attributed to Giotto (1266–1337) and shows Pope Boniface VIII proclaiming the first Holy Year in 1300.

Extraordinary Jubilees, called outside the normal liturgical calendar, may also be proclaimed for special events or purposes. From 1300 to the year 2000, eighty-six extraordinary Jubilees have been celebrated, either for the entire Church, or for individual countries, regions or even cities. The last extraordinary Jubilee, called by Pope John Paul II in 1983, observed the 1,950th anniversary of Human Redemption.

INDULGENCES

For the Jubilee of 1300 Boniface VIII proclaimed a plenary indulgence for pilgrims who visited the Apostles' basilicas in a state of true penitence, and the tradition has continued for Jubilees and Holy Years down through the centuries. According to Church doctrine, an indulgence brings about remission of the temporal punishment still due for sins after confession, and can be either partial or plenary.

The ideal is a sharing of special grace and forgiveness granted by the Church. In some periods of Church history, however, the practice (sales of indulgences, granting of political privileges) became a bone of contention among pious believers, and was even a predominant cause for the sixteenth-century Protestant Revolt. Jubilee indulgences still exist. For the Great Jubilee of the Year 2000, Pope John Paul II once more confirmed the 'gift' of the plenary indulgence. In November 1998, he decreed the conditions in a special Papal Bull: Confession, Communion, true penance and conversion, and a visit to one of the Jubilee basilicas (or the catacombs). For the first time, pilgrims unable to come to Rome can perform acts of charity (visits to the sick, elderly, imprisoned or handicapped) or of sacrifice or abstinence (fasting, donations, volunteer work) in order to receive the same remission.

LE SETTE CHIESE

Boniface VIII declared plenary indulgences for pilgrims who visited the basilicas of S. Pietro and S. Paolo during the Jubilee Year of 1300. By the time of the 1400 Jubilee two other basilicas, St John Lateran and S. Maria Maggiore, were added to the obligatory Holy Year itinerary. Each of the four major basilicas is provided with a Holy Door, to be symbolically opened at the beginning and closed at the end of a Jubilee year. According to tradition, the doors have been opened and closed simultaneously, by the Pope in St Peter's and by his three delegates in St John Lateran, S. Paolo Fuori le Mura, and S. Maria Maggiore.*

It was in the mid-sixteenth century that Rome's beloved patron St Philip Neri (1515–95) encouraged the pious and penitent to undertake a day long (occasionally two days) tour of the so-called Sette Chiese, or Seven Churches. The itinerary included not only the four Jubilee basilicas mentioned above, but also S. Lorenzo Fuori le Mura and S. Sebastiano (both built over the tombs of revered early martyrs), and S. Croce in Gerusalemme (containing relics of the True Cross). This pilgrimage became immensely popular with Romans and pilgrims alike. Visits to the Seven Churches are now the most important ritual for Jubilee visitors to Rome.

The Jubilee basilicas have always been Rome's – and Christendom's – most important shrines, and throughout history pilgrims have travelled from far and wide to pray at their altars. It is here that the different epochs of Christian history may be discovered, layer by fascinating layer.

S. PIETRO IN VATICANO
Christendom's Capital

The shining dome of St Peter's Basilica has become the emblem of the Roman Catholic Church throughout the world. Rome's greatest and grandest church is built above the tomb of the First Apostle.

MAJESTY AND TRADITION

Any visitor arriving for the first time before St Peter's Basilica immediately feels a sense of majesty and authority. For this is not only Rome's but also Western Christendom's, most important shrine. The immense proportions and imposing quality of the architecture aim to inspire joy and awe in all believers. The monument raised over the tomb of the Apostle chosen by Christ to be the visible head of his Church clearly affirms the pre-eminence and continuity of St Peter's succession – the Pope and the Papacy.

Concerning St Peter's, Vatican guides often quote the eighteenth-century traveller Charles de Brosses – who in fact

---

* For the Great Jubilee of the Year 2000, the Holy Door openings in St John Lateran and S. Maria Maggiore take place on Christmas Day, and in the basilica of S. Paolo Fuori le Mura for the Ecumenical Prayer for Christian Unity on 18 January. The Jubilee for the Year 2000 ends officially with the closure of the Holy Door in the Basilica of St Peter on the feast of the Epiphany, 6 January 2001.

was not particularly known for his piety. 'St Peter's is the finest thing in the universe…all is simple, natural, and august, consequently sublime,' the French magistrate wrote home to a friend. 'You might come to it every day without being bored…It is more amazing the oftener you see it.'

A Catholic tradition going back 2,000 years holds that Peter, the First Apostle, came to Rome, capital of the Empire, to preach the Gospel, that under the Emperor Nero (54–68) he suffered martyrdom and was buried in the area known as the Vatican, and that later the Emperor Constantine (*c.*288–337) built over his tomb a world-famous church, demolished in the sixteenth century to give rise to the present basilica.

PRINCE OF THE APOSTLES

What would be the reaction of Simon, the simple fisherman from Galilee, were he to stand under the vast dome and classical portico of the basilica built in his name, dwarfed by a statue of himself more than twice his size?

The New Testament tells us that Simon was a native of a small village (Bethsaida) on the Sea of Galilee, earning his living by fishing with his brother Andrew. From the Gospels, we can sense his amazement and reverence as Jesus summoned him, along with Andrew, James and John, from his humble boat on the Judaean shore, to follow him in his spiritual mission.

This simple and unlettered man, as he was described in the Acts of the Apostles (4:13), was both fallible and lovable. The Gospels show us that Peter was slow in understanding and impetuous in action. He fell asleep when he should have been keeping watch, and sliced off the ear of the High Priest's servant during Christ's arrest. He refused to let his Master wash his feet. His warm-hearted and impulsive nature prompted him to disagree with the necessity of Christ's humiliation and death. In fact, it is Peter's very human qualities, his alternating weakness (denial of Jesus during the Passion) and spiritual strength (recognition of Christ as the Messiah, Son of the living God), which endear him to us and make him the ideal leader of the earthly Church.

Upon Peter, Christ himself bestowed the Aramaic title of *kepha*, the term for both 'Peter' and 'rock' (*petros* and *petra*,

Inside St Peter's Basilica, Roman Catholicism's most important shrine, from Michelangelo's great dome. More than 2,500 different types of marble were used to decorate the interior.

respectively, in Greek and Latin), with these words from Matthew's Gospel (16: 18–19): 'And on this rock I will build my Church, and the gates of hell shall not prevail against it. I will give you the keys to the kingdom of heaven.' According to St John, Peter received three times from the Lord the pastoral charge to be the shepherd of his sheep. It was in fulfilment of this mission that Peter came to Rome.

An unbroken tradition from the first century, and later historical sources (the historian Eusebius, d. 340, and St Jerome, d. 420) suggest that Peter was martyred during Nero's persecutions after the great fire of Rome in AD64, in the Neronian Circus in the Vatican. (Declaring himself unworthy of suffering the same martyrdom as Christ, the Apostle was crucified upside down.) He was allegedly buried by pious Christians just beyond the arena, in an area already used as a pagan necropolis.

TRACES IN STONE

The memory of St Peter's burial on the very spot where his huge basilica now stands has lasted in Rome for 2,000 years. Sceptics will claim that no precise documentary or archaeological evidence irrefutably proves the location.

A view of the *Scavi*, or excavated section, under St Peter's Basilica, where archaeologists claim to have discovered St Peter's tomb, and St Peter's Square at night, with Gianlorenzo Bernini's two semi-circular colonnades, surmounted by statues of saints, martyrs and Doctors of the Church.

Nevertheless, a fervent and unbroken conviction remains in the hearts of the Christian faithful – and provides the very foundation of Catholic tradition.

Any visitor to the churches of Rome, and to St Peter's Basilica in particular, is advised to descend to the *Scavi*, or excavation site beneath the church, to judge first-hand the tradition of Peter's burial here. A guide leads small groups along a narrow underground passageway lined with house-like façades, opening to rooms decorated with paintings, mosaics and carved sarcophagi. These were the (mostly) second-century tombs of middle-class Romans, located at that time above ground and along a main Roman thoroughfare flanking the northern side of Nero's Circus. (This area was outside the prescribed city limits, or *pomerium*, and thus appropriate for burials).

could date the structure by seals on the bricks from the time of the Emperor Marcus Aurelius (161–180).

In the Scavi we can stand a few feet from that early monument. Peering through grates and past a jumble of walls and ruins, we glimpse sections of the 'red wall' and one of the trophy columns. Excavations carried out beneath St Peter's Basilica between 1939 and 1951 uncovered first a pagan, then an increasingly Christian graveyard, and finally a semi-circle of graves surrounding a central cavity – directly below the present altar. The central grave was empty, but covered with coins and other votives from the first and second centuries. Within the hollow 'graffiti' wall above, engraved with surnames, greetings and funeral invocations, was found a packet of bones, encrusted with dirt and wrapped in fine cloth.

These were the remains of an older man, broad-shouldered and short of stature, and were datable to the first century. Obviously they had been hidden away here for safe-keeping during a period of great danger. No great leap of faith was needed to convince the diggers – or those of us who visit the excavations today – that this was the burial place of Peter of Galilee, the Prince of Apostles.

A SPIRITUAL CONTINUITY

Now, entering the third millennium, pilgrims come to St Peter's to experience the continuity which links the Apostle to his successors, the Roman Popes. An important personage in that spiritual–historical thread was the Roman Emperor Constantine, who legalized Christianity and decided to build a great church on this very spot.

In order to execute his project, the Emperor had to level the Vatican Hill, slice off the tops of many of the mausoleums, and fill in the cemetery with 20,000 tons of dirt and rubble. Why would Constantine have taken on such a difficult task, even infringing Romans' deeply ingrained – and strictly regulated – respect for burial grounds, if he had not been firmly convinced of the sacredness of the site?

An oratory had been built here in the time of Pope Anacletus (79–91). Constantine replaced the shrine with a marble 'memorial', within which he enclosed St Peter's so-called trophy. Around this the Emperor raised (320–26) his immense basilica, with a great nave, four aisles, and a four-porticoed courtyard reached by a flight of thirty-five stairs.

Down through the ages, the basilica was richly embellished: pavements of coloured marble, stained-glass windows, hanging lamps of gold and silver, bas-reliefs and statues, Oriental

Most of the mausoleums were pagan; some have Christian symbols (the dove of peace, Christ as the sun-God) and inscriptions ('Rest in Peace'). Further along, on a slight downward incline (the necropolis was built upon the Mons Vaticanus, or Vatican Hill), was the area for poorer burials – which were made directly into the earth, often unmarked, and sometimes superimposed one above another.

According to tradition, Peter had a simple earthen grave. The site was the object of special care and veneration from the beginning; around the saint's tomb an extensive Christian burial ground sprang up in the second and third centuries. It seems that a small funerary monument, consisting of niches, small columns, a red retaining wall, and another wall covered with pious graffiti, was built around Peter's grave in the second century (the 'trophy of Gaius' noted earlier). Archaeologists

draperies and silken tapestries. Many great artists worked here. Popes crowned Kings and Emperors before St Peter's altar, notably Charlemagne on Christmas Eve in the year 800. Emperors and Pontiffs had their tombs built in the vicinity of the Fisherman's shrine. In the succeeding centuries, three new altars were built over Constantine's memorial to St Peter: by Gregory the Great (590–604), Calixtus II (1119–24), and Clement VIII (1592–1605).

For twelve centuries the Constantinian basilica was the centre of Christian worship and the destination of pilgrims from every corner of the globe. The church was sacked by Goths, Vandals and Saracens, and during the Avignon exile, when the Popes resided in France for over seventy years

(1305–78), the building suffered irreparable decay and disintegration. In the early sixteenth century the building was finally declared unfit – and it was progressively demolished during the sixteenth and seventeenth centuries.

The new St Peter's, without skipping a beat, continued to be a protagonist in every era of Church history, and a showpiece for the artistic genius of each age. It was the great Renaissance Pope Julius II who laid the first stone in 1506. 'His' church, conceived by the father of Renaissance architecture, Bramante, was continued by – among other artists – the premier painter of the age, Raphael.

The original Greek cross design (with nave and transept of equal length) was later modified, but the classical harmony and

Interior view of St Peter's Basilica, the largest Christian church in the world, which can hold at least 90,000 people.

humanist symmetry, so admired in the Renaissance, are prevalent even today. In 1546, the seventy-two-year-old Michelangelo became chief architect of St Peter's for Pope Paul III (preceded by Baldassare Peruzzi and Antonio da Sangallo the Younger), conceiving the resplendent dome which is now visible from almost every point in the Papal city.

By the time Paul V (1605–21) instructed Carlo Maderno to complete the basilica, almost a century had passed since Luther's Reform movement and the Sack of Rome. Returning to the plan of a Latin cross, with the longer nave riveting attention on the altar, where the Pope himself presided, Maderno joined the church of St Peter to the battle ranks of the Counter-Reformation.

A line of determined and munificent seventeenth-century Popes, especially Urban VIII (1623–44) and Alexander VII (1655–67), ushered St Peter's into the Baroque age. It was Gianlorenzo Bernini (1598–1680) who lavishly decorated the basilica – inside and out – in the Baroque style. Bernini and his contemporaries did not hesitate to appeal to all the senses in order to effect conviction and conversion in the hearts of Christian worshippers.

ST PETER'S SQUARE

We can thank Pope Alexander VII for deciding to construct St Peter's Square as we see it today. The Pope entrusted the task to Gianlorenzo Bernini, who worked rapidly between 1656 and 1667. This is certainly one of the world's most successful architectural spaces. The square has the shape of an immense – and immensely harmonious – ellipse. Pilgrims arriving to visit St Peter's feel they are embraced by the two huge arms of the curving colonnade, stretching around the square in rows of classical Doric columns, thirteen metres tall and four on each side.

Bernini's was an image of the Church welcoming all her faithful. In one of his architectural sketches the architect portrayed God the Father rising from the basilica dome, with his arms extended along the parapet (where now perch 140 statues of gesticulating saints and martyrs) of both branches of the colonnade. Bernini's clear intent is realized almost every Sunday, when, from his window in the Apostolic Palace, the Pope addresses the crowds of faithful in the square below.

The centrepiece of the piazza, a lofty obelisk first raised in Heliopolis by the Egyptian Pharaohs, was later transported to Rome by the imperial legions and set in the middle of Nero's Circus. Constantine topped it with a relic from the True Cross

brought from the Holy Land by his mother, St Helena. Finally, as part of a great urban renewal scheme, Sixtus V moved it to the square in 1586. Before this obelisk, we are again overwhelmed by that sense of historical and spiritual continuity. As one Vatican guidebook notes: 'The very obelisk which looks down on us today witnessed the martyrdom of St Peter, and in all probability, the exodus of Moses and the Jews, as they fled Pharaoh's Egypt.'

The obelisk stands between two monumental fountains, designed by Maderno and Carlo Fontana and placed here by Bernini. Two huge statues before the basilica are of the Apostles Peter and Paul; they were made in the nineteenth century and placed before the basilica in 1847. The basilica's massive classical façade by Carlo Maderno, completed in 1612, is a monumental example of human vanity. Although many Popes patronized St Peter's construction and decoration, it was Pope Paul V Borghese who emblazoned his name in huge letters across the entrance architrave.

INSIDE ST PETER'S

Upon entering St Peter's a visitor is first struck by the 'classical' harmony of the colours, proportions and light, just as the original Renaissance architects intended. The immense structure is pure and simple in design. The colours are few – marbled whites, and gleaming gold and bronze. Between the nave's Corinthian pilasters, or under Michelangelo's dome, can be sensed the influence of imperial Roman monuments such as the Pantheon, or the basilica of Maxentius and Constantine.

Yet, because of the splendour of Bernini's decorations, St Peter's is known as a Baroque church. And perhaps no other monument of the period can match the lavish exuberance of Bernini's bronze Baldacchino (materials taken from the Pantheon), towering over the altar and St Peter's grave, and of the Papal throne, upheld by Doctors of the Latin and Greek Churches beneath a great golden sunburst. Bernini and his contemporaries used all their theatrical talents to impart Catholic doctrine – and all their sensual gifts to stir impassioned devotion.

Volumes have been written on the monuments and artistic treasures of St Peter's Basilica, and any visitor should be equipped with detailed maps and guidebooks for a thorough visit. Here are just a few things not to be missed. After entering the basilica, the first chapel in the right aisle contains Michelangelo's *Pietà*, carved in 1498–9 when the artist was only twenty-four years old, and the only sculpture he ever signed (on the band crossing Mary's breast). Mary's youthful

appearance has been explained by the artist's remembrance of his own mother, who died when he was only five years old. The statue was vandalized in 1972 and is now protected by a special glass screen.

On the right aisle's left-hand wall are the funerary monuments of several amazing women: among others, the eccentric Queen Christina of Sweden (1626–89), who relinquished her throne to convert to Catholicism, and Countess Matilda of Canossa (1046–1114), Pope Gregory VII's champion against the Emperor Henry IV. The Blessed Sacrament Chapel has Pietro da Cortona's *Trinity* (1628–31) – the basilica's one and only oil painting; most of the basilica's art works are, in fact, mosaic copies of original paintings.

The four massive piers supporting the dome have large statues of Sts Longinus, Helena, Veronica and Andrew. They were designed by Bernini to host the basilica's holiest relics: Longinus' lance, a piece of the True Cross, Veronica's veil, and the head of the Apostle Andrew (all now gathered in the Veronica reliquary, except for St Andrew's skull, which Pope Paul VI returned to the Greek Church).

Tradition has it that the Barberini Pope Urban VIII commissioned Bernini's Baldacchino as a thanksgiving offering for the safe childbirth of his favourite niece. Close inspection of the bases of the canopy columns show the face of a woman in various stages of labour, and, finally, a cherub-like baby's head.

One of the basilica's last left-aisle tombs is the mournful memorial to the 'last of the Stuarts', attesting to the sad exile and end of this family of eighteenth-century Pretenders to the British throne. Throughout the church there are huge and elaborate funerary memorials to Pontiffs of every era. In the so-called 'grottoes', that is the crypts below the present church (entrances near the St Longinus pier of the dome), many art treasures from Constantine's demolished church have been preserved, as well as the tombs of recent Popes.

Perhaps the basilica's most visited monument is the bronze statue of St Peter in the nave near the main altar. Although created by Arnolfo di Cambio in the thirteenth century, the work breathes the spirit of an even earlier age. Peter, seated upon a simple throne, is solemnly imparting his blessing, and his right foot has been worn smooth by the kisses of pilgrims

down through the centuries. There is something so appealing and so humble about this figure that we immediately conjure the image of the Galilean fisherman buried below, in whose honour this magnificent temple has been built and enriched throughout two millennia of Church history.

Indeed, everything in the church speaks of St Peter. Written above the pilasters of the nave, and in gigantic letters on the golden band around the cupola, are the New Testament phrases upon which Peter's authority and his Apostolic succession are based. At almost every hour, rays of seemingly 'heavenly' light flow downwards from the dome, towards the Confession over St Peter's tomb. The altar above is framed by Bernini's Baldacchino against the brilliant amber light of the apse window. The effect is worthy of Western Christendom's most important shrine.

S. PAOLO FUORI LE MURA
A Martyred Apostle's Shrine
The basilica of St Paul Outside the Walls was built over the tomb of the missionary Apostle Paul, founder – along with St Peter – of the Roman Church. His memory has been honoured in this basilica as St Peter's in his – throughout two millennia of Christian history.

THE MISSIONARY APOSTLE
Two very Oriental palm trees stand in the courtyard before the basilica of St Paul Outside the Walls. This exotic suggestion – as palm fronds in medieval mosaics evoked far-away Jerusalem – eases the pilgrim beyond an initial disappointment to a hint of the modern building's origins in the early days of Christian martyrdom. For the basilica was originally constructed in 324, upon the express desire of the first Christian Emperor, Constantine, to commemorate the burial place of the martyred Apostle St Paul.

We know much about Paul (Saul), a Jew born in Tarsus and trained as a Pharisee, from the Acts of the Apostles and from his own Epistles. Intense and ambitious, he first persecuted Christians with fanatic determination, and even participated in the stoning of St Stephen in Palestine. Later, after his

Bernini's bronze Baldacchino covers the Papal altar, directly above the tomb of St Peter.

conversion on the road to Damascus, the new Apostle (by virtue of his personal vision of and 'calling' by Christ, as he himself wrote) pursued his worldwide evangelizing mission with the same boundless energy with which he had hunted down Christians. Less appealing than the fallible, lovable Peter, Paul's tireless missionary efforts and great theological contributions nevertheless gave Christianity its universal momentum.

Paul arrived in Rome under a type of 'house arrest' (for his revolutionary activities), preached for about two years, and was finally executed outside the Roman walls on the Ostian Way.

Since he inherited Roman citizenship from his father (the Acts do not say how or why), he was beheaded rather than crucified. Legend holds that three fountains sprang up where the Apostle's head bounced three times as it was cut off, and the area, where a Trappist monastery now stands, has since been called the Tre Fontane (Three Fountains).

According to tradition, St Paul was buried by the pious matron Lucina in her family vineyard–cemetery on the Ostian Way. There, from the first century, a *cella memoriae* (grave memorial) was venerated by early Christians and was even

The basilica of St Paul Outside the Walls has a nineteenth-century façade and a large garden.

mentioned along with St Peter's 'trophy', by the presbyter Gaius around AD200. In fact, during excavations in the nineteenth century, archaeologists found a typical first-century grave surrounded by many pagan and Christian tombs, similar to the necropolis unearthed under St Peter's Basilica.

A CONTINUOUS TRADITION

The *Liber Pontificalis* (biographies of the early Popes) tells us that the Emperor Constantine ordered basilicas to be built over the *cellae memoriae* which marked both St Paul's and St Peter's tombs. Furthermore, the *Acts of St Sylvester* record the consecration of the basilica of St Paul by Pope Sylvester (314–35) on 18 November 324, as well as Constantine's generous donations throughout the following years.

Several Emperors who jointly ruled the Roman Empire in the late fourth century – Valentinian II (375–92), Theodosius (375–95), Arcadius (377–408), and Honorius (395–423) – decreed that the church should be enlarged in accordance with its importance to pilgrims. That church, built with five aisles, eighty columns, and a huge porch, was completed in the early fifth century (as we are informed by an inscription on the triumphal arch inside). Many Popes restored and embellished St Paul's, and in time the basilica became the largest and most beautiful church in Rome, surpassing even St Peter's.

St Paul Outside the Walls continued through the Middle Ages as the largest Christian church in the world, until the new St Peter's was built in the sixteenth and seventeenth centuries. The basilica was a protagonist in centuries of agitated Church history. Pope St Leo the Great (440–61) commissioned additional mosaics; Pope St Gregory the Great (590–604) endowed the basilica with extensive lands. The Saracens attacked the church in 846, and in the late ninth century Pope John VIII (872–82) made it the centre of his new fortified town, Giovannopolis.

In the eleventh century the Emperor Henry IV (1050–1106) besieged St Paul's and destroyed its famous portico; the basilica's abbot, who became Henry's nemesis as Gregory VII (1073–85), restored the church and transformed it into a powerful monastery. During the later Middle Ages, until the time of the transference of the Papal residence to Avignon, St Paul's was beautified with some of Christendom's most magnificent art. Later enrichments included early and High Renaissance paintings and seventeenth-century chapels.

During the night of 15 July 1823, a terrible fire, set off by some careless workmen on the roof, reduced to rubble the ancient basilica of St Paul Outside the Walls, along with much of its rich artistic and historical patrimony.

The basilica was rebuilt quickly (it was finally reconsecrated in 1854) and the entire world assisted in its reconstruction. Mohammed Ali of Egypt sent over the six huge alabaster columns which flank the inside entrance. Tsar Nicholas I of Russia underwrote malachite and lapis lazuli decorations for altars in the right and left transepts. Collections were taken up on every continent for restorations of the mosaics.

A VISIT TO ST PAUL OUTSIDE THE WALLS

St Paul's mass towers above one of Rome's dingiest suburbs. Completely rebuilt after the 1823 fire, the Neo-classical re-creation greets the visitor with hulking grey walls, a huge foursided columned porch and gaudy mosaics on the façade. Disenchantment grows with the realization that the original church, housing the martyred Apostle's remains, was one of Rome's earliest and most beautiful, and, until the fire, had stood almost unchanged since its completion in the fifth century.

But the churches of Rome always manage to dazzle us with some unexpected treasure – and this Jubilee basilica has preserved some of the most delightful medieval rarities to be found in Italy. Once past the 'evocative' palm trees, a huge statue of St Paul with the sword of his martyrdom, and the massive porch, the pilgrim enters a different world. St Paul's interior gives an overwhelming impression of almost icy emptiness. Although all is (relatively) new here, we seem to experience a type of imperial Roman basilica upon which the earliest Christian churches were modelled. The great hall, with its forest of gleaming marble columns dividing five aisles, could easily have served as a meeting place for powerful Roman politicians and jurists in the days of Maxentius and Constantine.

In this immense and vacant space all attention is focused on a single point: underneath a graceful Gothic canopy, the Papal altar stands above the burial place of Paul the Apostle – the *confessio*, which is illuminated by rows of glowing candles and reached by descending a double staircase to a lower level. In this spot, the pilgrim senses the spiritual presence of the Apostle's sepulchre below.

Here, during excavations after the 1823 fire, archaeologists discovered not only the pre-Constantinian necropolis, but a columned monument resembling the 'trophy' of St Peter. On top of a bronze sarcophagus containing the Apostle's relics, dated to Constantine's era, were found two flat, joined marble slabs, bearing the letters PAOLO APOSTOLOMAR and two openings, one round and one square. Researchers claim that the round hole was used in ancient times for introducing an incense-holder into the Apostle's grave, while the square opening served the earliest pilgrims for lowering items to be blessed near St Paul's remains. A copy of this interesting panel can now be seen in the basilica museum.

Although the vast spaciousness of the 'new' St Paul's makes it appear quite empty, visitors should carefully explore its chapels, statues and paintings. Among these is a series of mosaic portraits of all the Popes (beginning with St Peter), which weaves its way high above the nave, transepts and apse. These are modern; the few which survived the fire are kept in the basilica museum. One of St Paul's earliest treasures is the pair of silver-inlaid bronze doors to the right of the main entrance, crafted in Constantinople in 1070 and presented to Pope Gregory VII by the wealthy merchant Pantaleon of Amalfi. This is S. Paolo's Holy Door, opened at the beginning of each Jubilee year and walled-up upon its conclusion.

The Blessed Sacrament Chapel, to the left of the apse, was the only chapel to survive the fire. Designed by Carlo Maderno (1556–1629), it hosts a crucifix attributed to Pietro Cavallini (*c.*1250–1330) which allegedly spoke to St Bridget of Sweden. The basilica museum has valuable paintings and frescoes saved from the pre-fire church.

MEDIEVAL TREASURES

In the devastation of the 1823 fire, some of Italy's most remarkable medieval treasures were miraculously spared: for a start, the twelfth-century Paschal candlestick and Arnolfo di Cambio's (*c.*1245–1303) altar canopy. No greater contrast in medieval styles and spirit could possibly be imagined.

Confronted by the colossal Romanesque candelabrum at the angle of the right transept and nave, we are alternately amused and terror-stricken. Signed by the artists, Nicola de Angelo and Pietro Vassalletto, and thus datable to the end of the twelfth or the beginning of the thirteenth century, this Dark Ages 'tree of life' winds upwards with a series of grotesques, arabesques and Christological figures. In the bottom section, strange Oriental animals with human heads denote Christian

Although St Paul Outside the Walls was almost completely restored after a fire in 1823, its interior preserves the spirit of an early Christian basilica.

control of animal passions; there follow plant and animal motifs, interspersed with strange foetal forms.

Next come three tiers with scenes from the Passion and the Resurrection. In these, rows of helmeted soldiers leer and gape at Pontius Pilate's side, while Christ is jostled by rude and frightening crowds. After Christ's ascension to heaven in a nimbus, plants and flowers climb to a row of upright monsters, supporting the candle-holder at the top. Our reaction is similar to that of the young seminarian described by Umberto Eco in *The Name of the Rose*, when he first experienced the terrifying Romanesque tympanum in the novel's sinister abbey.

Arnolfo di Cambio's gilded *baldachin*, dated 1285, stands over the altar above St Paul's tomb. Created about a century after the candelabrum, this work breathes the new Gothic spirit of refinement and elegance. In a style very rarely found in Italy (the same artist's *baldachin* in the church of S. Cecilia in Trastevere is another example), the tabernacle soars upward with a series of golden pinnacles, ogival and pointed arches, and airy spires. Elongated angels hover gracefully in the tympana and aristocratic heads peer from the richly carved capitals. Bible scenes and saints' statues cover all the available spaces, and even the canopy's underside is decorated with mosaics and carvings.

The partially restored mosaics of the apse and triumphal arch must also be mentioned. According to the inscriptions, the apsidal mosaics, showing Christ enthroned, flanked by Apostles and a lower register of saints and palms, were carried out between 1220 and 1230 by Venetian artists summoned to St Paul's by Pope Honorius III (1216–27). A minuscule portrait of the Pope shows him prostrating himself at Christ's feet.

The fifth-century mosaics in the triumphal arch were commissioned by Galla Placidia, sister of the Emperor Honorius mentioned above, while Pietro Cavallini (who frescoed the apse in S. Maria in Trastevere and S. Cecilia in Trastevere's choir) is believed to have executed the series in the arch's inner face.

By some miracle, St Paul's medieval cloister escaped the 1823 fire practically untouched. Constructed between 1193 and 1226, it combines elements of both Romanesque and Gothic styles. In fact, in the earlier section, we find the signature of that same Pietro Vassalletto who worked on the Paschal candlestick; his appealing contributions are the naive animals and small human figures between the columns.

Each of these columns is different from the others, and all are very beautiful: some have winding or zig-zagging bands of

gold and gem-like mosaics; others are in smooth, fluted or spiralling marble. The cloister has a marvellous atmosphere of peace and antiquity; no visitor should leave St Paul's without meditating a while in its green garden.

S. GIOVANNI IN LATERANO
Christianity's First Cathedral
St John Lateran was Christendom's mother basilica and home of the Popes for 1,000 years.

CATHEDRAL OF THE POPES
S. Giovanni in Laterano (St John Lateran) was Christendom's earliest Papal basilica. Commissioned by Rome's first Christian Emperor, Constantine the Great, it became the Popes' official residence and cathedral for the first millennium of Christian history. Today, standing before the basilica's ponderous eighteenth-century façade, assailed by ear-splitting Roman traffic on every side, we can hardly imagine this as the cradle of Christianity. A visitor should glance upwards. Towering against the (usually) cobalt-blue Roman sky, a seven-metre-

St John Lateran, the first cathedral of the Popes, now has an eighteenth-century façade topped with huge statues of the Saviour, Sts John the Baptist and John the Evangelist, and Doctors of the Church.

high statue of Christ triumphantly displays the Cross of Redemption. The Saviour is flanked by Sts John the Baptist and John the Evangelist, as well as Doctors of the Eastern and Western Churches.

'Omnium urbis et orbis ecclesiarum mater et caput' – this inscription from the basilica's earlier façade, now covering the space between the portico and the loggia, declares that the Pope and the Emperor wished this basilica to be considered the first and mother of all churches. It was to Jesus the Saviour that Constantine dedicated the original church, confirming Christ's superiority over the Capitol's pagan gods and assuring the worldwide expansion of the Christian religion.

THE EMPEROR CONSTANTINE

With the ascent of Constantine as Emperor of Rome (306–37), the days of bloody Christian persecutions came to an end. Placed at first on an equal footing with paganism, Christianity soon became the official religion of the Roman Empire.

Constantine was the son of Constantius Chlorus, Roman Emperor (Caesar) of the West (305–6), and Helena, a woman of obscure origins, whose fervent conversion to Christianity and alleged finding of the True Cross in Jerusalem won her sainthood. After defeating his rival Maxentius, son of the earlier Emperor Maximian (286–305), at the Milvian Bridge in Rome in 312, Constantine established himself as the undisputed ruler of the Western Empire.

The night before this battle, Constantine's earliest biographer, Eusebius, tells us, the Emperor saw a cross of light in the heavens and the words: 'By this sign you shall conquer.' His soldiers went into battle bearing the Christian monogram on their shields, rather than the Roman eagle, and with a standard of Christ's cross carried before them. From that time, as he won battle after battle, and consolidated his rule over the Empire in East and West in 324, the Emperor claimed to be fighting in Jesus's name, as the champion of the Christian faith.

The Edict of Milan (313) secured Christians' freedom and legal recognition. By imperial edicts, Constantine restored Christians' property and strengthened the Church hierarchy (without giving too much offence to Rome's influential pagans). He called the Council of Nicaea, which denounced the Arian heresy and promulgated the Nicene Creed.

Was Constantine a pious visionary or an ambitious opportunist? Historical opinions differ. Biographers report his late-in-life remorse for ordering the deaths of his wife Fausta,

son Crispus (by his first wife, Minerva), and several other relatives. It was only when he lay upon his deathbed that the Emperor asked to be baptized. At the age of sixty-four he died, clad in the white garment of a new convert.

The first Christian Emperor had ordered basilicas built over the *cellae memoriae* marking St Peter's, St Paul's, and other martyrs' tombs. And he donated his personal property, received in dowry from his wife, for the first Papal cathedral and residence in Christian history. So begins the story of St John Lateran.

HISTORICAL ITINERARY

It was to Pope Melchiades (311–14) that Constantine gave his Lateran Palace, so-called because it had earlier been the property of the patrician Laterani family, which his second wife Fausta (Maxentius' sister) had brought to the marriage. Soon after, the Emperor razed the adjoining imperial horseguards' barracks (allegedly the *equites singulares* had supported Maxentius against Constantine) and commissioned the construction of the world's first major Christian basilica on that site.

The Lateran Palace, known as the Patriarchate, was the Popes' official residence until the late fourteenth century. The basilica, consecrated in 324 by Melchiades' successor, Pope Sylvester I (314–35), was dedicated, by will of the Emperor, to Christ the Saviour. In the tenth century Pope Sergius III (904–11) added St John the Baptist, and in the twelfth century Pope Lucius (1144–5) added St John the Evangelist to the basilica's dedication.

In the course of its history, St John Lateran suffered just about as many disasters and revivals as the Papacy it hosted. Sacked by Alaric in 410 and Genseric in 455, it was rebuilt by Pope St Leo the Great (440–61) and centuries later by Pope Hadrian I (772–95). Almost entirely destroyed by an earthquake in 896, the basilica was again restored by Pope Sergius III (904–11). Later the church was heavily damaged by fires in 1308 and 1360.

When the Popes returned from their sojourn in Avignon (1305–1378), they found their basilica and palace in such disrepair that they decided to transfer to the Vatican, near St Peter's. (That basilica, also built by Constantine, had until then served primarily as a pilgrimage church.)

Pope Sixtus V (1585–90), in one of his frenzied urban renewal projects, tore down St John Lateran's original buildings, replacing them with late Renaissance structures by his favourite architect, Domenico Fontana (1543–1607). Later,

Pope Innocent X (1644–55) engaged one of the Baroque's most brilliant architects, Francesco Borromini (1599–1667), to transform St John Lateran's interior in time for the Jubilee of 1650. Finally, Pope Clement XII (1730–40) launched a competition for the design of a new façade, which was completed by Alessandro Galilei in 1735.

Of the original Lateran basilica and palace, only the Popes' private chapel, the Sancta Sanctorum, remains. Sixtus V removed this magnificently frescoed shrine to what has become a grimy traffic island. As an approach to the chapel, Sixtus moved from the Lateran Palace the Scala Sancta, the staircase which Jesus supposedly ascended to Pontius Pilate's palace in Jerusalem, and which, according to tradition, was brought to Rome by St Helena herself.

Many important historic events have taken place in St John Lateran, including five Ecumenical Councils and many diocesan synods. In 1929 the Lateran Pacts, which established the territory and status of the State of Vatican City, were signed here between the Holy See and the Government of Italy.

Since the late fourteenth century the Popes have resided in the Vatican, and St Peter's Basilica now hosts the most important Papal ceremonies. St John Lateran is still, however, Rome's only cathedral, the original and continuing church for the Pope as Bishop of Rome. In fact, the term cathedral actually refers to a bishop's church, more precisely a church with a bishop's throne (*cathedra*). Every year the Holy Thursday liturgy, when the Holy Father symbolically washes the feet of priests chosen from various parts of the world, is celebrated in St John Lateran.

The offices of the Cardinal Vicar of Rome now occupy the Lateran Palace. On the night of 27 July 1993, a bomb explosion (simultaneous with that in S. Giorgio in Velabro across the city, and likewise an act of Mafia terrorism) devastated the façade of the Rome Vicariate of S. Giovanni in Laterano. Repairs were completed in 1996.

A VISIT TO ST JOHN LATERAN

St John Lateran retains, internally at least, its original Constantinian arrangement: a large rectangular hall with an impressive nave, flanked by double aisles and terminating in an apse. The Emperor seems to have conceived an edifice to rival the Roman *basilicae,* or monumental public meeting-halls of the imperial city. As we have mentioned several times, the imperial basilica provided the model for the great majority of Roman churches, from the earliest to most recent.

Even Borromini's Baroque decor does not detract from the impression of an early Christian church. As usual, Borromini's genius is not immediately evident. But any visitor will be rewarded by a close examination of the details and architectural solutions this resourceful artist managed to execute. The massive statues of Apostles which line the main nave (by various late Baroque artists, some followers of Gianlorenzo Bernini) fill their marble-columned niches, fairly bursting with psychological and aesthetic power. The figures of Matthew and Bartholomew, carrying his flayed skin, are especially impressive.

Above these powerful figures, Pamphili doves (family insignia of Innocent X) are prominently displayed in the pediments, topped by reliefs by Alessandro Algardi (1595–1654) of Old and New Testament scenes, and by painted medallions with prophets. A gold-leaf coffered ceiling bears the coats-of-arms of its patron Renaissance Popes, Pius IV (1559–65) and Pius V (1566–72). The 'cosmatesque'-style pavement in polychrome marble, restored by Pope Martin V (1417–31), appears, somehow, much more recent.

St John Lateran contains artistic treasures from every historic period, a tribute to the important role the basilica has played in the history of Rome and of the Roman Catholic Church. The cathedral also boasts an especially important Jubilee memento. On the second pilaster, between the main nave and the far right aisle, is a fragment of a fresco, attributed to Giotto, of Pope Boniface VIII (1294–1303) proclaiming the first Holy Year in 1300 from the 'loggia of the blessings' in the medieval Lateran Palace.

During excavations carried out in 1934–5 beneath the central nave, significant pagan and early Christian remains were unearthed – floor mosaics, household implements, and even stretches of paved Roman streets. In a niche in the portico, an imposing fourth-century statue of the Emperor Constantine (from the Constantine Baths on the Quirinal) is a reminder of the basilica's origins, while the central bronze doors (second century) come from the Curia, or Senate, in the Roman Forum.

The Gothic altar in St John Lateran during the Holy Thursday liturgy, celebrated by Pope John Paul II.

The apse mosaic was commissioned by Pope Nicholas IV (1288–92) in 1292, using designs and fragments of the original Constantinian decorations. The mosaic includes, besides the bust of Christ the Saviour surrounded by angels (perhaps a remnant of the fourth-century work), figures of the Virgin and saints, a magnificent jewelled cross, and pleasant scenes of animals and children frolicking in the River Jordan.

In this charming work of art, there are also smaller figures of St Anthony and St Francis of Assisi (Pope Nicholas was a Franciscan), as well as tiny portraits of the medieval Franciscan friar artists Jacopo Torriti and Jacopo da Camerino, crouched between the Apostles in the lower level. The donor, Pope Nicholas, kneels at the feet of the Virgin, who gently places her hand on his head. Below the apse mosaic, the walls and Papal throne are decorated with beautiful panels and discs of porphyry.

Beneath the triumphal arch in the middle of the transept stands the Gothic Papal altar, which contains a wooden altar where the earliest Popes, from St Peter to St Sylvester, supposedly celebrated Mass, and silver busts with alleged relics from the heads of St Peter and St Paul. The tabernacle, known to be the last Gothic work executed in Rome, was designed by Giovanni di Stefano in 1367, and surmounted by bright frescoes painted by Barna da Siena in 1369. The *confessio* below contains the tomb of Pope Martin V (1417–31), responsible for many of the basilica's most important embellishments.

Entering the transept, we pass from the Middle Ages to the height of late sixteenth-century Mannerism. Pope Clement VIII (1592–1605) employed his favourite architect, Giacomo della Porta (1539–1602), and painter, Cavalier d'Arpino (1568–1640); (see his famous *Ascension* in the right transept altar) to direct the works. Top Mannerist painters of the day (Cesare Nebbia, Paris Nogari, Cristoforo Roncalli, Agostino Ciampelli, etc.) executed a series of frescoes around the entire left and right transepts, which tell the story of Constantine and St John Lateran.

After *Constantine's Dream* and *Victory at the Milvian Bridge*, come *Constantine's Search for Pope Sylvester I*, *Baptism of Constantine*, *Dedication of the Basilica*, *Miraculous Appearance of the Saviour in the Basilica*, and *Presentation of the Emperor's Gifts*. Much of this legend has been disputed by later historians (who claim that Constantine thought little of Pope Sylvester, and waited until after his death to be baptized).

To the left of the apse is the nineteenth-century tomb of Pope Innocent III (1198–1216), moved here from Perugia in 1891. It is fitting that Innocent's remains lie in St John Lateran for it was here that the powerful Pope approved the Franciscan Order, after a frightening dream in which he saw St Francis holding upon his shoulders a collapsing Lateran basilica.

SPECIAL SURPRISES

No visitor should miss the lovely cloister (1215–30), reached from a door off the left transept. This was designed by Pietro Vassalletto and his son, who also worked on the cloister in St Paul Outside the Walls. The abundant mosaics, delicate arches with paired spiral and smooth columns, and oddly 'primitive' animal and floral motifs are typical of the Vassalletto duo.

This is one of Rome's most peaceful and evocative spots. Bypassed by the tourist crowds, aired by soft breezes and the scent of flowers, the Vassalletto corridors also offer the pilgrim a wealth of unexpected surprises. Displayed along and upon the ancient brick walls are fragments from the original basilica, carved sarcophagi, a thirteenth-century Papal throne, and touching inscriptions from the earliest Christian burial sites.

The Baptistery, around to the back and right of the basilica, was originally built by Constantine, transformed into an octagonal brick building by Pope Sixtus III (432–40), and substantially restored by Pope Urban VIII (1623–44). This structure breathes the spirit of a different age, and should be enjoyed at length.

The bronze doors in the right-hand chapel have been praised by Dante and others down through the ages because of the wonderful 'singing' sound they make when they open and close. The left-hand chapel dates from the fifth century and has rich fifth-century mosaics on the vault. The shrine was built by Pope Hilarius (461–8) in fulfilment of a vow to St John the Evangelist, in whose tomb the then Papal legate had hidden during a dangerous riot in Ephesus.

The original narthex and entrance form another chapel (opposite the entrance), and here can be sensed the atmosphere of Constantine's days. To the left another chapel has seventh-century mosaics – very rare for Rome and partially obscured by a Baroque altar.

S. MARIA MAGGIORE
Honouring the Mother of God

S. Maria Maggiore is widely believed to be the most important church dedicated to Mary in Western Christendom. This explains the basilica's name – St Mary Major.

MARY'S GREATEST CHURCH

St Mary Major stands on the highest point of one of ancient Rome's 'seven hills', the Esquiline, and in the very middle of the present-day capital's busy centre. In the sixteenth century, the ambitious urban renewer Pope Sixtus V (1585–90) made the church the axis of a new series of radial streets, extending like the points of a star to connect with Rome's other major basilicas. An obelisk, which Sixtus removed from Augustus' mausoleum, was placed to the rear of the basilica's apse, and marked the focal point of this urbanist vision. Around the other side, in front of the basilica's façade, Sixtus' successor Pope Paul V (1605–21), erected a fifteen-metre-high column surmounted by a beautiful bronze statue of the Virgin and Child. That homage is our exterior preparation for the wealth of tributes to be encountered inside St Mary Major.

In the course of sixteen centuries all the arts have joined together to glorify this ancient basilica as the house of the Virgin Mary on earth. The church is a jewel box of art treasures of each epoch and style. Classical marble columns divide the nave and side aisles, while Byzantine mosaics glitter with gold in the apse. The main altar is a blaze of gilded bronze and porphyry, balanced by a wealth of other materials – marbles, agates and lapis lazuli – used for the various side altars. The basilica's architectural and artistic masterpieces, contributed by some of Catholicism's most powerful Popes, underline one constant theme: the pre-eminence of Mary, Mother of Jesus and true Mother of God.

Above and right: According to legend, S. Maria Maggiore, or St Mary Major, was built in the fourth century on the spot indicated by a miraculous summer snowfall. The event is depicted in a thirteenth-century mosaic in the loggia above the entrance.

BASILICA OF SUMMER SNOWS

Even today St Mary Major is known as the 'Liberian Basilica', in honour of Pope Liberius (352–66). According to legend, a miraculous summer snowfall, announced by the Virgin in a dream both to Pope Liberius and to a pious and wealthy Roman couple, who had decided to give all their earthly goods to the Church and needed a specific cause, fell on the night of August 4–5. Following Mary's instructions, Liberius traced the dimensions of a new basilica in the fallen snow, and there built a church to the Madonna in the year 358.

The legend of 'Our Lady of the Snows' can be traced back to an oral tradition in the seventh century, although the miracle was first recorded in writing by Fra Bartolommeo of Trento around 1250. Leaving legend aside, history recounts that Pope Liberius was a firm crusader against the Arian heresy, which denied the divinity of Jesus in his human person. It is known that in Liberius' time the Esquiline Hill had been settled by barbarian troops who were largely Arian. By constructing a church to the Virgin Mary, Liberius evidently wished to foster her cult as Mother of God against the spread of Arian beliefs.

Before stepping inside St Mary Major, the visitor should pass beyond the eighteenth-century façade and mount some stairs to the loggia above the façade. Here, guarded by four colossal angels with gilded draperies, a magnificent medieval mosaic recounts the story of the basilica's foundation. Pope Liberius and the patrician donor Giovanni are peacefully sleeping on a hot summer night, while Christ, enthroned on a blue background studded with golden stars, supervises the Virgin's apparitions and the miraculous snowfall. The work is signed by Filippo Rusuti, who worked in Rome between the end of the thirteenth and the beginning of the fourteenth centuries. Until the eighteenth century, these splendid mosaics graced the church façade and welcomed the countless pilgrims who came to visit Mary's basilica.

Modern archaeologists now hold that St Mary Major has nothing to do with Liberius' church, supposedly built on a different Esquiline site. The disclaimers are based on excavations carried out between 1966 and 1972, which unearthed, six metres below the church pavement, a private first-century Roman villa with a large portico and third-century frescoed calendar scenes.

The thirteenth-century mosaic in the apse of S. Maria Maggiore shows *The Glorification of the Virgin*.

VENI
ELEC
TA M
ETPO

NA M
TE TE
RONV
M GV

Nevertheless, the snowfall legend is still very dear to the hearts of the Roman people. Every year on 5 August St Mary Major celebrates the event with a showering of white flower petals from the ceiling of the nave in front of the high altar. The petals fall down slowly like snowflakes inside the basilica, and after the liturgical service, the faithful rush to the presbytery to collect the scattered petals as tokens of special grace.

A CHURCH FOR THE MOTHER OF GOD

Pope Liberius' basilica fell into ruin and disappeared. The St Mary Major we see today took shape in 432, when Pope Sixtus III (432–440) decided to build a new and more magnificent structure near the site of Liberius' former Marian church.

The time was ripe for Sixtus to forcefully reaffirm the Marian cult. In the late Empire a temple to the Roman mother goddess Juno Lucina was flourishing on the Esquiline Hill and was frequented by many Roman matrons approaching childbirth. It is highly likely that a church to the Virgin Mother of God was erected to supplant the enduring pagan cult of Juno Lucina. In fact, some of St Mary Major's marble columns probably came from the Juno Lucina temple, which was located, according to archaeological findings, about 300 metres from the basilica's present site.

Sixtus III had an additional incentive for the construction of his new church. In 431 the Church Council of Ephesus had condemned the Nestorian heresy, which denied the unity of the divine and human natures in the person of Christ. The

The Pauline Chapel in S. Maria Maggiore was commissioned by Pope Paul V in 1605 to house a miraculous icon of the Virgin, known as *Salus Populi Romani* (Salvation of the Roman People).

Council affirmed that the person of Jesus possessed both divine and human natures, and was thus truly God and truly man. Mary, being the mother of the divine person Jesus, was also the Mother of God.

It was Sixtus' intention, realized in a series of mosaics (*Annunciation*, *Adoration of the Magi*, *Flight into Egypt*, etc.) in the triumphal arch over the altar, to invite the faithful to meditate on the divinity of Christ and the Virgin's divine motherhood. In one touching panel, Joseph looks perplexed as an angel takes him aside to explain his role in the impending Nativity.

Another series of mosaic panels around the nave architrave depicts scenes from the Old Testament, emphasizing the link between Christ's birth and the Messianic prophecies. These are high up and very difficult to see in detail, but can be appreciated for their colouring and delicate composition.

MEDIEVAL TESTIMONIALS
In the Middle Ages, Nicholas IV (1288–92) replaced Sixtus III's apsidal mosaics with an even more splendid portrayal of the Virgin in Glory. A glittering gold and gem-coloured mosaic, *The Coronation of the Virgin*, executed by the Franciscan friar Jacopo Torriti around 1295, became the aesthetic focal point of the entire basilica. Pope Nicholas changed Sixtus' earlier representation of *The Madonna and Child* to a portrayal of the Virgin as a crowned and bejewelled Byzantine bride, enthroned side by side with Christ. This Marian iconography had first made its appearance a century earlier in S. Maria in Trastevere and coincided with the rapid spread of the Marian cult throughout twelfth- and thirteenth-century Europe.

Other mosaics in the band below recount events in the life of the Virgin (*Annunciation*, *Nativity*, *Dormition*, etc.). Nicholas IV and Jacopo Torriti had worked together on the apse mosaic in S. Giovanni in Laterano; the Pope's diminutive figure appears to the left, along with the equally tiny brother-Cardinals Pietro and Giacomo Colonna. The same donors, whose munificence must have been extensive and sustained, are also portrayed in the somewhat later 'loggia mosaics' we have already admired.

THE PRESEPIO ORATORY
A precious wooden relic, believed to be part of the Sacred Crib (*presepio*) and allegedly brought from Bethlehem by St Jerome in the fourth century, has been associated with St Mary Major from early times. In fact, an oratory reproducing the Bethlehem grotto may have housed the relic from the days of Sixtus III. First documented in the reign of Pope Theodore I (642–9), the chapel stood outside the basilica and was visited by pilgrims throughout the Middle Ages. Successive Popes endowed the oratory with a golden altar, jewelled statues, and silver gates. Towards the end of the thirteenth century, Arnolfo di Cambio (1245–1303) decorated the grotto with his world-famous Nativity statues.

Unfortunately, Sixtus V decided to transfer the Presepio oratory to his own newly-designed chapel inside the basilica. In the process the whole construction caved in and fell apart. The relic of the Sacred Crib, encased in a nineteenth-century reliquary, is now located under the main altar. Some of Arnolfo's statues (the original Madonna and Child have been replaced by sixteenth-century figures) can be seen in a subterranean room inside Sixtus V's chapel.

THE SISTINE AND PAULINE CHAPELS
The Sistine Chapel in St Mary Major's right transept is like a miniature church with its own large cupola, and is filled with marbles, gilded statues, and Mannerist paintings. It was commissioned by Sixtus V when he was still a Cardinal, designed by his favourite architect Domenico Fontana (1543–1607), and contains Sixtus' tomb, that of Pope Pius V (1566–72), who made Sixtus a Cardinal, and a chapel with the remains of St Jerome (341–420).

Across from Sixtus V's chapel, Pope Paul V built his own to match in 1611. The chapel hosts Paul V's tomb and that of Clement VIII (1592–1605, who made Paul a Cardinal), but the real purpose was to house a sacred icon of the Madonna and Child. All the famous artists of the day – goldworkers, architects, painters and sculptors – worked to realize the flamboyant spirit of the seventeenth century. We are overwhelmed by larger-than-life statues, contorted marble angels, and the contrasting shades of amethyst, agate and lapis lazuli.

According to a seventh-century tradition, the Madonna icon, said to have been painted by the Evangelist Luke (but dated by scholars to somewhere between the fifth and ninth centuries), was carried through the streets of Rome by Pope St Gregory the Great in the year 594, to pray for deliverance from a terrible pestilence. When the plague miraculously ceased, the grateful Roman population gave the icon the appellation of *Salus Popoli Romani* (Salvation of the Roman People), and its veneration as such continues to this day.

THE BASILICA TODAY

Today St Mary Major has an eighteenth-century façade designed and executed by Ferdinando Fuga (1699–1781) on the orders of Benedict XIV (1740–58). Fuga also gave a classical regularity and symmetry to the interior by making all of the columns uniform – paring, shortening and adding on, and providing all with Ionic bases and capitals. Even today St Mary Major's interior gives the impression of a classical basilica of the early Church. The 'cosmatesque' pavement dates from the thirteenth century.

The gold coffered ceiling over the nave was commissioned by the Borgia Pope Alexander VI (1492–1503), whose coat-of-arms is prominently displayed. Supposedly, Alexander used the first gold brought from America, a gift from Ferdinand and Isabella of Spain, as gilding for the ceiling. The Baroque artist Gianlorenzo Bernini is buried in St Mary Major, to the right of the main altar, along with his father Pietro, who worked as a sculptor in some of the chapels. Another chapel commemorates the descendants – who are supposed to be buried here – of Pope Liberius' first generous 'sponsor', the patrician Giovanni.

S. LORENZO FUORI LE MURA
Prince of Deacons

The basilica of St Lawrence Outside the Walls has been a martyrs' shrine, imperial oratory, medieval fortress, and several Popes' favourite sanctuary. Unravelling the monument's archaeological skein brings to light many treasures and a fascinating history.

FAITH BRIDGES CENTURIES

Except for the original Apostles and St Paul, no saint inspired as much devotion in the early Church as St Lawrence, arch-deacon of Rome and martyr of the third century. The Emperor Constantine built a basilica in his honour, S. Lorenzo Fuori le Mura (St Lawrence Outside the Walls),

Above and right: St Lawrence Outside the Walls has an evocative medieval portico, built in the thirteenth century and decorated with frescoes of the saint's life.
The church has been rebuilt several times in its history. It has one of Rome's most complicated and mysterious interiors.

which was transformed many times down through the centuries. Succeeding generations have rebuilt and re-orientated the shrine until it has become one of Rome's strangest and most baffling churches.

Before entering, the visitor should savour the mingling of past centuries under its shadowy portico. Pagan cupids frolic across Papal sepulchres; faded paintings recount the lives and martyrdoms of early saints; medieval lions guard the portals; and sober memorials honour the contributions of modern Popes and statesmen.

MARTYRS' TRACES, CHRISTIAN DEVOTION

In the third century, in spite of persecution, Christianity had already made many converts and was spreading rapidly through the Roman population. By the year 250, more than twenty Popes had organized and guided the primitive Christian community. Early bishops were assisted by deacons, who were elected to help with worship, collect alms and minister to the poor. St Lawrence Martyr was the most beloved of these and is considered the patron saint of all Church deacons.

Lawrence served under Pope Sixtus II (257–8), just as the Emperor Valerian (253–260) was abandoning his earlier tolerant attitude and beginning a severe persecution of Christians. The imperial edict of 257 ordered summary executions of all bishops, deacons and priests found worshipping, assembling the faithful, or visiting Christian cemeteries. On 6 August 258, Sixtus was surprised by Valerian's guards while saying Mass in the catacombs, and beheaded on the spot, along with six of his deacons. Several days later, Sixtus' seventh and Chief Deacon Lawrence was tortured and martyred,

A 'cosmatesque' throne, dated 1254, in the earlier (sixth-century) upper presbytery of the basilica of St Lawrence Outside the Walls.

allegedly by being roasted on a gridiron. St Ambrose (339–97) recorded that when Lawrence was ordered by the authorities to hand over the Church treasure entrusted to his charge, he gathered together and presented a multitude of the poor, declaring: 'Here is the Church's wealth.' The martyr was buried by the Roman matron St Cyriaca, in her own private cemetery, in an area called *Ager Veranus* (property of the wealthy Roman Lucius Verus), beside the Via Tiburtina, outside the city walls.

St Lawrence's tomb, on the busy Via Tiburtina thoroughfare, immediately began to attract Christian worshippers and pilgrims from far and wide. Many Christians wished to be buried near St Lawrence, and soon a new cemetery, the Catacombs of St Cyriaca, grew up around his grave.

IMPERIAL CELEBRATION, PAPAL VENERATION

As we have seen, Constantine the Great (306-37) built the first official Christian basilicas: S. Pietro, S. Paolo Fuori le Mura, S. Giovanni Laterano, S. Croce in Gerusalemme – and S. Lorenzo Fuori le Mura. According to tradition, Constantine held his memorial to St Lawrence dearest of all.

The Emperor Constantine is known to have been extremely devoted to the memory of St Lawrence (whether for personal or political reasons will never be known). He isolated the martyr's grave, surrounded it with a silver grating, and dug out an adjacent oratory. In 330, wishing to create the most splendid martyr's shrine in all Rome, Constantine raised over the sanctuary a *Basilica Maior* ('major' that is, in relation to the underground oratory) to accommodate the increasing numbers of faithful.

Constantine's basilica was embellished with several chapels and rich decoration, as well as a long portico which apparently extended all the way to the Porta Tiburtina. Several Popes chose to be buried in the complex (Zosimus, Sixtus III and Hilarius in the fifth century).

Thus we come to the sixth century, when Pope Pelagius II (579–90), finding the structure invaded by dampness and dripping water, decided to preserve the sacred spot. Leaving Constantine's church to moulder next door, Pelagius built another church facing in exactly the opposite direction, its apse contiguous to that of the earlier basilica. Contemporary accounts praise Pelagius' church as spacious and luminous, and sumptuously decorated with columns and sculptures taken from earlier classical monuments.

To this site Pelagius transferred the relics of two other revered martyrs: St Stephen and St Justin. St Stephen, stoned to death in Jerusalem in AD35, is often considered the Church's first martyr, and along with St Lawrence he was also patron of deacons; his remains had been transported from Constantinople to Rome in 415, and in 578 placed beside those of St Lawrence in this church. St Justin, known as the first Chris-tian philosopher, was martyred in 165 in the reign of another philosopher, Emperor Marcus Aurelius (160–80).

In the Middle Ages the monastery complex which had grown up about S. Lorenzo was turned into a veritable fortress, surrounded by thick walls and guarded by watch-towers. Called 'Laurentiopolis', the small fortified city was similar to that which spread around S. Paolo Fuori le Mura around the same time. Today all that is left of that stronghold is the twelfth-century Romanesque bell-tower and another tower, now used as a burial place for the Capuchin monks, who have been the custodians of St Lawrence since 1855.

A NEW ERA

The thirteenth century marked a new period of splendour for S. Lorenzo Fuori le Mura. Pope Honorius III (1216–27) decided to create one large basilica by demolishing the walls of the Pelagian apse; Pelagius' *Basilica Maior* became the presbytery of the enlarged thirteenth-century church.

It is to this later period that we owe the portico's frescoes. They cover all three walls with lively scenes from the lives and miracles of St Lawrence and St Stephen, and were proudly signed in the early thirteenth century by a certain Paolo and his son Filippo. The portico itself was built (1220) by Rome's most famous thirteenth-century architect, Pietro Vassalletto, already mentioned for the lovely cloisters of S. Paolo Fuori le Mura and S. Giovanni in Laterano.

Vassalletto was reported to be a member of the 'cosmatesque' school of mosaicists, who were active in Rome and Lazio in the twelfth and thirteenth centuries. We admire more Cosmati work inside the basilica: the mosaic pavement which spreads like a flowered carpet throughout the church; pulpits with glittering mosaic designs; a slender Paschal candlestick; and a marble bishop's throne.

A VISIT

As we approach the basilica of S. Lorenzo Fuori le Mura, the façade already impresses us with the spirit of another age. The wide and sober porch, with old columns and lions peering from the horizontal cornice, is decidedly medieval, and quite unusual for Rome. Massive classical sarcophagi in the portico have reliefs of bacchanalian cupids harvesting wine, and sombre Christian Bible scenes. (The first was used as a tomb for Pope Damasus II in 1048.) Worn stone lions – one has a child between its paws – guard the entrance. Some historians date these to as early as the eighth century.

Inside, thick columns rise heavily from the irregular pavement, as if bearing the weight of centuries on their Ionic capitals. At the end of the nave we ascend to a higher level, to the strange and mysterious area which formed Pelagius' original sixth-century church. Stocky columns sport Corinthian capitals with pagan garlands and imperial war trophies. Above these, antique sculpted blocks (from earlier Roman monuments and appearing about to crumble at any moment) support a higher level of arcaded galleries, the *matronea*, or women's section. Further up, small windows illuminate the area with an eerie, flickering light.

The pilgrim should sit in the 'cosmatesque' episcopal throne (1254) at the end of the presbytery, to fully experience the sixth-century Byzantine-style mosaic on the inner face of the triumphal arch. From the centre, the Saviour imparts his blessing from a blue globe. To either side, stylized saints stand in attendance: on the left, Pope Pelagius presents a model of his church, flanked by St Lawrence and St Peter; on the right stand St Hippolytus (St Lawrence's gaoler, who was converted, martyred, and buried in a nearby Tiburtina cemetery), St Stephen and St Paul.

Eight steps lead down to the *confessio*. Above is an inscription: 'Here lie the bodies of Blessed Stephen, proto-martyr, Blessed Lawrence, deacon, and Justin, presbyter and martyr.' Their sarcophagus is enclosed by a thick grating and almost impossible to see. On this level are the St Cyriaca Chapel (redone in the seventeenth century) and the funerary sanctuary of Pope Pius IX (1846–78). Pius restored the basilica by removing all unsuitable Baroque accretions – and then commissioned this Gothic Revival chapel, almost over-whelming in its mosaic display of saints and emblems of all the dioceses and institutions which financed the project.

The fascinating Catacombs of St Cyriaca and the peaceful Romanesque cloister in the former monastery of Clement III (1187–1191) are definitely worth a visit.

BACK TO THE PRESENT
Upon leaving the church, to the right of the main doorway we notice a huge block of marble commemorating the visit of Pius

XII (1939–58), to S. Lorenzo on 19 July 1943, three days after the basilica and piazza had been severely damaged by aerial bombardment. During his rare appearance in this heavily populated and suffering neighbourhood (the Popes almost never left the Vatican during the war), the Pontiff also dispersed money to the parish faithful. At that moment, Pius may have seemed the very reincarnation of St Lawrence, who had defended the Roman populace at another trying moment almost two millennia earlier. The tomb of the post-war Italian statesman Alcide de Gasperi is also in the portico.

S. Lorenzo was the only Roman church to suffer damage during the Second World War. Painstaking restorations were carried out from 1943 to 1949, when the basilica was finally reopened. It is thanks to the restorations and resulting excavations that S. Lorenzo's complicated building history is now known.

It is difficult to find a quiet moment to visit S. Lorenzo Fuori le Mura. Afternoons are best. The basilica is adjacent to Rome's official Campo Verano cemetery, where most Catholics (except Popes, Cardinals, and royalty) are buried. It seems fitting that today's funerals are held in the very shrine where some of Christianity's earliest martyrs are also buried.

S. CROCE IN GERUSALEMME
Shrine to the Holy Cross
This basilica has been a magnet for Christian pilgrims down through the ages.

SACRED RELICS
There is in Rome a church which, according to tradition, hosts Christianity's most precious relics: alleged fragments of the True Cross, upon which Jesus Christ suffered and died almost two millennia ago. For Rome's earliest Christians, this shrine represented a second 'Jerusalem', a sanctuary for evoking the Passion and the promise of eternal life. Even today, particularly during Lent, pilgrims flock to Rome from all over the world to say prayers in the presence of the sacred relics.

The approach to S. Croce in Gerusalemme is disappointing. For although the façade and oval atrium are declared by many guidebooks to be 'the most delightful Rococo monument in Rome', they do not really do justice to the church's ancient origins and spiritual heritage. The exterior was transformed in 1743–4 by Pietro Passalacqua and Domenico Gregorini for Pope Benedict XIV (1740–1758).

ST HELENA AND THE TRUE CROSS

The basilica of the Holy Cross in Jerusalem, usually known simply as Santa Croce (Holy Cross), recalls the presence of the holy relics and the fact that a portion of it is built upon soil brought back from Jerusalem. Some obscurity surrounds the origins of the relics (see below), but the church owes its foundation to St Helena (250–330), mother of the Roman Emperor Constantine the Great (306–37), who built most of the Jubilee basilicas discussed in this Pilgrimage.

We know very little about St Helena. Some biographers say she was an English princess, others that she was a serving girl or an innkeeper's daughter born in Bithynia. In any case, she married the Roman general Constantius Chlorus, who, upon becoming Caesar in 292, immediately divorced her for a bride

of more politically expedient lineage. Her son Constantine, however, respected and honoured her immensely. The date of Helena's conversion to Christianity is not known, but in about 326 she made a pilgrimage to the Holy Land, where she found and carried off several important relics – fragments of the True Cross, soil from Calvary, and the stairs believed to have been ascended by Christ in Pontius Pilate's Jerusalem palace (now the Scala Santa across from the basilica of St John Lateran).

Tradition holds that St Helena transferred the sacred relics to her royal residence near Constantine's Lateran Palace, and spread the Jerusalem soil upon the floor of her private chapel there. The first account (395) of St Helena's finding of the True Cross comes from St Ambrose (334–97). Strangely enough, Constantine's contemporary and biographer, Eusebius, Bishop

Rome's Shrine of the Holy Cross has a Rococo façade, added to the basilica in 1744.

of Caesarea (263–340), does not record Helena's discovery. St Cyril, Bishop of Jerusalem at that time, while alluding to veneration of the True Cross and other relics of the Passion in one of his *Catechetical Homilies* (347–8), makes no mention of Helena in that connection.

Despite these gaps in the historical record, it is still likely that Helena lived and prayed on this site. There are concrete historical accounts of her residence (between 317 and 322) in the imperial Palatium Sessorianum, built on this spot around the year 200. From earliest times the church was known as the Sessorian Basilica and associated with the cult of the True Cross. Archaeological research has revealed that a monu-mental basilica was built into the atrium of the palace. (More recently, the foundations of the palace's private amphitheatre were discovered beneath the next-door convent.)

Two small rooms (now on a lower level) have from the beginning been known as the chapel and bedroom of St Helena; the floors of these have been dug up by countless pilgrims who wished to take away holy soil from Calvary. During restoration of the church in 1492, relics, with

inscriptions describing them as fragments of the True Cross, were found walled into a niche in the triumphal arch before the apse. This is hardly surprising, since such items were susceptible to destruction or theft during the years of incessant barbarian invasions.

The shrine was allegedly consecrated to the Holy Cross by Pope St Sylvester I (314–35), who also consecrated St John Lateran, and the basilica was much visited and venerated in the early centuries of the Church. In the fifth century, the Emperor Valentinian III (419–55) adorned St Helena's Chapel, where the relics were undoubtedly kept at first, with famous mosaics (now disappeared) of himself, his mother Galla Placidia, and his sister Honoria. Medieval Popes celebrated the Good Friday liturgy in St Helena's Chapel, bringing in procession from St John Lateran a golden rose as the symbol of the radiant joy of eternal life.

THE CHURCH TODAY

St Helena's original basilica – one great hall, divided horizontally by huge granite columns, and probably open to the air – was very different from the building we see today. The existing structure is a normal three-aisled Roman basilica, reconstructed in 1144 by Pope Lucius II (1144–5), who also raised the Romanesque campanile and built a cloistered monastery next door.

The overall impression is of a Baroque interior, due to alterations commissioned by Pope Benedict XIV (1740–58) in the mid-eighteenth century. Corrado Giaquinto's pompous ceiling painting over the nave (1744) shows *St Helena in Glory*, as well as St Michael subduing the demon of heresy, and many other pious saints and Doctors of the Church. Many of the side-altar paintings depict episodes relevant to the Cistercian Order, reformed by St Bernard of Clairvaux (1090–1153), and custodians of the basilica since 1561 (*St Bernard Subjugates the Antipope to Pope Innocent II*, *St Bernard Miraculously Extracts a Tooth from the Dead St Caesarius*, and *Vision of the Founder's Mother*).

Left: This sculpture on the altar of St Helena's Chapel was actually a classical Roman statue of Juno. In the Middle Ages the addition of the missing head and arms, and a cross, transformed the work into a portrait of the Christian Empress St Helena.

Right: The Relics of the Passion, now in a modern chapel in the Shrine of the Holy Cross.

The sense of disappointment in the inappropriateness of all these Baroque surroundings finally dissipates as we approach the apse. Artists have left many magnificent renditions of the Finding of the True Cross, including Piero della Francesca's (1416–92) renowned frescoes (1460) in Arezzo's church of St Francis. Yet this basilica's portrayal is certainly one of the loveliest of all.

Besides, there is an intriguing mystery for art historians here. Who did these paintings? Earlier attribution to Antoniazzo Romano (1435–1508) has now been disproved. Three different expert 'hands' have been identified, with votes for Melozzo da Forli (1438–94), who worked on mosaics for St Helena's Chapel, Pinturicchio (1454–1513), and even Perugino (1445–1523). It is entertaining to listen to the streams of art experts and dilettantes who pass beneath the paintings, claiming the scenes are reminiscent of works by Benozzo

Gozzoli (1420–97), with hints of Botticelliesque draperies.

Versions of the Legend of the True Cross differ. Here we have, from left to right across the lower apse: St *Helena* [against a fairy-tale background of a fifteenth-century Italian hill town] *Discovers and Excavates the True Cross in Jerusalem*; *A Dead Youth, Placed Upon the True Cross, Is Brought Back to Life*; *King Chosroes II* [d. 614] *of Persia Conquers Jerusalem and Carries Away the True Cross*; *Emperor Heraclius* [610–41] *Defeats the Persians and Returns the Cross to Jerusalem*. Above, the Saviour, surrounded by cherubs, imparts a blessing from a glorious gold background. The entire work was commissioned by the Spanish titular Cardinal Bernardino Carvajal (d. 1522, shown kneeling beside St Helena and the True Cross in the middle of the fresco), when the relics were rediscovered in the church in 1492.

ST HELENA'S CHAPEL AND THE RELIQUARY
Now on a lower level (because of uneven sinking in the Roman soil), St Helena's Chapel is entirely vaulted by bright mosaics. Those commissioned by the Emperor Valentinian, which were so famous throughout the Middle Ages, were restored by Melozzo da Forli in the late fifteenth century, touched up by Baldassare Peruzzi (1481–1536) in the sixteenth century, and completely redone by Francesco Zucchi in 1593. This is regrettable – for although the colours are dazzling, the figures (Helena, Pope Sylvester, Peter, Paul, the Evangelists, and, of course, Cardinal Carvajal) are clumsy and awkward.

The chapel has one very interesting work. In the altar-niche is a classical statue of St Helena holding the Cross. What is wrong here? Well, actually this was a Roman (first century BC) image of the goddess Juno, which had lost its appendages. With the addition of head, arms, and a cross, the pagan goddess became a Christian saint.

Beside St Helena's Chapel there is an important Cistercian chapel, built and dedicated to St Gregory the Great by Cardinal Carvajal in 1520. Off the basilica's left aisle is the Reliquary of the Relics of the Passion, housed in a truly ugly modern chapel (1929–31). A portion of the Good Thief's Cross is on a left wall. A glassed aedicule at the back displays three fragments of the True Cross, a nail, two thorns, and a portion of the Cross inscription, fragments from the Holy Sepulchre, the column of flagellation, the Bethlehem Crib, and the index finger of the Doubting Apostle Thomas.

This is quite a lot of important relics for one church to offer, and is the explanation for the tourists' and pilgrims' buses which clog the streets of this slightly out-of-the-way quarter of Rome.

BIBLIOGRAPHY

A complete list of sources used for this book on the churches of Rome would be a volume in itself.
The following is only a very selected choice.

For individual churches: the churches themselves – their brochures, guidebooks and mouldy papers tacked up on walls or hidden away in dusty cupboards – are the best sources of information. Pastors, sacristans and elderly parishioners have wonderful stories to tell.

Otherwise, two series of small guides are helpful:
Le Chiese di Roma Illustrate; Istituto di Studi Romani, Fratelli Palombi Editori, Rome
Guide Rionali di Roma, SPQR Assessorato Alla Cultura, Fratelli Palombi Editori, Roma

For general background information the following were my constant and informative companions:
Coarelli, F., *Guida Archeologica di Roma,* Milan 1997
Hibbert, C., *Rome, The Biography of a City,* Harmondsworth 1987
Krautheimer, R., *Early Christian and Byzantine Architecture,* New York 1986
Krautheimer, R., *Rome, Profile of a City, 312–1308,* New Jersey 1980
Masson, G., *The Companion Guide to Rome,* Woodbridge, 1998

On Church history whole libraries exist on the subject. For me, some of the most useful were:
Bokenkotter, T., *A Concise History of the Catholic Church,* New York 1990
Crucitti, E. R., *The Christian Persecutions,* Rome 1978
Eusebius, *The History of the Church,* (Penguin), London 1989
Frend, W. H. C., *The Early Church,* Philadelphia 1984
Loeb Classical Library, *The Apostolic Fathers,* Volumes I&II, Cambridge 1985

Specifically on the churches of Rome, the following works were indipensable, although there are many others:
Armellini, M. and Cecchelli, C., *Le Chiese di Roma dal Secolo IV al XIX,* 2 vols., Rome 1942
Buchowiecki, W., *Handbuch der Kirchen Roms,* 3 vols., Vienna 1967-1974
Gunn, P. and Beny, R., *The Churches of Rome,* New York 1981
Huelsen, C., *Le Chiese di Roma nel Medio Evo,* Rome 1927
Kirsch, J. P., *Die Romischen Titelkirchen Im Altertum,* Paderborn 1918
Male, E., *Rome et Ses Vielles Eglises,* Rome 1992
Tylenda, J., (S.J.), *Pilgrim's Guide to the Churches of Rome,* Collegeville, Minnesota, 1993

Other favourites:
Blunt, A., *A Guide to Baroque Rome,* Rome 1982
Brezzi, P., *Gli Anni Santi nella Storia,* Milano 1975
Carpocini, J., *Daily Life in Ancient Rome,* Yale University 1940
Duffy, E., *Saints and Sinners,* Yale University, 1997
Farmer, D. H., *Oxford Dictionary of Saints, Oxford, 1987*
Fasola, U. M., *Peter and Paul in Rome,* Rome 1980
Johnson, P., *The Papacy,* London 1997
Kelly, J. N. D., *Oxford Dictionary of Popes,* Oxford, 1988
Llewellyn, P., *Rome in the Dark Ages,* London 1993
Pergola, P., *Le Catacombe Romane,* Rome 1998
Strinati, C., etc., *La Storia dei Giubilei,* Vol. I, Rome, 1997

INDEX